MULTICULTURAL PSYCHOTHERAPY

SECOND EDITION

MULTICULTURAL PSYCHOTHERAPY

An Approach to Individual and Cultural Differences

Manuel Ramirez III

The University of Texas at Austin

Allyn and Bacon

Boston   London   Toronto   Sydney   Tokyo   Singapore

Series editorial assistant: Susan Hutchinson
Manufacturing buyer: Suzanne Lareau

Copyright © 1999 by Allyn & Bacon
A Viacom Company
Needham Heights, MA 02494

Internet: www.abacon.com

A previous edition was published under the title *Psychotherapy and
Counseling with Minorities: A Cognitive Approach to Individual and Cultural
Differences.* Copyright © 1991 by Allyn & Bacon.

Library of Congress Cataloging-in-Publication Data

Ramirez, Manuel
      [Psychotherapy and counseling with minorities]
      Multicultural psychotherapy : an approach to individual and
  cultural differences / Manuel Ramirez III. — 2nd ed.
          p.   cm.
      First ed. published in 1991 under title: Psychotherapy and
  counseling with minorities.
      Includes bibliographical references and index.
      ISBN 0-205-28904-5
      1. Psychotherapy—Cross-cultural studies.   2. Cross-cultural
  counseling.   3. Minorities—Mental health services.   4. Family
  psychotherapy—Cross-cultural studies.   5. Cultural psychiatry
  I. Title.
  RC451.5.A2R36   1998
  616.89'14'089--dc21   98-31392
                                                                    CIP

Printed in the United States of America
10 9 8 7 6 5 4 3 2 1   02 01 00 99

To Susanne Doell and to my students and clients.
Thank you for making me a better multicultural
therapist and scholar.

CONTENTS

PREFACE

Pergamon Press first published this book in 1991, and Allyn and Bacon reissued it in 1994. It represents the culmination of my thirty-two years of experience in research and work in public education and in university, community, and clinical settings. My work has centered on the experiences of "the different"—those who, in some way, do not fit the preferred or idealized images of society; those who, because of their uniqueness, are subject to prejudice, oppression, and pressures to conform.

I began my work in this area thinking that only members of ethnic and racial minority groups suffered from the marginality syndrome related to feeling different. Through research and intervention work with people from all ethnic, religious, and socioeconomic backgrounds, as well as with people of varying physical abilities and sexual orientations, I have come to realize that the mismatch syndrome is common to people who live and work in diverse societies.

As I developed and implemented educational programs in schools; taught courses; lectured at different colleges and universities; and did psychological assessments, counseling, and psychotherapy with clients, I came to realize that no one fits society's ideal image perfectly.

For some, the lack of fit is due to external features—skin color, accent, physical appearance, or impairments. For others, the lack of fit is due to "invisible" characteristics—values, thinking style, emotional or expressive style, philosophy of life, or sexual orientation.

My work with the different gradually led me to the realization that traditional approaches to education, counseling, psychotherapy, and personality assessment are not adequate or appropriate for intervention; a new theoretical and research perspective, a new model of personality change was in order.

This new edition, like the one that preceded it, explores a model of counseling and psychotherapy based on the multicultural perspective that evolved from my work with the different. This book introduces five new case studies to supplement the five presented in the earlier edition. I have expanded the case studies to include an African American single mother, an Asian American young adult man, a Latina who has impaired vision and is a single mother, an elderly Latino who is retired and disabled, a multiracial male, an intact Latino family, and a single-parent family. This edition includes a chapter on family therapy and adds insights into counseling and/or therapy for mixed-race couples. I've also added a new chapter on how the multicultural model can be useful in meeting guidelines introduced through managed care.

The principal objectives of the model are to help people who feel different and alienated accept and understand their uniqueness. The model also seeks to enhance cultural values and to develop flexibility in cognitive styles. Although its primary focus is on ethnic/racial minorities, the model is appropriate for members of any group that differs from the societal ideal. I have varied gender pronouns in referring to clients and mental health professionals. No gender preference is intended.

The ultimate goal of this model is the development of a multicultural orientation to life. This orientation has the following five ideal characteristics:

1. The first is a striving for the maximum development of the personality, a striving for self-actualization. People with a multicultural orientation toward life are motivated to develop as many aspects of their personality as they can. Multicultural people recognize that interacting with diversity stimulates the evolution of underdeveloped areas of the personality. The multiculturally oriented recognize that stereotypes and notions of societal, cultural, and personality superiority or inferiority can block experience and learning filters and prevent them from valuing and respecting people, groups, and cultures who might otherwise act as teachers and catalysts for development. Culturally flexible people are willing to take diversity challenges, to risk situations totally unlike previous experiences. Such individuals learn by observation, by listening, and by exposure to different worldviews and life philosophies.

2. A second characteristic of multicultural orientation is adaptability to different environmental situations. Regardless of how work, educational, or other environmental conditions change, multicultural people are motivated to adapt and to flex in order to be effective.

3. Third, the person with a multicultural orientation enjoys the challenges of leadership roles in diverse groups. That person evolves innovative solutions for resolving conflict in groups with diverse memberships (Ramirez, 1998; Garza et al., 1982).

4. Another characteristic is the multicultural person's commitment to changing groups, cultures, and nations to guarantee social justice for all members and citizens. Such a person has a goal of helping to develop a perfect society. Although multicultural people may feel more comfortable in their native groups, they develop perspectives as world citizens (Ramirez, 1998). Adler (1974) observed that multicultural people can transcend families, groups, and cultures; that is, they have the ability to step back in order to take an objective look at the groups with which they are familiar and in which they have participated to determine what has to be modified to ensure social justice and equality for all members.

5. The final characteristic of people with a multicultural orientation to life is the motivation to get the most out of life. Multicultural people seek exposure to as much diversity in life as possible. They enjoy traveling and living in different environments such as different countries, different regions of the same country, or different areas within their communities. They enjoy knowing different people, whether in person or through biographies and autobiographies.

But how does the multicultural model fit into the overall psychotherapy and counseling picture? Although the words "therapist" and "therapy" are used throughout the book, the model is relevant to all mental health practitioners. Do counselors and therapists need to make major changes in the way they do therapy in order to be effective as multicultural therapists? The techniques and strategies of the multicultural model reflect an eclecticism, ranging from the intensive study of the client's life history and the use of insight, to the employment of cognitive behavioral as well as humanistic and cross-cultural approaches. Multicultural therapy, however, is unique in its theoretical concepts and goals for change.

The multicultural model of psychotherapy and counseling is eclectic with respect to techniques and strategies. The model borrows a focus on collecting a detailed life history from the dynamic approaches and theories of therapy. This life history helps the therapist understand the client's past and develop insight for making the unconscious conscious through interpretation.

From the humanistic perspective, the multicultural model borrows unconditional positive regard, that is, uncritical acceptance, to allow a client to accept her unique self. Also from the humanistic approach comes the use of phenomenology, or the therapist's attempt to see the world through the eyes of the client.

From the cognitive and behavioristic approaches and theories, the multicultural model incorporates an emphasis on reducing stress, on establishing behavioral goals, and on emphasizing homework and the client's active participation through role-playing. Finally, from the ethnopsychological, cross-cultural, and community schools, the multicultural model has adopted an emphasis on values and on the assumption that each cultural and environmental set of circumstances or conditions produces a unique set of coping techniques, or cognitive styles, crucial to personality development and functioning.

The theoretical base of the multicultural model of psychotherapy and counseling had its origins in cross-cultural mental health and in the psychology of equality and liberation that evolved from the psychologies of ethnic groups in the United States, of the colonized, and of women. The cross-cultural emphasis emerged from the application of psychoanalytic and behavioristic theories and intervention approaches in different cultures throughout the world (Triandis and Lambert, 1980).

The goals of multicultural psychotherapy and counseling are different from those of traditional schools of personality change. The multicultural model has two categories of goals: individual and institutional, or societal, goals. Individual goals emphasize self-understanding and self-acceptance. In addition, the model encourages understanding the effects of person–environment fit on personality development and adjustment. Multicultural therapy seeks to empower the client to produce significant environmental changes. Institutional and societal goals focus on the identification and elimination of barriers to multicultural development, and on replacing those barriers with the positive politics of diversity in families, interpersonal relationships, institutions, and in society as a whole.

Multicultural therapy and counseling work toward the creation of a truly multicultural society, striving to develop a world of peace, understanding, and cooperation in which each person's individuality is respected. In this model, the diversity of society is viewed as a potential teacher and catalyst to the total development of the personality.

In today's world, all people who live and work in diverse environments and societies are prone to feeling marginalized, confused, and perhaps threatened from time to time. The demands of both cultural and cognitive flexibility in a pluralistic society can be felt in all facets of life. They are part of daily interactions in business, personal relationships, education, community services, religion, and government. The multicultural model of psychotherapy provides a useful set of coping techniques as well as a worldview that is useful to everyone living and working in pluralistic environments.

ACKNOWLEDGMENTS

This book is the result of a team effort. Terry Foster edited and prepared the manuscript and also gave me valuable suggestions, which I incorporated into the text. She ensured the readability of the volume. Lisette Kunz did an excellent job of typing the manuscript and of pointing out inconsistencies and missing details. I owe her a debt of gratitude. I am also grateful to the graduate students who have taken my seminar on multicultural psychotherapy over the years, with special thanks to Floyd Berry and Douglas Campbell for making valuable suggestions for changes to the first edition.

I am also grateful to the first edition's reviewers who were commissioned by Allyn and Bacon: Maria Cecilia Zea, Ph.D., The George Washington University; Felipe G. Castro, Ph.D., Arizona State University; and John J. Echeverry, Ph.D., The George Washington University. Their incisive and timely suggestions, along with those made by Carla Daves, former editor at Allyn and Bacon, have made this edition a much better book.

I am thankful to the Center for Mexican American Studies at the University of Texas at Austin for awarding me a faculty development grant to help me complete the work on this manuscript.

1

FEELING DIFFERENT
A Major Mental Health Problem in a Diverse Society

CASE STUDIES

The people described here have one thing in common: They are in crisis because they feel different from those around them. The feeling of being different is accompanied by feelings of alienation and loneliness, depression, and anxiety. People who feel different feel misunderstood and undervalued. The feeling of being different is typical among members of minority groups.

Imelda M.

Imelda is a sixteen-year-old Latina high school student who attempted suicide. She was despondent because of the breakup of a three-year relationship with her boyfriend. During an interview in the hospital, she said, "I wanted to die because I am alone and I'm different. I've lost the only person who accepted me as I really am. I have always been different from my parents, from my teachers, and from the other students. My boyfriend was the only one who understood me. No one will accept me as I am. They are always trying to change me."

Raul B.

Raul is a thirty-five-year-old multiracial man (Latino, African American and Native American). He sought therapy because of depression and anxiety. Raul was also suffering from flashbacks and nightmares related to his experiences as a serviceman in Vietnam. His sense of failure in his relationships with women added to his crisis. He said, "I fall in love with women who cannot love me as much as I love them."

Tara W.

Tara, a twenty-six-year-old African American college student, is a single mother. She presented for therapy feeling depressed and suffering from insomnia. She sought counseling because of her ambivalent relationship to her parents (particularly her mother) and her live-in boyfriend. She said, "I am confused about the way my life is going. I love my mother, but I also resent her telling me how I should be. Like my boyfriend, she tries to control me."

Alex S.

Alex is a twenty-one-year-old college student of Vietnamese descent. Born in Vietnam, he immigrated to the United States with his parents and siblings when he was six. At the time he sought counseling, Alex was feeling guilty and distraught. He was lying to his parents about his major in college and his future plans—they wanted him to attend medical school, but he was planning to pursue graduate studies in social work. He had also withheld the fact that he is gay and has a live-in partner. Alex said, "I feel like I am living two different lives. When I go home, I am the good Vietnamese son; I date my old girlfriends from high school; I talk about my plans to attend medical school and to get married and have a family. It makes me feel terrible to have to do this, but they just would not accept me as I am."

Rose A.

Rose, a thirty-five-year-old Latina with impaired vision, is married and has three children. She is a survivor of a tornado that struck the small town where she lived and worked as a Head Start teacher. The storm hit when she was at the Head Start center, killing several of Rose's colleagues, members of the community, and children in her class. Rose suffered injuries that resulted in her loss of vision. She said, "I feel bad about being alive when many of my friends and children whom I loved are dead. I'm angry with God, but my family and friends don't understand my feelings. They keep telling me how lucky I am to be alive. I'm not. I wish I were dead."

Harold H.

Harold, a thirty-five-year-old Anglo engineer and co-owner of a computer software company, came to therapy in distress. He explained, "I don't feel I'm as effective and capable as I used to be. I don't really belong anywhere—not with my family, not with my partners, not even with my own parents." During the initial psychotherapy session, he talked about how he had always tried to win his father's love and admiration: "Dad always preferred my older brother; nothing I did changed that. I tried to show him that I could be successful in business, because that is what I thought he wanted.

And to be a success, I had to ignore my wife and kids. Well, I'm a success now, and this hasn't changed anything with my father. Now I'm in danger of losing my family while my partners are complaining that I don't seem to have my heart in my work anymore. I honestly don't know what's happening. My entire world is falling apart, and I can't do anything about it. I just don't feel like I belong anywhere anymore. I'm so alone."

Wanda and Javier J.

A mixed-race couple, Wanda is Anglo and Javier is Latino. They have been married for eight years and have two children. Their marital problems began two years before they sought couples counseling. Wanda said, "I feel that Javier does not support me in what I am trying to do in my career. He is also too strict with the children." Javier's perspective was different: "Wanda is too wrapped up in her world to care about what is going on in our family. The children don't have enough direction from us, and they are having problems in school because of the prejudice they feel from the Anglo kids. Wanda doesn't seem to care."

The Rosales

The Rosales are a Latino family consisting of the parents—forty-five-year-old Anna and forty-six-year-old Jesse—and two children—Nancy, fourteen, and Tati, twelve. The Rosales have been married for seventeen years. They sought therapy because Anna and Jesse had been threatening to separate. The children are having adjustment problems: Tati is not doing well in school and he wants to drop out; Nancy took one of the family cars without permission and was involved in an accident. Anna reported, "Nancy and I are like two peas in a pod. We get along very well and understand each other. Jesse and Tati seem to be from another world." Jesse, on the other hand, observed, "Anna is always criticizing Tati and me. She feels that we don't do anything right."

Tony G.

Tony is a sixty-five-year-old Latino who has a physical disability. Born in Mexico, he immigrated to a city in the southwestern United States when he was forty-one years old. He was holding down three different jobs when he was injured in an automobile accident that incapacitated him, forcing him to retire. The accident left him with limited use of his right arm and leg. He also suffers from severe muscle spasms in his neck, many lasting for several minutes at a time. The spasms are triggered by stress and fatigue. He is divorced and has four children. He lives alone. Tony told the therapist, "I feel useless now because I can no longer work. People see me and think I'm exaggerating my problems. Not even my family understands the pain I feel or my unhappiness and feelings of uselessness."

Camilla and Her Two Daughters

Camilla, Lavis, and Tracy are members of a single-parent family. Camilla, a thirty-three-year-old Latina, has been divorced from Robert, who is white, for two years. Their two daughters, Lavis, six years old, and Tracy, eight, are biracial. Camilla and Robert have been having conflicts and their differences are exacerbated when Tracy and Lavis visit with Robert.

FEELING DIFFERENT

The feeling of "differentness" is familiar to anyone who has felt pressured by society to conform. The common dynamic in the "differentness syndrome" is mismatch. Those who suffer *mismatch* feel alienated from individuals, groups, family, cultures, and institutions that play important parts in their lives. What are the causes of mismatch? The cultural and individual differences that make each of us unique are also responsible for making us feel mismatched to others and/or to our environment. The majority of society imposes pressures on us to conform, to abandon our individuality, and to force ourselves into the fictional ideal molds and patterns created by those who have power and influence (Katz and Taylor, 1988; A. Ramirez, 1988).

Because few of us fit these patterns in every way, we feel different and inferior, as if there were something wrong with us. The end result is that we reject ourselves, or at least part of our true selves, in order to "fit in" and to appear less different.

The Mismatch Syndrome

The clients described earlier in this chapter felt mismatched to the important people and institutions in their lives. They felt alone, hopeless, angry, and misunderstood. They exhibited a number of common traits: self-rejection, depression, anxiety, emphasis on the negative, and rigidity of thinking and problem solving. All of these are symptoms of mismatch syndrome. Let us examine the cases in more detail to see how pressures to conform are related to the syndrome.

Imelda. Imelda was reared in a traditional society, typical of rural communities in the U.S.–Mexico border region. Atypical of the traditional pattern, however, were her parents' divorce and her interest in sports. She was a member of the varsity basketball and volleyball teams. Imelda felt mismatched to the important authority figures in her life—her father, stepmother, grandparents, and teachers. Her parents and grandparents pressured her to abandon her involvement in sports because it was not consistent with their perception of how a proper young woman should be-

have. Her teachers did not like Imelda's attempts to make classes more relevant to herself and to her fellow students. When she asked her teachers to
relate what they were teaching to her own experiences and to those of her
classmates, they interpreted her behavior as rebellious and lacking in respect. Although Imelda's peers admired her feats on the basketball and volleyball courts, they saw her as an oddball, as not being feminine enough,
and rarely included her in their social activities. Thus, Imelda was often
lonely, isolated, and misunderstood. Only with her boyfriend did she feel
comfortable and accepted. When he broke up with her, she felt her life had
come to an end.

Raul.   Raul grew up in a predominantly Caucasian city. His parents were
both biracial—his mother was African American and Latino and his father
was Native American and African American. During his childhood and
adolescence, his family lived in subsidized government housing in the inner
city. In late adolescence he lived with relatives in a rural community in the
U.S.–Mexico border region of the state in which he lived. When he left
home, he joined the armed forces and traveled widely throughout Europe
and Asia, particularly in Vietnam.

Raul felt different from his peers in the housing development where his
family lived; almost all were either Latino or African American and none
were multiracial like his family. Since the time he was twelve, his mother
had to work full time; because he was the oldest, he had to take over the role
of supervisor to his younger siblings. Additional feelings of differentness
emerged when Raul had to attend a middle school in which whites were in
the majority. At that time he was not only diagnosed as being dyslexic and
placed in special classes, but he also experienced rejection when he approached white girls.

Feelings of differentness were exacerbated in the year that he lived in a
border community; his Latino relatives and peers criticized him for his accent, for his inability to speak Spanish fluently, and for his lack of familiarity with traditional Latino culture. Raul felt pressured to conform from the
institutions of a segregated community in which Caucasian people were in
the majority and mixed-race dating and friendship were discouraged. He
also felt pressured to be a traditional Latino when he later went to live in a
border community while he was in high school.

When Raul returned to his home community after his military service,
he again encountered prejudice and lack of acceptance. His siblings were resentful of him because they felt he had been a harsh disciplinarian when he
had been left in charge of them. He felt sexually attracted to white women,
yet he felt that they could not love him as much as he loved them.

Tara.   Tara, an African American, grew up in a small semi-rural town,
which was predominantly Caucasian and Latino. Tara had two older brothers. Her father was a farmer and her mother a nurse. She had a difficult time

being accepted by her older brothers and her father because they were very involved in the work of the farm. She remembered feelings of abandonment when she was young and her mother worked long hours at the hospital. Tara's feelings of differentness began when she attempted to gain the acceptance of her father and brothers. Her attempts at doing farm work, such as driving a tractor, only amused them. Her feelings of differentness were exacerbated by her appearance as an adolescent—she was tall and thin. She was uncoordinated, and her peers made fun of her awkwardness when she tried to participate in sports. It was also difficult for Tara because African Americans were in the minority in her home community. She didn't date in high school.

Her feelings of differentness continued when she attended college in a segregated town close to her home community. Caucasians predominated, and she felt prejudice against African Americans. By this time she had become an attractive woman, successful at volleyball and basketball. She started to date an African American basketball player and became pregnant. She dropped out of college to return home. Her parents were angry with her, feeling that she had caused them to lose face in their small community. Tara faced strong conformity pressures to be the perfect mother, and her parents wanted her to marry.

She started therapy after she moved to a city two hours away from her hometown to complete her college education. She was confused about a relationship in which she was involved. Her mother was pressuring her to marry her boyfriend so her child would have a father. Tara was having a difficult time juggling the many responsibilities that went along with being a single mother, a student, and an employee.

Alex.   Alex was born in Vietnam and spent the first few years of his life there. He was the youngest of five children. Before immigrating to the United States with his family at age six, Alex had been reared largely by his grandparents because his father was an officer in the South Vietnamese Army and his mother was a businesswoman in Saigon. When South Vietnam fell, his family immigrated to a large U.S. city with a substantial Asian population. He had many members of his extended family, including uncles, aunts, and grandparents living in his neighborhood.

Alex first began to feel different when he entered school. His dominant language was Vietnamese, and he was confused about the behaviors, values, and attitudes of his teachers and classmates. His feelings of differentness increased during his high school years when he became aware that he was sexually attracted to men rather than to women. He felt guilty and confused about these feelings. Although some uncles and aunts in his family were not married, the predominant emphasis in his home culture was to marry and to have a family.

Feelings of differentness became more acute when Alex went to college and discovered that he felt mismatched to the course of study his parents had encouraged him to choose—premed. He found his real interest was in social work. In college he developed some important homosexual relationships and had a live-in partner. Alex felt that he was living a double life and was uncomfortable about this. He was a junior and preparing to apply to graduate school in social work, yet his parents thought that he was applying to medical school and did not know about his sexual orientation.

Rose.   Rose grew up in a small predominantly Latino town in a rural area. She had always been the most independent child in her family of six, and she had been closer to her father than to her mother. Although Rose aspired to attend a university away from home, she gave in to family pressure and attended the community college in her hometown to get her associate's degree in child development. She worked as a teacher and assistant director of the local Head Start center. She had three children, but was not happy in her marriage. She was often physically and emotionally abused by her husband, a heavy drinker.

Rose's feelings of differentness began when she discovered that, unlike her siblings, she was independent and her ambitions extended to completing a four-year degree and law school. These feelings of differentness became even more intense when she started considering getting a divorce—something no one else in her family had done. These feelings intensified when she survived a tornado, which resulted in the loss of her vision. The Head Start center she worked for was holding a graduation ceremony when a tornado struck the town and leveled the school gymnasium. Several of her colleagues and children in her class and their parents died in the disaster. Rose was struck in the back of the head by a steel beam and lost her vision. She suffered a severe depression following the disaster. She felt guilty for surviving while others had died. With her loss of vision, she lost her job and her identity. She had to endure the anger of her husband, who told her she was now useless. It took great determination for her to make the decision to leave her children with relatives and to travel hundreds of miles to go to a rehabilitation center.

Harold.   Harold grew up in the suburban–modernistic world of the San Francisco Bay Area. His feelings of being different began when he started to compare himself to his older brother and when he tried to win his father's love and approval. His father and brother were well matched to each other; they were both competitive and interested in electronics. Harold, on the other hand, was cooperative in orientation, with interests in art and music.

Pressures to conform increased for Harold after his brother's death. To please and comfort his father, he changed his academic focus. His own personality prevailed, however, with his choice of a wife and with his attempts to establish a sense of community and leadership in his place of work. At home, however, he became more like his father—distant and uninvolved with his children.

Because he felt pressured by his wife and children to become more involved with them and more sensitive to their needs, Harold began to feel increasingly uncomfortable about neglecting his partners. When he came to therapy, he was confused, believing it was impossible to please all of the important people in his life. He also felt like a failure because, despite making what he considered to be superhuman efforts to please his father, he had not succeeded: The relationship between father and son was fraught with conflict and misunderstanding.

Tony.   Tony was born in Mexico and settled in a city in the southwestern United States when he was forty-one years old; he sought and was granted U.S. citizenship. He became disabled and had to retire at the age of sixty-two when the injuries he suffered in an automobile accident left him incapacitated and with severe muscle spasms resembling epileptic seizures. This is when his feelings of differentness and mismatch began. These feelings were exacerbated when his wife left him and when he was forced to deal with government agencies, institutions, and insurance companies to get the medical help and financial aid he needed to survive from day to day.

Wanda and Javier.   Wanda and Javier, an interracial couple, grew up in families and communities that were quite different from each other. Wanda had been reared in an urban, modernistic sociocultural environment. Her feelings of mismatch and differentness had begun in adolescence when she first realized that her father was an alcoholic. She did not feel that she could invite her friends over to her house, because she never knew when her father would be drunk. There was always tension between her parents, and she came to resent her mother for not leaving her father. Her friends didn't understand her father's varying moods—he would be friendly to the point of being intrusive when he had been drinking but irritable and distant when he was sober.

Javier grew up in a traditional, urban Latino cultural environment with emotional closeness in his extended family. Most of his relatives lived in his neighborhood, so there were frequent family get-togethers. Feelings of differentness and experiences with mismatch first began for Javier when he was bussed to a predominantly Caucasian middle school. He had done well academically and had been socially active in elementary school; in the new school, however, his grades suffered and he became withdrawn. There were few members of minority groups at the new school, and he was the only Latino in college-bound classes.

The Rosales.   In the Rosales family, feelings of mismatch for the individual members were related to different life circumstances. When Jesse was growing up in a medium-sized, semi-urban community with a very traditional Latino orientation, he felt different because he was emotionally closer to his mother than to his father. He was teased by his peers because he would prefer to stay at home rather than play in the neighborhood or hang out at the mall. Anna, on the other hand, felt mismatched because she was closer to her father than to her mother. She was good at sports and preferred playing traditional male games in the multiracial, bicultural neighborhood where she grew up. She preferred male to female friends and was ostracized by the girls in her neighborhood, who called her a tomboy.

Tati's experience with mismatch began when he started experiencing academic difficulties because of learning disabilities that surfaced in the second grade. He was also taller and more uncoordinated than most of his peers, so he did not do well at sports. When teams were chosen for sports on the school grounds or in his neighborhood, he was the last one chosen.

Nancy's mismatch surfaced when she was first made aware of her phenotype by her classmates. Her skin was darker than that of her brother, her parents, and most of her classmates. She became painfully aware of this difference when one of her friends asked her, "Are you adopted? You don't look like the others in your family."

Camilla and Her Daughters.   Camilla, a Latina woman, felt most different starting in about the fourth year of her marriage to Robert, an Anglo. She began to feel guilty about abandoning her goal of completing college. Robert felt different when Camilla became involved in community projects and social events in the Latino community where he was practically the only non-Latino in the group. Tracy and Lavis felt different when their parents divorced and the family's income dropped. They were no longer able to keep up with schoolmates in dress and extracurricular activities. They would also feel alienated at school events when parents were asked to participate and their friends would ask about their father.

SUMMARY

The mismatch syndrome—feelings of differentness, of depression, of not belonging or being accepted—is common in societies that stress conformity to certain ideals. Although women and members of minority groups have been the most frequent victims of this syndrome, in one way or another almost everyone has had this experience. How can therapists help the victims of conformity pressures? Developments in the psychology of differentness have introduced a new paradigm and models of personality and counseling based on the realities of adjustment to a pluralistic society. These new developments encourage multicultural development in an atmosphere of peace and cooperation.

2

EMERGENCE OF A PSYCHOLOGY OF DIFFERENTNESS AND PLURALISM

The Multicultural Person–Environment Fit Paradigm

The task facing the therapist trying to help a victim of the mismatch syndrome is a challenging one. This task is all the more difficult because mainstream theories and techniques of counseling and psychotherapy often ignore cultural and individual differences.

PSYCHOLOGY AND COLONIZATION

Although psychology began as the science of individual differences, it has, over the years, abandoned its original mission and become the science of the mean and of the mode. In the years since the publication of the first edition of this book, psychology in the United States has taken a decidedly biological perspective as more emphasis is being given to behavior genetics, neuropsychology, and evolutionary psychology. For the most part, the uniqueness of people has been forgotten while the emphasis moved to what the people in power have felt was the most desirable composite of personality or adjustment or on what was considered a standard of adjustment and health.

Because of the redefinition of its mission, psychology has been used by conformists and enculturationists to force those who are disenfranchised—the colonized, the recent immigrant, the poor—to become like the mythical ideal valued by those in power.

European Powers and Colonization

The colonization programs of France, England, Portugal, and Spain made use of psychological theories, concepts, and techniques. These programs reflected the colonizers' belief that their culture and lifestyle were superior to those of the colonized (Collins, 1954). Detribalization and the accompanying enculturation were essential to European colonizing efforts. The detribalization and enculturation efforts programs attempted to break up old loyalties and allegiances of the members of colonized populations to families, tribes, religions, regions, and countries.

The principal objective of these efforts was to replace old loyalties with a total allegiance to the culture and religion of the colonizer. The enculturation program adopted by the British government was particularly thorough. It involved sending members of the native populations to England, where they were taught English, trained in Christianity, instructed in British history, and introduced to British culture. After several years, these people were returned to their homelands to assist the British in the enculturation process. This emphasis on the use of psychology to ensure the success of colonization programs provided some of the early impetus for the development of cross-cultural psychology in Europe.

The colonization programs undertaken by European countries in general, and the application of psychological concepts to understanding the behavior of members of the colonized populations in particular, helped shape a worldview of those peoples whose cultures and lifestyles differed from those of the colonizers. This worldview has had a significant impact on the development of personality and clinical psychology, as well as of psychiatry, with respect to individual and cultural diversity.

The United States—From Inclusive to Exclusive Melting Pot

In the early history of the United States, there was an initial acceptance of individual and cultural differences. Conditions unique to the American continent produced changes in the class-bound institutions brought by British colonists. Institutions brought by immigrants from non-British homelands were similarly modified by the new environment. The evolution of institutions, which were uniquely American in an environment that was more accepting of cultural and individual diversity than Europe, inspired the French writer Crevecoeur (1904) to posit a new social theory: America as a melting pot. Crevecoeur conceived of the evolving U.S. society not as a slightly modified England, but as a totally new cultural and biological blend.

The genetic strains and folkways of Europe mixed indiscriminately in the political pot of the emerging nation and were fused by the fires of American influence and interaction into a distinctly new American personality. This inclusive version of the melting pot was transformed into a more exclusive version as more people from Eastern Europe, Asia, and Latin America began to immigrate into the United States.

What finally emerged was a forced conformity model. The major principles of this exclusive melting pot are best described in the words of E. P. Cubberly (1909), a leading American educator. Describing the new immigrants from Southern and Eastern Europe as illiterate, docile, and lacking in self-reliance and initiative, he identified the goals of the American public education system for immigrant parents and their children:

> ... Everywhere these people settle in groups or settlements, and ... set up their national manners, customs and observances. Our task is to break up these groups or settlements, to assimilate and amalgamate these people as part of our American race, and to implant in their children, as far as can be done, the Anglo-Saxon conception of righteousness, law and order and our popular government, and to awaken in them a reverence for our democratic institutions and for those things in our national life which we as a people hold to be of abiding worth (pp. 15–16).

Psychology as a Source of Tools for Enculturation and Conformism

Psychology became a prime source of tools for educators and mental health professionals who forced conformity on "the different." One of the major tools borrowed from psychology by conformists and enculturationists, and still widely used today, is the intelligence test. As Guthrie (1976) observed in his book *Even the Rat Was White*, tests of intellectual ability have been used by both psychologists and educators to try to prove that African Americans and Mexican Americans are intellectually inferior to European Americans, and that recent immigrants are of lower intelligence than mainstream Americans.

The first attempts to demonstrate that members of minority groups were intellectually inferior to Caucasians were encouraged by Terman, the psychologist who revised the original scales for assessing intelligence developed by Alfred Binet in France. Terman (1916) stated that mental retardation "represents the level of intelligence which is very, very common among Spanish-Indians and Mexican families of the Southwest and also among Negroes. Their dullness appears to be racial" (p. 92). In addition, Terman went on to predict that when future intelligence testing of the aforementioned groups is undertaken, "there will be discovered enormously significant racial differences which cannot be wiped out by any scheme of mental culture" (p. 92). More recently, in their book *The Bell Curve*, Herrnstein and Murray (1994) argue that the low intelligence of people of color burdens all of society (*dysgenesis*). The authors state, "Latino and black immigrants are, at least in the short run, putting some downward pressure on the distribution of intelligence" (pp. 360–361).

The effort to use measures of intelligence to push enculturation conformity and the ideas of cultural and racial superiority extended to the so-called "culture free" tests such as the Raven Progressive Matrices (Raven, Court, and Raven, 1986). Cohen (1969) and Ramirez and Castaneda (1974) observed that even these tests are biased in favor of learning and problem-solving styles that are more characteristic of the culture typical of the European American middle class.

Another tool borrowed from psychology and used extensively for encouraging enculturation and conformism was the psychoanalytic theory of personality. Psychoanalytic theory was used extensively by European powers to justify their programs of colonization. Mannoni (1960), a French psychoanalyst, published a paper on the psychology of colonization in which he concluded that colonization was made possible by an inherent need in subject populations to be dependent. He believed that this need for dependency was satisfied by the high degree of individualism and self-sufficiency characteristic of Europeans. In fact, Mannoni made it appear as though colonized populations were characterized by an unconscious desire for colonization: "Wherever Europeans have founded colonies of the type we are considering, it can be safely said that their coming was unconsciously expected—even desired—by the future subject peoples" (1960, p. 644).

Psychoanalytic theory has also been used to force conformity on women. The most widely used aspect of the theory was Freud's (1925) conceptualization of the sexual development of women that led him to conclude that women's superegos were not as highly developed as those of men and that women suffered from "penis envy" (Freud, 1961).

Still another tool borrowed from psychology by enculturationists and conformists was behavior-modification techniques and approaches. Going hand in hand with the misuse of behavior modification with "the different" is the misclassification of children, adolescents, and adults of minority groups (Malgady, Rogler, and Constantino, 1987) who are incorrectly diagnosed as having attention deficit disorder, conduct disorder, oppositional defiant disorder, or as having learning disabilities. A person so categorized is subjected to "behavior shaping" or "behavior management" programs that attempt to change behavior and to make it conform more closely to the mythical mode of the mainstream middle class.

These enculturation–conformity programs are being widely used in schools, prisons, mental hospitals, and institutions for the mentally retarded or disabled. In her book *Black Children: Their Roots, Culture, and Learning Styles*, Hale-Benson (1986) observed:

> The emphasis of traditional education has been upon molding and shaping Black children so that they can fit into an educational process designed for Anglo-Saxon middle-class children. We know that the system is not working because of the disproportionate number of Black children who are labeled hyperactive (p. 1).

In a similar vein, Snowden and Todman (1982) postulated:

> In assessing assertiveness, some of the variety encountered will have cultural origins. . . . Those evaluating assertiveness are prone to standardize their conceptions of situations and behaviors, making unwarranted uniformity assumptions. As cultural differences are only dimly understood, they may be particularly easy to overlook (p. 221).

ORIGINS OF THE PSYCHOLOGY OF DIFFERENCES

Despite the strong conformist and enculturation trends in the United States and Europe, voices of dissent began to make themselves heard in the early 1900s. A new psychology of differentness, of respect for individual and cultural differences, was being born.

Founders of the Psychology of Differentness

DuBois. The first pioneer in the development of the psychology of differentness was W.E.B. DuBois, an African American sociologist who did extensive research with African Americans in urban and rural areas of the United States in the late 1800s. DuBois was the first social scientist to promote the goal of multicultural orientations to life. In his book entitled *The Souls of Black Folk*—first published in 1903—DuBois, in referring to African Americans, said (1989 edition):

> One ever feels his two-ness—an American, a Negro; two souls, two thoughts, two unreconciled strivings. Two warring ideals in one dark body, whose dogged strength alone keeps it from being torn asunder. The history of the American Negro is the history of this strife—this longing to attain self-conscious manhood, to merge his double self into a better truer self (p. 3).

DuBois went on to observe:

> He would not Africanize America, for America has too much to teach the world and Africa. He would not bleach his Negro soul in a flood of White Americanism, for he knows the Negro blood has a message for the world. He simply wishes to make it possible for a man to be both a Negro and an American, without being cursed and spit upon by his fellows, without having the doors of opportunity closed roughly in his face (p. 3).

Thus, the research and writings of DuBois laid the foundation for a psychology of differentness and diversity.

Horney. Another early pioneer in the development of the psychology of differentness was Karen Horney, one of the first women psychoanalysts.

Horney's story is truly a profile in courage. She grew up in Germany, and although she was reared in a traditional Victorian family with an authoritarian father, she succeeded in overcoming the conventions of her time by going to medical school and becoming an independent thinker. She emigrated to the United States in the 1940s and worked with many female patients whose problems centered around oppression in a sexist society. Her own personal experiences, along with what she learned from her patients, led her to conclude that Freud's emphasis on penis envy in the dynamics of women's sexuality was inaccurate.

She also discovered that the biological orientation of Freud's theory ignored important cultural realities: the powerless position of most women in society and the central role of culture in personality dynamics. Horney (1937) wrote:

> One can diagnose a broken leg without knowing the cultural background of the patient, but one would run a great risk in calling an Indian psychotic because he told us that he had visions in which he believed. In the particular culture of these Indians the experience of visions and hallucinations is regarded as a special gift, a blessing from the spirits (pp. 14–15).

Sanchez. George I. Sanchez, a Latino psychologist and educator, was another early contributor to the psychology of differentness. Born and reared in northern New Mexico, he received his doctorate from the University of California at Berkeley. Criticizing efforts by Caucasian psychologists and educators to prove that Latino and African American children were intellectually inferior to white children, Sanchez (1932) asserted that racial and ethnic superiority could not be claimed. In a review of the literature, he showed intellectual testing indicated that environmental and linguistic factors were related significantly to performance on intelligence tests.

Sanchez objected to those who would simply translate a test from English into Spanish and expect it to accurately assess the intelligence of bilingual children. He repeatedly pointed out that the validity of any test was limited to the normative sample on which it was based. Sanchez also claimed that data on genetics and heredity were being garbled in order to champion the superiority of one group over others. He directed his efforts against those who blindly accepted the doctrine of genetic superiority while disregarding the importance of such fundamental factors as personal, social, economic, and environmental differences and their effects on intellectual assessment.

Sanchez's views were supported by the research findings of an African American educator, Horace Mann Bond. In a classic research study, Bond (1927) selected African American children from the professional and the middle classes rather than from the laboring class, the favored source of subjects for Caucasian psychologists. Using the Stanford Binet Test, he showed that 63 percent of the African American children achieved scores above 106; 47 percent had intelligence scores equal to or exceeding 122; and 26 percent had scores of over 130. Bond concluded that these children "were not out of the ordinary . . . the same sort of group could be selected in any Negro community" (p. 257) provided that the sociocultural backgrounds of the subjects were similar to the one he tested.

Fanon. The African Martiniquean psychiatrist Franz Fanon was another pioneer in the differentness movement in psychology. He emphasized the importance of sociocultural realities and especially the influence of racism and oppression in the personality development of colonized peoples (Bulhan, 1985). Fanon criticized the psychoanalytic theories of Freud, Jung, and Adler for their Eurocentric orientation. In his book *Black Skins: White Masks,* Fanon (1967) rejected Freud's ontogenetic perspective and Jung's phylogenetic speculations: "It will be seen that the black man's alienation is not an individual question. Beside phylogeny and ontogeny stands sociogeny" (p. 13). He also rejected the notion of the Oedipus Complex and sought to explain personality dynamics in terms of sociohistorical and cultural realities.

Fanon rejected Freud's argument that neurosis was an inescapable consequence of all cultures. He instead saw neurosis as the expression of a given culture: "Even neurosis, every abnormal manifestation, every affective erethism . . . is the product of the cultural situation" (p. 152).

NEW WORLDVIEW OF MENTAL HEALTH AND PSYCHOLOGICAL ADJUSTMENT

In the 1960s and 1970s, new developments in psychology began to incorporate the ideas of DuBois, Horney, Fanon, and Sanchez. One of these movements was the development of community psychology as a legitimate area of study within psychology. Community psychology, seen as a true "psychology of the Americas" (Ramirez, 1998), reflected the unique ideology emerging from the experiences specific to peoples of the Americas. This ideology was reflected in the melting-pot philosophy in the United States and that of the *Mestizo*—the cultural and genetic mixture of Native Americans and Europeans in Mexico and other regions of Latin America.

Specifically, community psychology had its roots in the community mental health movement and in applied sociology. One of the major contributions of community psychology to the psychology of differentness was what Julian Rappaport (1977) referred to as the paradigm of *person–environment fit*, rather than of incompetent or inferior people, or inferior psychological or cultural environments.

The major impact of this new paradigm on psychology was most felt in Latin America (Ardila, 1986; Ramirez, 1998), where psychologists began to turn to their own cultures and to the experiences of their own countries and peoples to develop new approaches to psychological research and intervention, as well as new conceptual frameworks for interpreting the data they collected.

The earliest developments in the psychology of differentness came in the area of women's psychology in the United States. The Civil Rights Movement of the 1960s provided the impetus for the development of ethnic psychologies, as well as a psychology of women based on the writings of W.E.B. DuBois, Karen Horney, Franz Fanon, and George Sanchez. These perspectives were true psychologies of the Americas. These new approaches disclaimed the emphasis on universals in psychology, instead looking to the importance both of sociocultural environments and the effects of minority status and oppression on personality development and functioning. They emphasized values as reflected in socialization practices and examined how these values affected personality development.

In addition, there was an emphasis on how oppression and minority status were related to the development of pathology and problems of identity. In the case of women, the emphasis was on development of self-in-relation—that is, the conflict between attachment and separation because of the way in which women are socialized and because of expectations placed on them by society.

These movements in psychology led to a new paradigm that now guides the work of the psychology of differentness—the multicultural person–environment fit paradigm. This paradigm represents an extension and amplification of the person–environment paradigm. It assumes that it is important to synthesize and amalgamate diversity to arrive at multicultural identities and perspectives on life and to new approaches to solutions of problems. These new outlooks can lead to understanding among different peoples and groups—the basis of peace and cooperation.

CHARACTERISTICS OF THE MULTICULTURAL PERSON–ENVIRONMENT FIT WORLDVIEW

The multicultural person–environment fit worldview is based on a number of assumptions, as follows:

- There are no inferior peoples, cultures, or groups in terms of gender, ethnicity, race, economics, religion, disabilities, region, sexual orientation, or language.
- Problems of maladjustment are not the result of inferior peoples or groups, but rather of a mismatch between people, or between people and their environments.
- Every individual, group, or culture has positive contributions to make to personality development and to a healthy adjustment to life.

- People who are willing to learn from others and from groups and cultures different from their own acquire multicultural *building blocks* (coping techniques and perspectives) that are the basis of multicultural personality development and multicultural identity.
- The synthesis and amalgamation of personality building blocks acquired from different peoples, groups, and cultures occur when the person with multicultural potential works toward the goals of understanding and cooperation among diverse groups and peoples in a pluralistic society.
- The synthesis and amalgamation of personality building blocks from diverse origins result in the development of a multicultural personality and in psychological adjustment in a pluralistic society.

SUMMARY

The struggle against the idea that some cultures, groups, or peoples are superior to others has led to the development of the multicultural person–environment fit worldview. In recent years, a model of psychotherapy and counseling based on this new paradigm has begun to evolve. This new model not only helps the victims of mismatch, but it also empowers them to help create a better world—a world in which individual and cultural differences will be respected and in which pluralism will be viewed as a resource for the development of mutual understanding, cooperation, and self-actualization.

3

THE COGNITIVE
AND CULTURAL THEORY
OF PERSONALITY

In her book *Neurosis and Human Growth*, Karen Horney (1950), the psycho-analyst and pioneer feminist psychologist, introduced the idea that a person becomes neurotic because of his or her attempts to live up to the *tyranny of the shoulds*. That is, the neurotic person develops a self-image based on what others would like him or her to be, an idealized image, instead of developing a "true self." The person becomes neurotic, developing a false self based on the shoulds of parents, societal institutions, and important others. This false self is an idealized image that forces the person to conform to certain imposed idealized standards and results in the disavowal and suppression of the true or real self.

The "different" in society are most vulnerable to the tyranny of the shoulds because it is they who are most often targets of conformity and assimilation pressures. The autobiography of Richard Rodriguez (1983), *Hunger of Memory*, is a good example of how the tyranny of the shoulds works. Rodriguez tells a story of when he was in elementary school in Sacramento, California. The primary language of his family was Spanish, and he struggled in school because he did not know English very well. One day his teachers visited his parents and implied that if they wanted Richard to succeed in school, they would have to start speaking English at home. Convinced of the validity of this, his parents began speaking to Richard only in English. However, they continued to communicate with each other in Spanish. The change resulted in academic success for Richard at the price of his psychological disorientation and emotional alienation from his family. He remembered that, "once I spoke English with ease, I came to feel guilty. I felt that I had shattered the intimate bond that once held the family close" (p. 30).

SCHOOLS AND CONFORMITY

For the "different" the strongest agents of conformity in society are often the schools. In their book *Cultural Democracy, Bicognitive Development and Education*, Ramirez and Castaneda (1974) argued that schools force conformity onto children of minority groups through their assimilationist philosophies and predominant orientation, a Caucasican, middle-class teaching style, and curriculum content. The message of the schools to minority children is very much like that given to Richard Rodriguez: If you want to succeed, you must reject your true self and be like us.

But the pressures to assimilate and to conform are not restricted to members of minority groups. Anyone whose personality, lifestyle, gender, value system, or physical characteristics makes her different from the majority becomes the target of the assimilation and conformity pressures of society—the tyranny of the shoulds. A newspaper feature article entitled "Being Different Can Be Difficult in the Classroom" makes a strong case for the conformist trends in many schools. The article quotes Tom Yamokoski, a psychologist, who observed: "The school system is absolutely not designed for creativity. Quietness, going with the flow, keeping order—that is encouraged. It's tough to find a school system that encourages not being the same" (Austin, TX, *American Statesman*, May 25, 1997, p. E11).

CULTURES, COMMUNITIES, FAMILIES, AND THE UNIQUE SELF

In *Cultural Democracy, Bicognitive Development and Education*, Ramirez and Castaneda (1974) pointed out that people have unique intellectual strengths, abilities, and skills. Additionally, people develop learning and problem-solving styles to reflect the values and belief systems of the culture, community, and family in which they are reared. For example, Stodolsky and Lesser (1967) compared children of different ethnic groups on intellectual skills, finding that Chinese American children did better at problems involving spatial skills. Jewish American children, on the other hand, did better at tasks and problems requiring verbal ability.

Ramirez and Castaneda (1974) proposed that, in order to ensure respect for the intellectual strengths and styles of learning of all children, schools need to adopt a philosophy of cultural democracy as well as teaching styles and approaches to accommodate individual and cultural differences in learning styles. The authors defined cultural democracy and the teaching–learning and cultural styles match as follows:

1. *Including an educational philosophy of cultural democracy.* The opposite of assimilation, cultural democracy encourages schools to respect cultural,

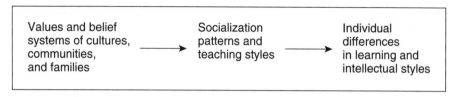

| Values and belief systems of cultures, communities, and families | Socialization patterns and teaching styles | Individual differences in learning and intellectual styles |

FIGURE 3.1 Relationship between values and personality

community, family, and individual differences in values and lifestyles. Values influence socialization and teaching styles, which in turn affect the development of certain learning and problem-solving styles. Figure 3.1 summarizes the relationships between sociocultural systems and individual differences in intellectual styles.

2. *Matching the teaching style with the cultural style.* Teaching styles and styles of curriculum and testing are tailored to match the cultural styles of the students. Students and teachers are encouraged to develop multicultural orientations to life in a pluralistic learning environment.

3. *Matching the teaching style with the learning style.* Teaching styles and styles of curriculum and testing are tailored to match the individual learning and problem-solving styles of the students. To achieve this, individual students and school personnel are encouraged to become flexible in their intellectual styles by learning unfamiliar teaching and learning styles in a supportive and accepting educational environment.

THE LINK BETWEEN CULTURAL AND COGNITIVE STYLES

Cultural Styles

Ramirez and Castaneda (1974) proposed that cultures, communities, and families can be classified on a traditionalism–modernism continuum with respect to their cultural styles. Modern lifestyles and belief systems encourage separation from family and community early in life. Modern orientations to socialization emphasize individual competition and give science great importance in explaining the mysteries of life. Traditional lifestyles, on the other hand, emphasize close ties to family and community throughout life. Traditional orientations emphasize cooperation and give spiritualism a greater importance in explaining life events. The following list describes thirteen domains within the traditionalism–modernism dimension.

1. *Gender-role definition.* Traditional environments tend to emphasize strict distinctions between gender roles, whereas modern environments encourage more flexible boundaries between these roles.

2. *Family identity.* Family loyalty and identification are emphasized in traditional communities while individual identities are more valued in modern societies.

3. *Sense of community.* Traditional cultural styles encourage a strong sense of community while modern environments emphasize individualism.

4. *Time orientation.* People reared in traditional communities have a stronger past- and present-time orientation while people who are more modernistic are oriented toward the future.

5. *Age status.* Traditional societies associate increasing age with increasing wisdom, whereas modern societies value the vitality of youth.

6. *Importance of tradition.* Traditional environments value traditional ceremonies as a reinforcement of history, whereas modern value orientations tend to view tradition as a potential barrier to progress.

7. *Subservience to convention and authority.* In traditional societies, people are socialized to follow norms and conventions and to respect authority; in modern societies people are encouraged to question authority.

8. *Spirituality and religion.* Traditional societies emphasize the importance of spirituality and religion in life events; modern societies are characterized by an emphasis on science and secularism.

9. *Sexual orientation.* Traditional societies generally accept a literal interpretation of the Bible concerning sexual orientation and family; modern societies are more likely to view decisions about sexual orientation as part of the individual's right to chose her own lifestyle. Also definitions of what constitutes a family are less conventional.

10. *Death penalty.* Traditional values usually uphold the belief of "an eye for an eye" when it comes to meting out punishment for major crimes. The view is that the person who is believed to have committed the crime is completely responsible for his actions. Modern cultures view the death penalty as a barbaric practice. For most crimes, the view is that circumstances, such as reduced mental capacity, the influence of addictive substances, limited opportunity in society, and abuse in childhood, need to be taken into consideration when decisions about punishment are made. Rehabilitation is emphasized over payment of a debt to society.

11. *Role of the federal government in education.* Traditional belief systems usually emphasize local control over the schools, while modern values emphasize the importance of meeting national standards in educational opportunities.

12. *Benefits to single mothers and noncitizens.* A traditional belief system emphasizes that single mothers, particularly those who are not U.S. citizens, and their children should not be eligible for economic aid because this is likely to encourage sexual behavior outside of marriage. Modern belief systems view some single mothers as likely victims of sexual abuse and rape and see payment of benefits as a way to prevent criminal behavior and addiction.

13. *Abortion.* Traditional societies view termination of pregnancy as a crime, as interference with the right to life. Modern societies view abortion decisions as part and parcel of a woman's right to decide what happens to her own body.

Even though rural environments are most commonly associated with traditional cultural orientations and urban lifestyles usually reflect modernistic orientations to life (Panday and Panday, 1985; *see also* Tharakan, 1987), research (Ramirez, 1987) has shown that some people who live in urban environments tend to adhere to traditional values and, similarly, that there are residents of rural areas who tend to be modernistic in their cultural styles.

Cognitive Styles

The hypothesized relationship between values and cognitive styles is summarized in Figure 3.2. Ramirez, Cox, and Castaneda (1977) identified the following learning behaviors as characteristic of children who tended to be field sensitive or field independent These are clustered into four categories, as shown in Table 3.1.

Additional research on the relationship of sociocultural environments to intellectual styles in children and college students led Ramirez and his colleagues (1977) to expand the theory of learning styles *flex* (the ability to switch styles to conform to environmental demands) to include other characteristics of personality. They posited that a person's unique self is made up of much more than just learning and intellectual styles.

They were able to show that field independent and field sensitive styles are also reflected in the ways in which people communicate and relate to others; in the rewards that motivate them; and in the manner in which they teach, parent, supervise, and counsel others, as outlined in Table 3.1. The behaviors that differentiate field sensitive from field independent personality styles are listed in Table 3.2.

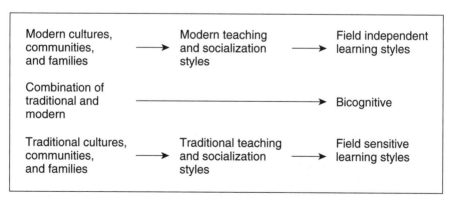

FIGURE 3.2   Relationship between values and cognitive styles

TABLE 3.1 Characteristics of Field Sensitive and Field Independent Children

Domain	Field Sensitive	Field Independent
Relationship to Peers	1. Likes to work with others to achieve common goals 2. Likes to assist others 3. Is sensitive to feelings and opinions of others	1. Prefers to work independently 2. Likes to compete and gain individual recognition 3. Task-oriented; is inattentive to social environment when working
Relationship to Teacher	1. Openly expresses positive feelings for teacher 2. Asks questions about teacher's taste and personal experiences; seeks to become like teacher	1. Avoids physical contact with teacher 2. Interacts formally with teacher; restricts interactions to tasks at hand
Instructional Relationship to Teacher	1. Seeks guidance and demonstration from teacher 2. Seeks rewards that strengthen relationship with teacher 3. Is highly motivated by working individually with teacher	1. Likes to try new tasks without teacher's help 2. Impatient to begin tasks; likes to finish first 3. Seeks nonsocial rewards
Thinking Style	1. Functions well when objectives are carefully explained or modeled 2. Deals well with concepts in humanized or story format 3. Functions well when curriculum content is relevant to personal interests and experiences	1. Focuses on details and parts of things 2. Deals well with math and science concepts 3. Likes discovery or trial-and-error learning

Ramirez, Castaneda, and their colleagues (Ramirez, Cox, and Castaneda, 1977) discovered that the personalities of most individuals are a unique combination of field independent and field sensitive elements. Nevertheless, each person seems to have a definite preference for one style or

TABLE 3.2   Personality Characteristics of Field Sensitive and Field Independent People

Domain	Field Sensitive	Field Independent
Communications	1. Tends to personalize communications by referring to own life experiences, interests, and feelings 2. Tends to focus more on nonverbal than verbal communications	1. Tends to be impersonal and to-the-point in communications 2. Tends to focus more on verbal than nonverbal communications
Interpersonal Relationships	1. Open and outgoing in social settings 2. Presents as warm and informal	1. Reserved and cautious in social settings 2. Presents as distant and formal
Motivation	1. Values social rewards that strengthen relationships with important others 2. Motivation is related to achievement for others (family, team, ethnic/racial group, etc.)	1. Seeks nonsocial rewards 2. Motivation is related to self-advancement
Teaching, Parenting, Supervisory, and Counseling Relationships	1. Focuses on relations with student, child, supervisor, or client 2. Is informal and self-disclosing	1. Focuses on task or goal 2. Is formal and private

the other. Style preference at any given time was often dependent on the type of demands made by the setting or task. For example, a person might be preferred field sensitive in a learning or problem-solving situation, but be preferred field independent in a social setting.

Research revealed (Ramirez, 1998), however, that successful children and college students tended to be more flexible in their styles as compared with their less successful peers. It was also discovered that the more successful students were flexible in both the cultural and cognitive domains; that is, these children, adolescents, and young adults could shuttle between different cognitive and cultural styles.

Life history and family and community research (Ramirez, Cox, and Castaneda, 1977; Ramirez, 1987) with students having different degrees of flex showed that those subjects who were the most flexible had been influenced by cultures, communities, and families whose lifestyles and institutions represented a mixture of traditional and modern values (see Figure 3.2). It was also discovered that in certain families, evidence of the ability to flex can be found in members of different generations (Buriel, 1981). A strong possibility exists, then, that propensity for flex is inherited.

Personality Flex

Research focusing on personality flex led to the identification of its three components: (1) the degree of development of the major cognitive (field sensitive or field independent) and cultural (traditional or modern) styles, (2) the ability to shuttle between the major styles within the cognitive and cultural domains, and (3) the ability to combine these major cognitive and cultural styles to develop multicultural cognitive (combination of field independent and field sensitive) and cultural (combination of traditional and modern) styles. All three characteristics of flex were found to be important in determining coping effectiveness: People who were found to be well developed in only one of the two cognitive and cultural styles were not as effective in coping as those who were able to shuttle between the two styles or to combine the major cultural and cognitive styles to arrive at new multicultural combinations.

Cognitive Flex

Ramirez and Castaneda (1974) identified three components of cognitive flex or bicognition: (1) the maximum development of all domains of field sensitive and field independent cognitive styles, (2) the ability to shuttle between the field sensitive and field independent styles to meet different environmental demands, and (3) the ability to combine elements of both field sensitive and field independent styles to develop new multicultural cognitive styles.

To assess the degree of cognitive flex, Ramirez and Castaneda (1974) developed observation instruments and personality inventories that assessed bicognition. These instruments, briefly described in the following paragraphs, are presented in their entirety in the appendices. The cognitive styles Behavioral Observation Instrument is an observational rating scale that lists field independent and field sensitive behaviors in these five domains:

1. Communications
2. Interpersonal relationships
3. Motivation
4. Teaching, parenting, supervising, and counseling
5. Learning and problem solving

Cognitive flex is defined by both degree and type. Degree can be assessed by examining behavioral ratings, which indicate how developed a person is in both of the styles—the degree of balance within the five domains listed here. Type of flex is determined in two ways: (1) the extent to which a person can combine behaviors that are characteristic of each of the styles to develop multicultural coping techniques (a composite of elements of both styles), and (2) the extent to which a person can use field sensitive and field independent behaviors in different domains. (For example, the person is competitive in a setting in which individual competition is emphasized, such as testing, and is cooperative in situations where working with others to achieve a common goal is required.

The Bicognitive Orientation to Life Scale (BOLS) is a personality inventory composed of items that reflect the degree of preference for field sensitive or field independent cognitive styles in different life domains. Cognitive flex is assessed by determining the degree of agreement (from Strongly Disagree to Strongly Agree) with items that reflect preference for either field independent or field sensitive cognitive styles. For example:

1. I have always done well in math and science courses. (field independent)
2. I have always done well in social science and history courses. (field sensitive)

Flex is also determined by arriving at a balance score, obtained by adding points (Agree = 1, Strongly Agree = 2, Disagree = −1, and Strongly Disagree = −2), and examining the difference between total field independent and field sensitive scores.

The type of flex is assessed by examining the life domains (family, education, world of work, and so on) in which agreement between field independent and field sensitive items is equally strong. The extent to which field sensitive and field independent characteristics are combined to develop new styles of coping cannot be assessed with the BOLS.

Cultural Flex

Ramirez and Castaneda (1974) identified the following four components of cultural flexibility:

1. Subscribing to values and belief systems that are representative of both traditional and modern cultures, groups, and families.
2. Being able to shuttle between traditional and modern groups and situations or activities.
3. Being able to combine traditional and modern values and belief systems to evolve new multicultural styles.
4. Feeling identified with both traditional and modern families, cultures, and institutions.

Three approaches have been developed to assess cultural flex: the Traditionalism–Modernism Inventory, the Multicultural Experience Inventory, and a Life History Interview Schedule.

The Traditionalism–Modernism Inventory, developed by Ramirez and Doell (1982), is a personality inventory that assesses the degree of identification with traditional and modern values and belief systems. The instrument yields scores indicating the degree of agreement with items reflecting traditionalism or modernism, as with the BOLS. The degree of flex can be determined by examining the difference between the total traditionalism and total modernism scores, as well as by looking at the degree of agreement with the traditional and modern items in the different domains of life (family, gender roles, time orientation, and so on). Type of flex can be assessed by examining the degree of flex within each domain. For example, a person whose personality is characterized by cultural flex in the child socialization domain could express that with both of these items:

1. Children should be taught to be loyal to their families. (traditional)
2. Children should be taught to be independent of their families at an early age. (modern)

The Multicultural Experience Inventory (Ramirez, 1983) is a questionnaire that focuses on personal history and behavior in three areas: (1) demographic and linguistic, (2) socialization history, and (3) degree of multicultural participation in the past as well as in the present. The degree of cultural flex is determined by the extent to which a person has been exposed to certain languages and value systems and the degree to which the person has participated in and is actively participating in and interacting with people of different cultures and groups in his or her social environment.

The Life History Schedule focuses on development and expressions of cultural flex in different periods of life, as well as on the extent of actual participation in both traditional and modern families, cultures, groups, and institutions. In addition, the Life History instrument also identifies the type of cultural flex by examining the degree to which a person has been able to combine modern and traditional values and belief systems to arrive at multicultural values and worldviews.

A COGNITIVE AND CULTURAL FLEX THEORY OF PERSONALITY

Life history research (Ramirez et al., 1978) with people who scored high in both the cultural and cognitive flex domains led to the finding that socialization and life experiences were related to the development of personality flex. Socialization and life experiences are two subcomponents of life history. Information on socialization history obtained from life histories of people who scored high in cognitive and cultural flex showed that, as compared with those with low scores, they had had parents and other socialization agents (teachers, employers, coaches, peers, and neighbors) whose attitudes toward diversity had been positive.

Not only did their socialization agents tend to hold positive attitudes toward diversity, the origins of those with high scores also reflected diversity:

They were members of different ethnic, racial, religious, regional, and socioeconomic groups. In terms of the life-experiences component of their personal history, what seemed to be most important was the degree of exposure to diversity challenges. That is, situations in which the person had to learn a new language; a new way of relating to others; or a new way of solving a problem because the language, relationship style, or problem-solving approach to which they were accustomed was not effective in a new setting (Ramirez, 1983).

The people who were the most flexible were those who had lived in many different cultures, communities, or regions and had attended schools with a diverse student body and staff. In addition, the number and type of positive or negative experiences with diversity seemed to play an important role in the development of flexibility. For example, a person who had always been accepted by others different from herself tended to show more flex development than a person who had been rejected or discriminated against.

History also appeared to have a direct relationship to the second major component in flex development—motivation. Life-history data (Ramirez, Cox, and Castaneda, 1977) showed that both the degree of attraction to diversity and the degree of openness of the person's learning–experience filter were critical subcomponents of motivation. That is, people who were the most flexible also seemed to be those who were the most attracted to diversity, as well as those who were the most willing to learn from diversity when exposed to it.

Motivation appeared to be reflected in a person's degree of willingness to take risks in diversity challenges. The person whose early history had provided him with positive attitudes toward diversity, and with a basic foundation for multicultural development, was also the one most likely to seek diversity challenges and to benefit from these experiences.

The third major component in the development of flexibility concerned the nature of the pool of resources available for personality development and for coping with the demands of life. This reservoir of resources could vary both in size and in degree of heterogeneity and diversity—the ethnic, racial, religious, age-related, regional, and socioeconomic mix. The more experience individuals had had with different peoples, cultures, groups, communities, and families, and the greater the variety of diversity challenges they had taken, the greater the size and heterogeneity of their personality resource pool.

The fourth major component of the flex theory of personality concerned multicultural patterns of behavior. That is, once a person had a heterogeneous mix of personality resources in her repertoire, she was able to behave like a multicultural person—to flex culturally and cognitively (Garza et al., 1982). In the early phases of development, personality-building elements and resources in the individual's repertoire are exclusively linked to the cultural, socioeconomic, sexual, racial, religious, political, and geographic contexts in which they were learned. Therefore, adaptation to new cultural

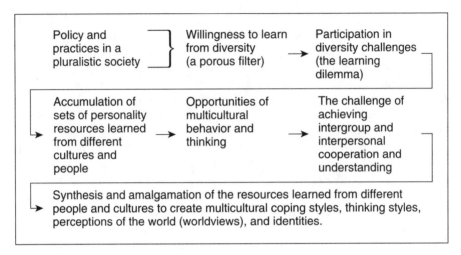

FIGURE 3.3   **Model of multicultural personality development**

environments and situations is an important precursor to the development of multicultural lifestyles and identities.

This sort of challenge encourages the individual to reorganize and synthesize the resources and elements in her repertoire so that efforts to adapt involve the formation of combinations of resources and elements learned from different cultures, environments, and peoples. The resultant coping techniques and orientation to life are pluralistic. For example, to achieve consensus in a group whose members are diverse, the leader must arrive at a pluralistic perspective of the problems that is representative of the diversity that exists in the group (Garza et al., 1982).

The fifth and final component of the flex theory is the development of multicultural identities. Being exposed to diversity and challenges for multicultural adaptation, a person continuously modifies both her self-picture and philosophy of life. Eventually, the person makes a definite commitment to growth by continuing to seek such challenges (Adler, 1974; Ramirez, 1998). It is at this point that people begin to develop a multicultural identity. That is, they express a strong, lifelong commitment to the well-being of all peoples, cultures, and groups (Ramirez, 1983). Figure 3.3 summarizes this process.

SUMMARY

The critical concepts of the cultural and cognitive flex theory of personality are traditional and modern cultural styles and field sensitive, field independent, and bicognitive styles of cognition. These concepts are useful in understanding multicultural personality development and functioning.

4

CULTURAL AND COGNITIVE MATCH AND MISMATCH IN PSYCHOLOGICAL ADJUSTMENT

The flex theory of personality looks to the levels of match and mismatch between individuals and their environments to explain problems of maladjustment. In the flex theory of personality, match and mismatch are assessed in two domains: cognitive and cultural.

Both of these domains have several subdomains, or areas. It is possible for a person to be well matched in certain subdomains while mismatched in others. A person can, for example, be well matched to peers in communication and interpersonal relationship styles but, at the same time, be mismatched in learning and problem-solving styles. A couple can be well matched in personal relations styles, yet mismatched with respect to communication styles. Similarly, members of a family can be matched in motivational styles, but mismatched in their teaching and learning styles. In fact, some members of the same family can be matched with respect to cultural and/or cognitive styles, yet mismatched to other members, resulting in alliances that are manifested in family conflicts and in the lack of effective communication. Frequently, one parent and one or more of the children who are well matched develop alliances against the other parent and mismatched children (see Chapter 12).

Examining some of the case histories introduced in Chapter 1 in more detail will help to demonstrate how the flex theory of personality can be used to assess the degree of psychological adjustment in degrees of match and mismatch in the cognitive and cultural domains of a person's life.

CASE HISTORIES

The specific focus of this chapter is on trying to understand the problems of adjustment that developed for Imelda, Harold, Raul, Tara, and Alex. The following information was obtained from life history interviews done with the individual clients. (The life history approach is discussed in detail in Chapter 7.) Although the principal focus of this book is on cultural and cognitive factors of maladjustment, general clinical considerations for each case are included to show that these were also of vital importance in the assessment of the clients.

Imelda

Background. Imelda was born and reared in a rural community located in the U.S.–Mexico border region of Texas. She was an only child. Her father, an accountant, and her mother, a homemaker, divorced when she was two years old. Following the divorce, Imelda's mother moved to a city in the northern part of Texas. Imelda and her father moved in with his parents.

When Imelda was twelve years old, her father remarried and the three of them moved to a house located next door to Imelda's grandparents. Imelda was shuttled between the two residences. Two years later, when she was fourteen, Imelda's half sister Claudia was born. As her half sister grew, Imelda began having conflicts with her stepmother. Imelda claimed that Claudia was spoiled and that the child would do things to aggravate her. Whenever she called the child's transgressions to the attention of her stepmother, Imelda and she would argue. Imelda's perception was that her father would side with his wife against her. Gradually, Imelda became increasingly alienated from her parents and started to spend more and more time at her grandparents' home.

Imelda's grades plunged after her father remarried. Her teachers reported that she acted out in class. Her only solace was sports and her relationship with Robert, her boyfriend. Her interests in sports, however, caused conflicts with her grandparents and most of her peers who felt that her activities were not proper for a girl. Her relationship with her boyfriend had started when she was fifteen. Her boyfriend's parents did not approve of the relationship because of Imelda's interest in sports and because she came from a broken home.

Imelda and Robert got along well because they both felt alienated from their teachers and their parents. However, after much pressure from his parents, Robert succumbed to their wishes and reluctantly broke off the relationship with Imelda. This precipitated Imelda's attempt on her life.

Imelda was socialized in a very traditional Mexican American community. After the divorce of her parents, she was socialized primarily by her grandparents, who strongly identified with traditional Hispanic culture. This culture encourages separation of gender roles and strict obedience to parents and other authority figures. This type of cultural and familial setting tends to encourage the development of a preferred field sensitive cognitive style in female children.

Imelda's father's chosen profession—accounting—requires analytical thinking and great attention to detail. This indicates that his preferred cognitive style is probably field independent, or bicognitive with a preference for field independence. In the elementary grades, Imelda's teachers had used field sensitive teaching styles and had encouraged cooperation and a sense of community. When she began junior high school, however, Imelda encountered a decided shift in teaching style toward field independence. This style had a pronounced emphasis on individual competition and on analytical thinking.

Imelda's relationships with her father, stepmother, and teachers were fraught with conflict. Her relationship with her natural mother seemed to be better than that with her father and stepmother, but the two rarely visited or telephoned each other. As Imelda became more involved in sports, her relationship with her grandparents began to deteriorate. Her only supportive relationship was with Robert, who, like Imelda, seemed to be preferred field sensitive in cognitive style. Robert was also supportive of Imelda's interest in sports. Imelda often said, "Everyone but Robert seems to be against me. They're always criticizing me and trying to force me to live like they do. Why don't they accept me as I am instead of trying to change me?"

Symptoms.   Imelda exhibited alienation from parents, teachers, and grandparents. She invested most of her time and energy in her relationship with her boyfriend at the expense of peer relationships.

General Clinical Considerations.   Imelda should be evaluated for appropriateness of antidepressant medication. It should also be considered that her attempt on her life places her at risk for future suicidal behavior.

Analysis of Cultural Style Mismatch

Imelda was modernistic in terms of gender roles as related to sports and in challenging the authority of teachers. She was traditional with respect to cultural loyalty and religion.	Imelda's parents and grandparents and Robert's parents were traditional with respect to gender roles. Imelda's teachers were traditional with respect to expecting subservience to authority.

Analysis of Cognitive Style Mismatch

Imelda was preferred field sensitive style.	Her grandparents were more field sensitive and less bicognitive than Imelda was.
	Her father's and teachers' styles were preferred field independent.

Harold

Background. Harold was born and reared in an upper middle-class, sub-urban community in the San Francisco Bay Area. Frank, a brother who was two years older than Harold, died when Harold was sixteen. Harold's father was an engineer and an executive with a major computer electronics firm in the Silicon Valley. Harold's mother taught elementary school.

Throughout childhood and early adolescence, Harold developed strong interests in art and music. He was closer to his mother during these years, and she encouraged his interests, providing solace from the constant frustration Harold felt because his father seemed to prefer his older brother.

Harold's father and Frank both had strong interests in sports, fishing, building model airplanes, and working with audio and television equipment. Harold had done his best to impress his father with his achievements in photography, painting, and music; his father did not seem to appreciate these things.

When Frank died in an automobile accident, Harold renewed his efforts to win his father's love and approval by trying to fill the gap Frank had left. Harold abandoned his old interests, becoming more involved in sports and working harder at doing well in math and science. Harold's shift in interests did bring him closer to his father, but he never succeeded in developing the close relationship he longed for. To compensate for this, he vowed to prove to his father that he could be successful in business, something his father had always wanted for Frank.

When Harold went to college, he majored in engineering and computer science. When he was at the university, he met Jan, whom he later married. Jan had been reared in a mid-sized southern city. Her large family had close ties. Jan's major in college was art history. Through her, Harold could maintain a vicarious interest in art and music. While in college Harold also met the two friends who would later become his partners. The three of them worked at the same computer and electronics firm as Harold's father did for four years before they decided to establish a software company of their own.

Because the startup of the new company was so demanding of Harold's time and energy, he made an informal agreement with Jan: If she would agree to give up her career temporarily and do most of the parenting of their two children, he would assume most of the family responsibilities once the company was on solid footing. Jan could then return to her career with Harold's full support. When Harold sought therapy, four years had passed since he had made his pact with Jan, and by then the company was successful, with two branch offices in Southern California.

Socialization and Life Experiences. Harold was socialized in a modernistic community, but his home included both traditional and modern values. Harold's father was traditional in terms of rigidly defined gender roles, yet

Harold's mother had a career, albeit one that was gender appropriate in terms of traditional cultural values.

Harold's father had a preferred field independent cognitive style, as reflected by his interests in electronics and engineering. His mother, a music major in college and an elementary school music and art teacher, had a preferred field sensitive cognitive style. Thus, Harold was exposed to both cognitive styles and to both major cultural value systems.

His early interests in art and music attested to his preference for field sensitivity. It was not until his brother's death that he turned to field independent pursuits. His preference for field sensitivity and traditional values were again manifested in choosing Jan for his wife. It was also fortunate for Harold that he could express and develop some of his interests in field sensitive areas in his work through the development of computer graphics programs and through his leadership of the mid-level managers and workers.

Pattern of Adjustment. Harold's relationship with his father had remained strained. Harold felt that his many efforts to win his father's love and approval had ended in failure. A major rift developed in their relationship when Harold and his partners established their company. Harold thought his father would lend him money for the company and was devastated when, at the last minute, his father changed his mind. Although Harold maintained contact with his mother, he cut off all communication with his father.

Over the years, Harold and Jan lost the intimacy they had enjoyed in their early years of marriage. The long hours and many weekends that Harold devoted to the company, as well as the extensive traveling he had to do as part of his work, made him feel like he was an outsider at home. As Harold said, "It got to the point that I had nothing to say to Jan or the kids. When I came home from work, I would just fix a drink and sit in front of the TV until it was time for supper. After supper, I would go back to work and come in after they had all gone to bed."

He rarely did anything with his children. At the time he came to therapy, Jan told him that if the situation did not change soon and that if he did not live up to his side of the bargain, she would divorce him. This shock brought Harold to the realization that his behavior with his own children and wife was not unlike that of his father when Harold was young—he, too, was acting indifferent toward his family.

Harold's business partners were becoming unhappy with Harold's interest in moving the company in the direction of computer graphics. They were also noticing signs of burnout in Harold—the charisma and leadership so important to employee loyalty and morale were disappearing as Harold retreated more and more into his own world.

Symptoms. Harold felt lonely, disoriented, and misunderstood. He was shocked by the ultimatum from Jan and by the realization that he had been acting just like his father toward his family. Harold was concerned with the fact that he had lost interest in technical software programs, the mainstay of the company's business over the years. He did not understand why the only things to excite him now were developments in computer graphics.

He also was concerned because he felt more and more alienated from his partners, who were not supportive of his interests. As a result, it was difficult for him to be enthusiastic about the future of the company. Thus, Harold was not investing as much time as he had in maintaining the sense of community within the company. As he said at his first therapy session, "My world is falling apart, and I don't know where to go from here."

Analysis of Cultural Style Mismatch

Harold's preferred cultural orientation was modernistic–urban, but he did acquire some traditional values from his parents, particularly in the gender role and interpersonal domains.

Jan's cultural orientation was semi-urban, traditional.

Harold's partners had all been reared in cities on the East Coast of the United States, so they were more modern–urban in their orientations than was Harold.

Analysis of Cognitive Style Mismatch

Harold's preferred cognitive style had been field sensitive in childhood and early adolescence, as demonstrated by his interests in art and music. In late adolescence and early adulthood, he had rejected this style and switched to the field independent style (through computer science and engineering) to please his father and to fill the void left by Frank's death. At home with Jan and the children, Harold was behaving as though he were preferred field independent, modeling his father's behavior. At work he had made use of his suppressed field sensitive style to provide leadership and a sense of community in maintaining a high level of employee satisfaction in the company. His interests in computer graphics were beginning to show that he was "field sensitive in field independent clothing." Actually Harold had the potential to be a balanced bicognitive. At the time he came to therapy, he was in a state of mismatch in different aspects of his life: He needed to be field sensitive in his behavior at home and to recognize his resurgent field sensitive interests in the domain of work and career.

Harold's father's preferred field independent cognitive style, particularly in the interpersonal domain, mismatched Harold's although Harold did try to match his father in the areas of work and career.

Jan's preferred style was probably field sensitive, and in recent years as Harold moved more in the direction of field independence, her style became increasingly mismatched to his.

Harold's partners' preferred styles were probably field independent, and he became increasingly mismatched to them as his field sensitive interests resurfaced.

Raul

Background.   Raul, a multiracial (African American, Latino, and Native American) man, was born and reared in a medium-sized city in the southwestern United States. The city was predominantly white with pronounced segregation when Raul was growing up. Even though there was a minority of Latinos, African Americans, Native Americans, and Asian Americans in the community, there were very few multiracial people.

Raul was the oldest of five children in an intact but dysfunctional family. He recalled that his father was a heavy drinker and had multiple extramarital affairs during Raul's childhood and adolescence. The family lived in government-subsidized housing; Raul was rejected by his peers because of his multiracial appearance. He was often told, "You are not one of us." He often had to fight to gain respect and acceptance. Eventually, through his prowess in fighting, he gained recognition as a leader.

In early adolescence Raul's life changed dramatically when his father's absence from home and gambling losses contributed to serious financial problems for the family. His mother held down two jobs, so Raul was forced into the role of authority figure for his younger siblings. He felt resentful because he was not able to spend time with his peers in the neighborhood and in school extracurricular activities when his interest in art was just developing. His resentment contributed to his becoming a strict disciplinarian; he was often demanding and harsh in the treatment of his siblings.

When Raul began to date in his middle and high school years he encountered rejection from white women. Although the schools he attended were integrated, both parents and school authorities discouraged cross-racial dating. Another major blow to Raul's self-esteem centered around his poor academic performance. He was diagnosed as having learning disabilities and placed in special education classes. By this time his father had developed health problems and had stopped gambling and discontinued his extramarital affairs. With the increased stability of the family, his parents felt that Raul would do better academically if he were to live temporarily with relatives who resided in a rural community located in the U.S.– Mexico border region.

Raul remembered this time with mixed emotions—his grades improved and his artistic interests were much influenced by Mexican, Native American, and Mestizo art. At the same time, he experienced rejection from relatives and Latino peers who chided him for his inability to speak Spanish fluently and for "acting like an Anglo."

Shortly after he graduated from high school and returned to his family, he was drafted and sent to Vietnam. In the military, he found acceptance from Vietnamese women and their families and he explored Asian and African art styles. However, Raul's combat experiences led to serious posttraumatic stress disorder symptoms. When Raul was discharged from the

Analysis of Cultural Style Mismatch

Raul was bicultural (Native American and Latino traditional values and Caucasian modern values). He was predominantly traditional with respect to spirituality, sense of community, and family identification while preferring modern in gender-role definition and subservience to convention and authority.

The traditional value system he identified with originated in the Native American culture of his father's family (he was close to his paternal grandparents), who took Raul to powwows and family gatherings. His traditional values also had their origin in the Latino belief systems, particularly in the area of the religion of his parents and his maternal external family. His extended family on his mother's side also introduced Raul to the rural traditional values of African–Latino culture (their origins were in the state of Veracruz in Mexico). Raul's modern values had originated in his contacts with Caucasian male peers during adolescence, Caucasian coworkers and friends in the military as well as from urban African American, Filipino, Asian, Latino, and multiracial peers he met in the military.

Raul's mother was mismatched to Raul in the area of human relational and communication styles.

Raul's father was bicognitive. He mismatched Raul in the area of learning style.

Raul's Caucasian girlfriends were mismatched to him on communication and interpersonal relationship styles (the principal reason for the failure of his relationships). His siblings were mismatched to him because of his preferred field sensitive style (he was directive with them).

service, he returned to his hometown and went to work for a print shop. He set up a studio at his home and continued to work on his art. On a limited basis, he began to show and sell some of his work—Raul was only willing to show it to his coworkers, family members, and best friends.

The general atmosphere concerning racial/ethnic relations in his home community reawakened the feelings of rejection he had experienced as a child and an adolescent. Even though he dated African American, Native American, Asian, and Latino women, he was most attracted to Caucasian women with blond hair and blue eyes. When he came to therapy, Raul reported that all of his relationships with Caucasian women had failed. He felt discouraged, confused, misunderstood, and used by the women he had developed intimate relationships with.

Symptoms.   Raul's self-esteem was low. He blamed himself for the failure of his relationships. He felt misunderstood and was having to contend with feelings of rejection and lack of acceptance that had their origin in his childhood and adolescence. He was also suffering from symptoms of posttraumatic stress disorder related to his combat experiences in Vietnam. Further, he was confused about his multiracial–multicultural identity, particularly because he was back in his hometown where multicultural and multiracial relations are not encouraged.

General Clinical Considerations. Raul should be evaluated for appropriateness of medication for amelioration of depressive and posttraumatic stress disorder symptoms. He also needs to be evaluated for his addictive tendencies and encouraged to return to Alcoholics Anonymous (in which he has participated in the past). The therapist also needs to evaluate his risk for suicide.

Tara

Background. Tara, a twenty-six-year-old African American woman, was born and reared in a semi-urban middle-sized community in a state in the southwestern United States. The community was predominantly white and Latino with African Americans and Filipino Americans in the minority. Tara is the youngest of three children—she has two brothers. Her mother is a hospital administrator and her father is a farmer who owns his own farm.

Tara's mother was often absent from the family home when Tara was young because of the demands of varying work shifts and because of her promotions, first to supervisor of nurses and then to hospital administrator.

In elementary and middle school and for the first three years of high school, Tara was self-conscious because of her physical appearance—she was much taller than most of her peers and was slight of build. She remembered that in those days her physique gave her a gangly and "string bean" appearance. She also recalled that she was uncoordinated when she tried to play sports or participate in gymnastics or dance.

At home Tara did her best to fit in with her brothers and her father when her mother was at work. She remembered wanting to be included, even if it meant doing what her father referred to as "men's work." She also remembered spending a lot of time alone making up imaginary friends and taking care of pets and farm animals.

In the last year of high school, Tara's physical appearance changed dramatically, and she was considered by the boys at school to be attractive. She also became more coordinated and was successful as a basketball player. In therapy, however, she still felt negatively about herself. She said, "I still felt that I was awkward and unattractive."

She left home to attend a community college, which was located about two hundred miles from her hometown. For the first time she found herself in a sizable African American community. She began to date and became pregnant during the second semester of her freshman year. Tara was surprised and ashamed about her pregnancy. She did not feel close to the biological father of her child and her academic performance suffered. She eventually left college in the middle of the second semester of her first year and returned to her parents' home. Her parents felt that, because of Tara's pregnancy and leaving college, they had lost face in the traditional community where they lived and in which they were well respected. Tara remembered tension in her family during her final months of pregnancy, but this finally eased when her child, Tamisha, was born. Two years after the birth, Tara moved about three hundred miles from her hometown to a city where she continued her college education and found part-time employment. She received some economic support from her parents.

Within a few months of her arrival in the new community, Tara established a relationship with a boyfriend who related well to Tamisha and who assumed the role of father to the child. Tara, however, had mixed feelings about the relationship. She described this man as controlling, jealous, and intrusive of her privacy. She recalled that he would hide a voice-activated tape recorder in the apartment to monitor who had visited or phoned when he was not there. He would go through her personal papers when Tara was away from the apartment. At times he would show up unannounced at her workplace or at her college. Eventually she broke up with him, and he moved out of their apartment. Nevertheless, he continued to call her and harass her in other ways—he would drive by her apartment and show up unannounced at her child's day-care center to try to urge Tamisha to convince Tara to take him back.

A few months after the breakup with her boyfriend, Tara began to date an African American man who had immigrated from the Bahamas. He was a college graduate and owned his own business. Tara developed intense feelings for him, but he kept giving her signals that he was not interested in a committed relationship. Tara's mother had met her new boyfriend and liked him so much that she kept pressuring Tara to marry and settle down for the good of Tamisha. Tara was very torn and confused. She was still being harassed by her former boyfriend and the behavior of her new boyfriend reawakened the feelings of rejection she had experienced as a child and an adolescent. Her academic performance began to suffer again and she lost her job; she was completely dependent on her parents economically.

Symptoms.   Tara was confused and angry that she had to be economically dependent on her parents: "My mother tries to run my life." She was frustrated by the mixed signals she was getting from her new boyfriend and was concerned about the harassment from the old one. She felt pressured to be a good mother to her daughter, to be successful in college, and to find a new job.

General Clinical Considerations.   Tara should be assessed for the need for medication. She also needs to learn stress-reduction techniques in order to manage stress more effectively.

Analysis of Mismatch in Cultural Styles

Tara developed as a bicultural (African American traditional and bicultural values and Caucasian modern values) although her traditional and modern styles remained separate (almost like two separate personalities) much the same as those of her mother.

Tara's father had traditional values, particularly in the area of gender-role definition.

Tara was mismatched to her mother in the area of time orientation and subservience to authority. Tara felt that her mother did not give her the quality time she needed and that she was trying to tell her how to live her life.

The mismatch with her professors was largely in the areas of her preference for professors who could take an interest in her personally—she felt she lacked a sense of community in the first college she attended. Mismatch with peers was with respect to her traditional values when it came to identification with the family.

Having been reared in urban settings, most of her peers emphasized separation from the family.

Tara mismatched her former boyfriend with respect to her modernistic orientation toward gender-role definition; he did not approve of her friendships with male and female coworkers and of her active role in community sports.

She was mismatched to her parents and siblings on the subservience to convention and authority domain; she felt comfortable being a single parent, while they insisted that she should marry so her child could have a father.

Analysis of Cognitive Style Mismatch

Tara's cognitive style was mixed. She was preferred field sensitive in the motivational domain (she preferred social rewards), but she was dominant field independent in learning/problem-solving style (she enjoyed finding new ways to do things and to solve problems in her work).

Tara's predominant learning style was field sensitive.

Tara's father was predominantly field sensitive. Tara felt partly mismatched to him on communication style.

Tara's mother was very field independent in the area of human relations style, so they were mismatched. Tara was mismatched to her mother with respect to motivational style (her mother kept pressuring her to be more concerned with financial success). She was mismatched to her boyfriends because of the strong field sensitive teaching–parenting–supervisory–counseling style they used with Tamisha.

Tara felt mismatched to the teaching style of most of the professors at her previous college, leading to her sense of frustration. She felt her present college was a better match to her preferred learning style.

Alex

Background.   Alex is a twenty-one-year-old college student of Vietnamese descent who was born in Vietnam and immigrated with his family to the United States at the end of the war. His family eventually settled in a large city in the southwestern United States. During the first six years of his life, Alex was reared primarily by his grandparents who lived in the family home. Alex's parents had been largely absent from the home during the family's years in Vietnam—his mother was a businessowner and his father was an officer in the South Vietnamese military. Alex remembered the time in Vietnam as a very happy period in his life—he attended a Catholic private school and his classmates were Vietnamese and children of American embassy personnel.

Coming to the United States resulted in a complete change in lifestyle and a severe culture shock for Alex. His parents, grandparents, and siblings moved into a small house. He had a very difficult time learning English when he first attended school in the United States. He found that the few words of English he had learned in Vietnam were not adequate to properly communicate with his teachers and peers in the public school he attended. He struggled academically and was placed in a "slow group" for a year.

He also felt that most of his Anglo peers were prejudiced against Vietnamese and used racial slurs. He also found the teaching styles of his new teachers very different from that of the French Catholic nuns in the school he had attended in Vietnam. It shocked Alex to see the emotional decline of his grandparents. His mother was not able to find work immediately, so she stayed at home and became a homemaker for the first time. She assumed a dominant role because Alex's grandmother appeared to be depressed and confused in the new culture. His grandfather stayed in his room most of the time.

While at middle school and high school Alex began to develop a bicultural orientation to life. His English language skills had improved considerably, and he continued to speak Vietnamese at home and in the predominately Vietnamese neighborhood where he lived. However, it was at this time that he began to feel different for other reasons—he felt sexually attracted to males rather than to females. This was confusing to him, and he did not have anyone to discuss it with.

Going to a large state university was a turning point in Alex's life—he was finally able to understand and accept his sexual orientation. He befriended others who were Asian and gay. Together they formed a support group to focus on family issues. However, he developed feelings of differentness in another area—his major in college. Alex's parents had encouraged him to become a physician since he was very young, so he came to the university as a premed major. He remembered feeling confused during his first two semesters of college—he felt positive about being homosexual for the first time, but he felt very mismatched regarding the major he had chosen.

Analysis of Cultural Style Mismatch

Alex had been very traditional prior to his family's immigration to the United States, because of the early influence of his grandparents and of the Catholic school he had attended. Like Tara, his two cultural styles remained separate. After coming to the United States, his mother, who was multicultural, became more influential in his life, so he developed an identity with modern values. In middle school and in high school, he developed close friendships with Caucasian, African American, and Latino peers who were also more modern. By the time he went to the university, Alex was multicultural, but remained preferred traditional in his values orientation.

Alex was mismatched to his grandparents and parents on subservience to convention and authority and on sexual orientation.

As Alex became more modern, he became more mismatched to his grandparents, who remained very traditional.

Alex was mismatched with his heterosexual Asian peers on acceptance of homosexuality. He was mismatched to the professors of his premed courses and to the other premed students because of his tendency to be more cooperative than individually competitive.

He was mismatched to most of his gay peers, particularly those who were not Asian, Latino, Native American, or African American because of his strong feelings of family identity and loyalty.

Analysis of Cognitive Style Mismatch

Alex's behavior reflected a mixed cognitive style; he was dominant field independent in communication style and preferred field sensitive in learning/problem-solving style. He reported that he never felt comfortable in the required natural science and math courses he took when he was a premed student. He felt his learning/problem-solving style was better matched to the requirements of social science courses and the social work courses that he was taking.

Both of Alex's parents were bicognitive, preferred field independent. His father had an engineering degree and his mother a degree in accounting.

Alex's preferred field independent communication style was mismatched to the strong field sensitive style of his peers in the Vietnamese American Student Association. His preference for a field sensitive learning/problem-solving style was mismatched to the orientation of most of the premed courses he had taken and also to the teaching style of the professors in the statistics–research design course he was having problems with.

He struggled in all the required premed science courses, and he could not relate well to most of the other premed students. During this time he took an elective course in social work and felt as if he had found his true calling. He did volunteer work at a facility near campus that offered counseling and support services to college students who were gay. He decided to change his major but did so without consulting his parents. His sexual orientation and his academic interests were secrets to his family.

Symptoms. Alex felt guilty about withholding information from his parents. He suffered from insomnia and from an approach–avoidance conflict regarding visits to his family. He was uncomfortable about "living a double life."

General Clinical Considerations. Alex should be evaluated for symptoms of adjustment disorder, mixed type, and consideration should be given to possible need for medication.

SUMMARY

The flex theory of personality helps to identify those areas of mismatch in the cultural and cognitive domains of life that are related to barriers in the development of multicultural personality styles. The analysis of the areas of mismatch suggests goals for psychotherapy. Cultural and cognitive styles mismatch analyses for Imelda, Harold, Raul, Tara, and Alex help to pinpoint the origins of the feelings of differentness and of the symptoms of the mismatch syndrome. Furthermore, the concepts of the flex theory of personality help to identify those areas of mismatch in the cultural and cognitive domains of life that interfere with the development of multicultural personality processes and lifestyles. The therapeutic approach of choice for adjustment problems associated with mismatch is multicultural psychotherapy.

The focus of multicultural psychotherapy is on the development of personality flex and multicultural orientations to life. In addition, clients gain an awareness of how they have experienced mismatch shock and suffered from the feelings of differentness. Clients are empowered to change the environment, helping to create a multicultural society, sensitive to diversity and oriented toward peace and cooperation.

The flex theory of personality was applied to information obtained through the life histories of Imelda, Harold, Tara, Raul, and Alex in order to understand how the mismatch syndrome developed in these clients. The life histories also helped to identify general clinical considerations as well as some of the goals to be addressed in multicultural therapy.

5

THE MULTICULTURAL MODEL
OF PSYCHOTHERAPY
AND COUNSELING
An Overview

In the previous chapter, the principal concepts of the cognitive and cultural flex theory of personality were applied to show how Tara, Raul, Alex, Imelda, and Harold were mismatched with people and institutions in their environments and how mismatch was associated with feelings of different-ness, alienation, and despair. This chapter introduces an approach to psychotherapy and counseling which evolved from the experience of treating clients who, like those in the case studies, were suffering from feeling different and from mismatch shock.

The multicultural model of psychotherapy and counseling differs from other treatment approaches in the following ways:

- It views every client as having the potential for multicultural development. It encourages the therapist to respect the client's origins as reflected in unique cultural and cognitive styles, because these are the foundation for multicultural development and for the development of maximum potential in the personality.
- It views the therapist as also having preferred cognitive and cultural styles. It encourages the therapist to become aware of his unique cultural and cognitive styles and to learn how to flex in order to best match the unique styles of clients.
- The therapist makes use of the opportunities for multicultural growth offered by the client's immediate environment and by encouraging the client to accept that diversity. The helping professional also encourages the client to recognize and use advantages for multicultural development present in the diverse society in which the client lives.
- Clients are encouraged to become multicultural educators, peer counselors, and ambassadors. They are also encouraged to become active change agents,

not only to enhance their own multicultural development, but also to help develop a society of social justice, peace, and cooperation that will be responsive and sensitive to the individual differences of all its citizens.

TASKS OF THE MULTICULTURAL THERAPIST

Specifically, the multicultural therapist or counselor has seven major tasks during therapy, as described in the following sections.

Matching Clients in an Atmosphere of Acceptance

The therapist provides a nonjudgmental, positive, accepting atmosphere devoid of conformity or assimilation pressures. In this climate, clients feel free to express their uniqueness in the form of their preferred cognitive and cultural styles. This accomplishes several objectives:

- It helps clients overcome feelings of differentness and of mismatch shock, which negatively affect their adjustment and prevents openness to multicultural development.
- It allows clients to abandon the false self and to express the unique self, thus allowing the therapist to know how best to match the preferred styles of the client. This helps the client to feel validated and accepted.

The therapist continues to match the client to further eliminate the effects of the mismatch syndrome and to continue to gain the client's trust. The most important initial area of match is communication style because it is important for the client to feel totally understood by the therapist. Continued match procedures gain the trust of the client by reducing alienation. Matching also helps in the assessment of clients' preferred styles as the false self recedes and the unique self emerges. Additionally, matching by the therapist helps to remove those barriers to learning from diversity that have kept clients from achieving their multicultural potential.

Making a Formal Assessment of Preferred Styles

As a cross-check on the assessment done through observations, the therapist administers three personality inventories that assess the client's preferred cognitive and cultural styles. These inventories accomplish three goals:

1. To indicate how well behavioral observations match the client's self report of preferred styles;
2. To provide materials for discussion of important therapeutic issues; and
3. To encourage client participation in goal setting and in gaining a firsthand understanding of the unique self reflected in their preferred styles.

Conducting a Life History Interview

The life history interview with the client (discussed in detail in Chapter 7) identifies a time or times in the client's life when the pressure to conform or assimilate caused a suppression of a preferred style. The life history helps to identify those people and institutions to which the client has felt most matched and mismatched. It also helps to isolate barriers to multicultural development such as Imelda's strong negative feelings toward mainstream European Americans and Tara's alienation from her parents. In addition, the life history interview helps to identify personality building blocks that can be used in multicultural development. An example is Raul's learning about other cultures by studying their artistic forms and styles and using these in his artwork. Finally, the life history interview helps to survey the resources and potential opportunities present in the client's environment that could facilitate multicultural development.

Making a Self-Assessment

In multicultural therapy it is necessary for the therapist to evaluate his own preferred styles to determine areas of match and mismatch with the client, allowing the therapist to flex in order to better match the client. This self-assessment is important to determine whether the therapist has a sufficient range of flex to provide an adequate match to the client's preferred styles. It also helps the therapist identify personal biases, prejudices, and preferences. In this way, it can be ascertained whether there are any stereotypes or negative attitudes that might interfere with establishment of rapport. Finally, self-assessment provides the therapist with an opportunity to identify those areas of cognitive and cultural styles in which he will need additional multicultural development.

Introducing Cognitive and Cultural Flex and the Multicultural Model

The clients' active participation in therapy is an essential component of this model. For this reason, the therapist introduces clients to the major concepts of both the flex theory of personality and the multicultural model of psychotherapy. The clients' knowledge and awareness of these concepts enables them to monitor progress. Clients also become more invested in the success of therapy during the process of setting personal goals. In the larger scheme, clients' involvement empowers them to become agents of change. Introducing mismatch to the client's preferred cultural and cognitive styles is the beginning of the development of cultural and cognitive flex. This introduction is done in the context of match. Clients are encouraged to participate in social situations and relationships that can foster the development of new cultural and cognitive styles.

Mismatch is practiced in the safe atmosphere of therapy through the writing of scripts and role-playing. This practice serves to develop cognitive and cultural flex as well as to encourage clients to learn how to empathize with people whose cultural and cognitive styles differ from their own. Through the use of homework assignments clients experiment with scripts in the world outside the therapy room and evaluate individual progress in these efforts. This phase continues the development of cognitive and cultural flex as well as the development of the clients' preferred styles. Further, clients develop self-confidence in interacting with people and situations that require the use of different styles.

To assess the progress of clients as they proceed through the therapy, the therapist makes ongoing observations of the client, noting progress on the Preferred Cultural and Cognitive Styles Observation Checklists (Appendices E and F). These ratings are compared to the ones made by the therapist in the initial stages of therapy to note the degree of change.

This ongoing comparison helps the therapist determine the degree of progress on the goals established for therapy and helps clients to see how much progress they are making as therapy proceeds. The comparison also enables the therapist and client to develop new goals or to modify existing ones.

Assessing Progress in Flex Development

Once the mismatch phase of therapy is well under way, the therapist assesses client progress in the different domains of cultural and cognitive styles. The data obtained from readministration of the paper-and-pencil inventories and from the observation instruments are compared to those obtained in the initial stage of therapy. These comparisons help to determine whether it will be necessary to make changes in the therapeutic plan. Feedback to the client ensures continued involvement and commitment to the goals of multicultural therapy and counseling.

Encouraging Clients to Become Change Agents

Clients learn how to encourage changes in the environment to ensure the best match to their preferred styles from others and from those institutions and agencies that most affect their daily lives. Clients also learn how to become multicultural educators and peer counselors for those who are suffering from feeling different and from mismatch shock. At the same time, they learn how to become multicultural ambassadors, facilitating the development of a multicultural society.

Transforming clients into change agents empowers them to gain control over their destinies. Also, clients become more committed to multiculturalism by helping others faced with mismatch. Working to introduce other individuals and institutions to the advantages and benefits of multiculturalism helps to promote the development of a society of peace and cooperation, stimulating the maximum development of the individual potential of all its citizens.

GOALS OF MULTICULTURAL PSYCHOTHERAPY AND COUNSELING

The multicultural model of psychotherapy and counseling has four major goals, as described in the following sections.

Overcoming the Mismatch Syndrome

The first goal of multicultural therapy is to reduce alienation and feelings of helplessness and despair. As long as clients suffer from the negative effects of mismatch, they cannot learn from other people and groups who are different. They are unable to discover their unique selves and to develop that uniqueness to its fullest. A person in mismatch shock cannot take full advantage of opportunities offered by a multicultural society. Mismatch shock closes experience and learning filters, causing clients to repeat old behaviors, attitudes, and values that have led to failure in the past.

Recognizing and Accepting the Unique Self

The client in mismatch shock has serious identity problems. The "tyranny of the shoulds," reflected in the conformist and assimilationist approaches of society, forces the client to reject the unique self in favor of a false self. Multicultural therapy helps clients identify the self that may have been suppressed earlier in life and to recognize how pressures from others and/or from society have forced them to try to be someone other than the unique self. This makes clients aware of how they became victims of conformity and/or assimilation. Multicultural therapy then helps clients to accept themselves and develop to the fullest extent possible by learning how to flex cognitively and culturally.

Achieving Cognitive and Cultural Flex

Once clients accept the unique self and understand how mismatch has led to alienation and unhappiness, and once they recognize the advantages offered by a multicultural society to personal development, multicultural therapy approaches proceed to help in the development of cultural and cognitive flexibility, which facilitates the development and expression of the unique self.

Empowering Clients to Become Change Agents, Peer Counselors, and Multicultural Ambassadors

The multicultural model of psychotherapy teaches clients the concepts and procedures of the flex theory of personality and the multicultural model of psychotherapy so that they can create change in their environments. By encouraging people and institutions in their environments to become more sensitive to diversity, clients ensure a better match for their unique styles as well as for the unique styles of others. Empowerment also encourages clients to become multicultural peer counselors and ambassadors for the development of a cooperative and peaceful multicultural society.

The preceding major goals are dependent on the accomplishment of a series of subgoals. The first two subgoals are (1) identifying the relationships of pressures to conform and assimilate to choice of cultural and cognitive styles; and (2) identifying possible attitudes and values associated with ethnocentrism and the development of negative stereotypes, which have prevented clients from participating in and learning from diversity. The goals and subgoals identified here can be accomplished by following the steps of multicultural psychotherapy. The therapeutic process generally consists of sixteen sessions and follow-ups. Each session focuses on specific goals, including the following:

- Helping clients recognize that they have been subject to the pressures to conform and assimilate, a product of the tyranny of the shoulds.
- Helping clients to overcome potential barriers to multicultural development. First, clients have to become aware of forces and factors in their histories that may have resulted in closing learning–experience filters and in an adherence to rigid cognitive and cultural styles that have isolated them from diversity and have resulted in alienation. Closed learning–experience filters are usually associated with ethnocentric attitudes and with negative stereotypes of those who are different from oneself.
- Encouraging clients to try out new values, worldviews, and cognitive styles in the safe environment of match provided in the therapeutic setting and relationship. This initial experience with match helps clients to eliminate barriers that have blocked their multicultural development. It also motivates and prepares clients to participate in diversity challenges that can give them the opportunity to develop the cultural and cognitive flex essential to multicultural personality development.
- Helping clients learn the strategies and concepts of both the flex theory of personality and the multicultural model of psychotherapy. This knowledge can make them active change agents so that people and institutions around them can better match their unique styles as well as those of other citizens. The therapist also empowers clients to become multicultural educators, peer counselors, and ambassadors.

SESSION-BY-SESSION DESCRIPTION WITH A FOCUS ON THERAPY GOALS

Session 1

The first session lasts about ninety minutes and focuses on the development of an atmosphere of acceptance and respect, encouraging the expression of the client's unique self through preferred cultural and cognitive styles. During this session the therapist must keep in mind that, because of the effects of pressures to conform and of mismatch shock, the client may not initially be open to self-expression. It is during the initial session that the therapist performs a preliminary assessment of the unique self through observation of the cultural and cognitive styles of the client. The therapist also begins to match and to monitor the effects of match on the client using behavior observation checklists.

The therapist administers four personality inventories to establish the client's preferred cognitive and cultural styles: the Traditionalism–Modernism Instrument (TMI, Appendix B), the Bicognitive Orientation to Life Scale (BOLS, Appendix G), the Family Attitude Scale (FAS, Appendix C), and the Multicultural Experience Inventory (MEI, Appendix A). While the client is completing the instruments, the therapist examines her self-observations and compares them to ratings of the client's preferred cultural and cognitive styles. The therapist then evaluates whether she possesses the range of flex necessary to maximize the chances for success with the client or whether the client should be referred to another therapist.

Session 2

In the course of the second session, the therapist continues to match the client and conducts a brief life history. During this session the therapist explains the principal concepts of the flex theory of personality and offers feedback on the results of the assessment instruments the client completed during the initial session. It is during the second session that the therapist and the client set the goals for therapy. The second session lasts approximately seventy-five minutes while all remaining sessions are approximately fifty minutes each.

Sessions 3 and 4

While the therapist continues to match the client's preferred cultural and cognitive styles, she obtains a more detailed life history from the client, with a focus on match and mismatch. The therapist introduces scriptwriting exercises and empathy projection. During these sessions there is continued discussion of the principal concepts of the flex model as well as discussion of the possible diversity challenges available to the client. At this time, the

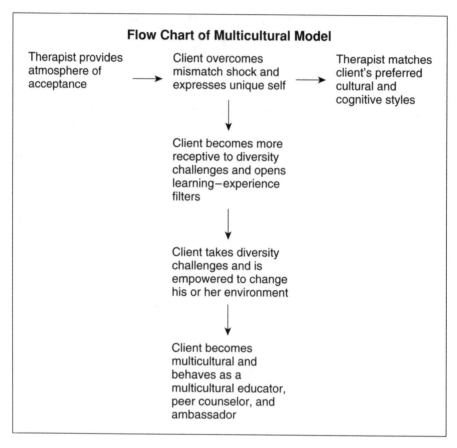

Flow Chart of Multicultural Model

Therapist provides atmosphere of acceptance → Client overcomes mismatch shock and expresses unique self → Therapist matches client's preferred cultural and cognitive styles

↓

Client becomes more receptive to diversity challenges and opens learning–experience filters

↓

Client takes diversity challenges and is empowered to change his or her environment

↓

Client becomes multicultural and behaves as a multicultural educator, peer counselor, and ambassador

FIGURE 5.1 The major stages of the multicultural model of psychotherapy and counseling

therapist attempts to reduce any negative stereotypes and possible negative attitudes toward diversity. In those cases where the client had been "forcing" himself to use nonpreferred cultural and cognitive styles (the false self), the unique self begins to emerge, thus the therapist may want to reassess the client using the Preferred Cognitive and Cultural Styles Observation Checklists (see Appendices E and F). Any differences in the ratings can be discussed with the client during the feedback session.

Sessions 5 through 10

While continuing to match the client's preferred styles, the therapist introduces mismatch through match, using scriptwriting, empathy projection, role-playing, and diversity challenges during the sessions, as well as in homework assignments.

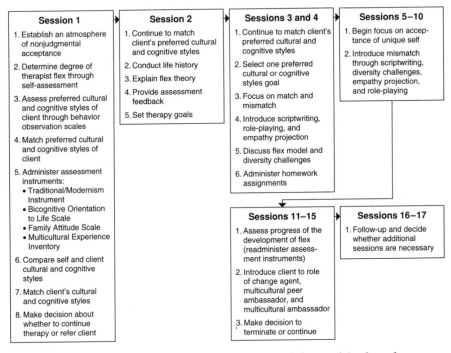

FIGURE 5.2   **Session-by-session description of the multicultural model of psychotherapy**

Sessions 11 through 15

Session 11 is used to assess the progress of the development of flexibility. The remaining sessions of this phase are used to work on areas of flex not yet mastered. It is during these later sessions that the client is introduced to the role of change agent, multicultural peer counselor, multicultural ambassador, and multicultural educator. Session 15 focuses on assessing the progress of the growth of the client in these areas. Depending on the client's progress, more sessions may be scheduled; otherwise regularly scheduled therapy sessions are terminated at this point.

Follow-up

Six months after the last regularly scheduled session, the client and therapist meet in Session 16 to follow up and to determine the necessity for additional sessions. Six months after Session 16, or after the final session of the series of follow-up sessions planned after Session 16, the client and therapist meet for an additional follow-up and to evaluate the need for additional sessions. Figure 5.1 summarizes the major stages of the multicultural model of psychotherapy and counseling, and Figure 5.2 presents a session-by-session summary in graphic form.

SUMMARY

The multicultural model of psychotherapy and counseling evolved from the experience of doing therapy and counseling with clients who experienced feeling different and who suffered from the symptoms of the mismatch syndrome. The model is a unique treatment approach that views every client and therapist as having the potential for becoming multicultural and for fostering the development of a multicultural society. This chapter presented the major concepts, tasks, and goals of the multicultural model of psychotherapy.

6

THE THERAPIST

Most psychotherapy and counseling models ignore the powerful impact that the therapist's personality has on the outcome of therapy. Witkin and Goodenough (1977) showed that the preferred cognitive style of therapists was reflected in their therapeutic styles. For example, therapists who were preferred field independent tended to talk less and to be less directive in therapy than were their field sensitive colleagues.

The cultural styles of therapists have also been found to be important in mental health service delivery for the "different" (Torrey, 1973; Sue and Zane, 1987; Sue and Sue, 1990). When therapist and client share the same cultural worldview and the same values, therapy is more effective.

Research by Lubrosky and colleagues (1985) showed that the therapist is much more than just the transmitter of a standard therapeutic approach: The mental health professional is actually an important independent agent of change, with the ability to magnify or reduce the effects of therapy. These authors found that an early in-treatment measure of the patient–therapist relationship, the Helping Alliance Questionnaire, yielded significant correlation with outcome measures. The researchers concluded, that "the best, i.e., most effective therapists, were those who also happened to form the better helping alliances with their patients" (p. 608).

Thus, it could be concluded that a cultural and cognitive styles match between therapist and client is likely to enhance the development of the therapeutic alliance. Therefore, focus on the therapist's preferred styles and on the degree of match between the cognitive and cultural styles of the therapist and the client are of central importance to the multicultural model of psychotherapy. When the therapist matches the client, mismatch shock and the feeling of being different can be reduced. This increases the client's trust and feelings of self-efficacy, which in turn increases the willingness to explore diversity and to learn from it by opening up learning–experience filters.

This chapter focuses on the preferred cultural and cognitive styles of the therapist. Further, it examines the degree to which the therapist can and should flex in order to match the client and serve as a multicultural model.

THE THERAPIST AS A PRODUCT OF HISTORY

The therapist's preferred cultural and cognitive styles and degree of flex have been shaped by personal history, vis-à-vis diversity. Thus, therapists need a systematic approach for determining how their preferred styles and ability to flex have been shaped by socialization and life experiences. One technique for learning this is through a self life history.

The Self Life History

The following sample questions can serve as a general guideline for developing a self life history:

- How much cognitive and cultural diversity was reflected in the make-up of my nuclear and extended families? Were parents, blood relatives, and relatives by marriage with whom I interacted extensively as a child or an adolescent members of different ethnic, racial, religious, regional, or socioeconomic groups? Did they represent different values (as reflected in the different value dimensions listed on Chapter 3), ideologies, and philosophies of life? Did they represent different cognitive style preferences as reflected in their jobs or professions and in their preferred communication, teaching, and learning/ problem-solving styles?
- How cognitively and culturally diverse were the countries, communities, and neighborhoods where I grew up and in which I have lived?
- How diverse were the student and staff populations of the schools I attended?
- How diverse were the teachers, clergy members, mentors, employers, and other influential authority figures?
- How diverse were the people I dated or those I considered to be close friends?
- How diverse were the places—homes, communities, regions, countries—I visited?
- How much diversity was reflected in the courses I had in college and in graduate school? in the novels, biographies, and autobiographies I have read?
- How much diversity is represented in my hobbies and pastimes?
- What is the nature and the frequency of the diversity challenges I have undertaken?

By answering questions like these, the therapist can gain insight into personal attitudes toward diversity. These questions also help to inventory the size and heterogeneity of the pool of personality resources (see Chapter 3) the therapist has available for cultural and cognitive flex in therapy and counseling.

In addition to the self life history, therapists can do self-assessments of their preferred cultural and cognitive styles and of the degree of their capability to flex in these two domains. The assessment instruments described in the following sections and provided in the appendices of this book can be used for this purpose.

Self-Assessment of Cultural Flex

The therapist can evaluate her cultural flex with several instruments. The Multicultural Experience Inventory (MEI, Appendix A) is a tool that can be used for the assessment of cultural flex. This instrument provides an indication of the degree of exposure the therapist has had to diversity in the past, as well as to the degree to which she is exposed to diversity in the present.

The Traditionalism–Modernism Inventory (TMI, Appendix B) assesses the degree of identification with traditional and modern values and belief systems. This instrument yields a score indicating the degree of agreement with traditional or modern values, as well as indicating the degree of flexibility—that is, the degree of identification with both sets of values and belief systems.

The TMI, the Family Attitude Scale (FAS, Appendix C), and the Multicultural Experience Inventory (Appendix A) can be used in still another way to assess the therapist's degree of cultural flex. Immediately after concluding a therapeutic session, the therapist can review the items of the instruments and identify those that were related to interpretations she made in the course of a therapy session. The therapist can also check her responses to the items with those made by the client to gauge their degree of match or mismatch.

Self-Assessment of Cognitive Flex

Therapists are also encouraged to assess their cognitive style preference and the degree to which they can flex cognitively by doing a self-assessment with the Therapist's Cognitive Styles Observation Checklist (Appendix D) and with the Bicognitive Orientation to Life Scale (BOLS, Appendix G).

The Therapist's Cognitive Styles Observation Checklist is used in much the same way as the Cognitive Styles Observation Checklist that is described in Chapter 7. Table 6.1 describes the field sensitive and field independent therapist behaviors that have been identified. By keeping this instrument in front of them during the course of therapy, therapists can monitor personal behaviors frequently used in the sessions and then check these against observations made of the client's behavior. A comparison of the two identifies areas of match and mismatch.

The BOLS (Appendix G) assesses the degree of preference for field independent or field sensitive cognitive styles as well as the degree of cognitive flex.

TABLE 6.1 Field Sensitive and Field Independent Behaviors

Field Sensitive	Field Independent
Communication Style	
1. The therapist does more talking than the client during the session.	1. The therapist talks less than the client during the session.
2. The therapist personalizes communications; is self-disclosing.	2. The therapist remains a "blank screen" for the client.
3. The therapist uses both verbal and nonverbal modes of communication.	3. The therapist emphasizes verbal communication.
Interpersonal Relationship Style	
1. The therapist is informal and establishes a close personal relationship with the client.	1. The therapist is formal and maintains a "professional" distance.
2. The therapist focuses on the nature of the therapist–client relationship in therapy.	2. The therapist emphasizes self-reliance and is problem-focused.
Motivational Styles	
1. The therapist emphasizes social rewards to the client.	1. The therapist emphasizes self-rewards.
2. The therapist emphasizes achievement for others as one of the goals of therapy.	2. The therapist emphasizes achievement for self.
Therapeutic Teaching Styles	
1. The therapist becomes a model for the client in teaching new behaviors, values, and perspectives.	1. The therapist uses the discovery approach.
2. The therapist uses direct interpretation.	2. The therapist uses reflection, encouraging clients to arrive at their own interpretations.
3. The therapist uses a deductive approach (global to specific) to teaching in therapy.	3. The therapist uses an inductive (specific to global) approach to teaching in therapy.

BECOMING A FLEXIBLE THERAPIST

It is important for the therapist to keep in mind that cultural and cognitive flex are processes, not fixed personality characteristics. Therefore, therapists should consider themselves as always being in the process of moving toward, but never reaching, the goal of total cognitive and cultural flexibility.

Because flexibility is constantly in process, it is important for therapists to work continuously toward the development of cultural and cognitive flex by using some of the same procedures and techniques they use with their clients. These will be described in more detail in Chapters 7, 8, 9, and 11, but they are introduced here with a brief discussion focusing on development of therapists' flexibility.

Empathy

Viewing the world through the eyes of someone whose cultural and/or cognitive style is different from the therapist's is an exercise for developing flex. The procedure that can be used is what is referred to as *empathy projection*—trying to understand the point of view and the feelings of someone whose values and cognitive styles may differ from those of the therapist.

A good place to start is with loved ones, family members, friends, and colleagues whose values and cognitive styles are different from the preferred styles of the therapist. Another approach is to read the biographies and autobiographies of people whose cultures and values are different from the preferred styles of the therapist. (A list of biographies, autobiographies, and novels written by authors of various ethnic or racial groups is included in Selected Readings at the end of this book.)

Scriptwriting and Role-Playing

Focusing on someone they know well, therapists should develop scripts that attempt to match that person, role-play the script with friends, and then try out the script with the person whom they want to match. After trying out the script, therapists can evaluate themselves by using the Homework Effectiveness Assessment Instrument described in Chapter 8, and provided in Appendix H, and by reviewing the categories of the Cognitive Styles Observation Checklist (see Appendices D and E). Therapists can then rewrite the script and make another attempt if necessary.

Modeling

Therapists can make changes in their friendship patterns in order to have opportunities to interact with people who have cognitive and cultural styles different from their own. By observing and then modeling the behaviors and values they observe and by attempting to communicate and relate effectively to these new friends, therapists can learn unfamiliar cognitive and cultural styles.

Diversity Challenges

Therapists can try out new tasks and activities or hobbies to create diversity challenges. Making new friendships can also stimulate the development of cultural and cognitive style flex.

Travel

Therapists can broaden cultural and cognitive horizons by visiting different neighborhoods or communities in their immediate area, as well as by traveling to different regions or countries in order to gain familiarity with other lifestyles and perspectives on life.

LIMITS TO THERAPIST FLEX

There are limits to the extent to which the therapist should attempt to flex in order to match clients: Every therapist has an effectiveness–comfort range of flex within which she can match clients while feeling comfortable, genuine, and effective. There are limits imposed by moral and ethical considerations—it would not be appropriate to match the client in situations in which matching would reinforce the client's pathology.

The Effectiveness–Comfort Range

Each therapist needs to become familiar with her effectiveness–comfort range through experience and self-evaluation. The greater the diversity of the therapist's caseload, the greater the opportunities for self-evaluation under different conditions of match. Therapists should take the issues in the following sections into consideration when determining the extent of their effectiveness–comfort range.

Therapy Goals. The therapist needs to be cognizant of the match requirements of the goals that have been established for the client. The therapist, through experience, comes to recognize that certain client goals require complete shifts in style during the course of therapy: A client who is suffering from a posttraumatic stress disorder, for example, may require a field sensitive match in the initial stages and a predominant field independent orientation in the later stages of therapy. Thus, when the therapist and client develop the goals of therapy in the second session, the therapist needs to decide whether she will have the required range of flex to meet the client's needs during the entire course of treatment. If the demands required by the therapeutic plan cannot be met, then the therapist must be prepared to refer the client to another professional who might have the range of flex required to work effectively with that client.

Limit-Setting and Confrontation. Some clients, such as those with borderline and antisocial personality disorders, may require the establishment of firm limits and the use of confrontation (behavior typical of a field independent therapy orientation) during the course of therapy. Therapists must know if their effectiveness–comfort range will allow them to be comfortable and genuine with limit-setting and confrontation.

Structure. Some clients, such as those with oppositional and conduct disorders, may require a very structured type of therapy—one that is typical of an extreme field independent type of therapeutic style. Therapists must ask themselves how comfortable and effective they can be in employing a structured approach to treatment.

Empathy.   Clients who have been physically and/or sexually abused may require strong and deep empathy. Therapists must determine if their effectiveness–comfort range will permit the degree of field sensitive orientation in therapy required by victims of abuse.

Moral and Ethical Issues

The therapist needs to be cognizant of the fact that, in some situations, matching behavior may inadvertently be interpreted by the client as support for pathological behavior. This is particularly difficult in cases in which clients need to establish good rapport with the therapist before they can gain the confidence they need to initiate cognitive and cultural style changes. Matching needs to be done with the clear message to the client that it does not imply approval of values and lifestyles that are potentially damaging to the client or to others.

Another area of therapy in which moral and ethical issues are paramount concerns the degree to which the therapist should encourage the client to develop unfamiliar styles. Clients, like therapists, have ranges of flex within which they feel comfortable at certain stages in their lives. The therapist needs to be aware that at some times in their lives clients may be unable to develop the degree of flex that will lead to perfect balance.

For example, encouraging Imelda in the direction of an extreme modernistic and field independent style could have resulted in the greater alienation of members of her family and her peers. The therapist had to consider that this client was living in a traditional community, emphasizing traditional values and a field sensitive orientation to life. When Imelda leaves her home community for a community more representative of modern values and field independent styles, it may become easier for her to further explore the development of the field independent and modernistic domains of her personality. Thus, in determining the degree of flexibility of both therapist and client, it is important not to lose sight of the principal paradigm on which the multicultural model is based—multicultural person–environment fit.

SUMMARY

Therapists, like clients, are the products of their socialization, histories, and life experiences. The multicultural model of psychotherapy requires that the therapist, as well as the client, be cognizant of personal preferred cultural and cognitive styles reflected in behaviors, thinking patterns, and lifestyles.

Therapists are encouraged to do short self life histories and self-assessments using the same instruments they use to assess clients preferred styles and degree of flex. Therapists are also asked to use the same techniques and procedures employed to encourage the development of flex in clients so that they too can develop greater flex and thereby become more effective with a wider variety of clients.

There are, however, limits to which the therapist can and should flex to match clients. Therapists should not match the values of clients whose actions clearly threaten the lives or the well-being of themselves or others. It is the therapists who must be the ultimate judges of the limits of their willingness and ability to match certain clients. They need to be aware of how entrenched they are with respect to preferred cognitive and cultural styles. Therapists must know when the demands of match would carry them beyond the range in which they feel comfortable, genuine, and effective.

7

THE FIRST STAGE OF MULTICULTURAL PSYCHOTHERAPY AND COUNSELING
Preferred Styles

The principal goal of the initial two sessions of multicultural psychotherapy and counseling is to match the preferred cultural and cognitive styles of the client. During the course of the first session, the therapist establishes an atmosphere of nonjudgmental acceptance in which the client can begin to overcome the effects of the mismatch syndrome and to express the unique self—the preferred cultural and cognitive styles that have been rejected and suppressed. The therapist then proceeds to match the client's preferred styles.

Another task of the first session is to administer assessment instruments to the client. In the second session, the therapist continues to match the client's preferred styles. In addition, the therapist completes a short life history with the client. It is also during the second session that the therapist introduces the client to the flex theory of personality and gives the client feedback concerning the findings of the assessment done during the first session in preparation for identifying the principal goals to be addressed in therapy.

THE INITIAL SESSION

The therapist establishes an atmosphere of nonjudgmental acceptance and begins the process of client assessment in the initial session. It is during this session that the client explains why therapy is being sought and what the client hopes to gain from it, while the therapist describes what the client can realistically expect and what the general course of therapy will be. In the first session the therapist evaluates the client both casually through observation and more formally by using evaluation instruments.

Categorizing Initial Observations of Preferred Cultural Styles

The professional can gain early clues to the preferred style of the client from informal observations. The client who has a traditional orientation is likely to be dressed more formally, although this can vary depending on socio-economic class. The traditional client may initially appear to be self-conscious, deferent, and shy. The client who is more oriented toward a modern system of values, on the other hand, is likely to be dressed more casually, with a behavior more reflective of assertiveness and self-confidence. While the traditionally oriented client is likely to be deferential and more likely to address the therapist by using an appropriate title, the modernistic client usually tries to relate to the mental health professional as an equal and may immediately begin to use the therapist's first name or at least inquire whether it is acceptable to do so.

The client with a traditional orientation will often expect the mental health professional to take the lead in therapy, expecting that the therapist will do most of the talking in the initial stages of the first session. The client with a modern orientation is likely to begin talking without much encouragement from the therapist. The client with a traditional orientation is usually sensitive to the social environment and may comment on how the therapist's office looks or on particular items in it. The traditional client is also likely to express an interest in the personal interests or background of the professional. The client with a modernistic orientation is usually less attentive to the social environment and to any nonverbal cues the therapist may project. This client is more likely to focus on the education, training, experience, and general qualifications of the professional.

When explaining why therapy is sought, the traditionally oriented client will usually focus on relationships with intimate partners, family members, peers, colleagues, or others. The modernistic client, however, is more self-focused, emphasizing self-efficacy rather than interpersonal relationships. Of course, most clients do not fall clearly and totally into one category or the other. For example, a culturally flexible client could be self-confident and assertive during the session while at the same time indicating that therapy is being sought because of a need to improve personal relationships. It should be kept in mind that some clients with mismatch are likely, at the first session, to present with the nonpreferred cultural and cognitive styles, which they have adopted in their attempt to comply with the pressures of the tyranny of the shoulds.

The Preferred Cultural Styles Observation Checklist is an instrument composed of behaviors that have been found to be typical of clients with either modern or traditional orientations. It is useful in helping the therapist define the client's orientation. Reference to the checklist during the initial session will help the therapist make appropriate observations and notes about the preferred style. If the client is suspected of presenting with nonpreferred styles, the therapist should wait until a stage during the ini-

TABLE 7.1 **Typical Observations from the Preferred Cultural Styles Observation Checklist**

Traditional	Modern
____ Behaves deferentially toward the therapist	____ Seeks to establish equal status with therapist
____ Expects the therapist to do most of the talking	____ Does most of the talking
____ Appears shy and self-controlled	____ Appears assertive and self-confident
____ Is observant of social environment	____ Seems to ignore social environment
____ Focuses on important others when relating reason(s) for seeking therapy	____ Focuses on self when relating reason(s) for seeking therapy

tial session when the client is feeling more comfortable and more likely to be using the preferred styles. Typical observations from the checklist are shown in Table 7.1. The Preferred Cultural Styles Observation Checklist is provided in Appendix F to facilitate duplication for use by therapists and counselors.

Manifestation of Preferred Cultural Styles in Case Studies

The individual cases presented earlier—those of Imelda, Raul, Tara, Alex, Rose, Harold, and Tony—reflect a variety of preferred cultural styles.

Traditional. Imelda's preferred traditional values were reflected in her manner of dress and in the way she related to the therapist. She was neatly dressed in a sportsshirt and dress slacks and wore her school jacket with a prominent athletic letter. Imelda was self-conscious during the initial stage of the session, initially avoiding eye contact with the therapist. In response to what she hoped to gain from counseling, she focused on improving her relationships with others and on trying to overcome the feeling of loss that she had about the breakup with her boyfriend. She was deferential and respectful, referring to the therapist as "Doctor" and "Sir."

Modern. Harold's strong modern orientation was conveyed in his air of self-confidence and assertiveness. He walked into the therapist's office with a notepad and pencil. Before the therapist had an opportunity to be seated, Harold began with, "May I call you Manuel?" He then announced that he had a number of questions, and proceeded to read from his notepad. When he reflected on the reasons for coming to therapy, Harold focused on his concerns about his self-efficacy. He made it obvious that the goal of improving relationships with his family and business associates was secondary to that of regaining feelings of creativity and effectiveness.

Traditional. Tara's traditional values manifested themselves in her parenting style with her four-year-old daughter, who accompanied her to the therapist's office. She told her, "I would like you to be very quiet and to play with your coloring books while I am in the other office. If you need anything, you can ask the lady behind the desk. I will be back in about an hour." Tara also asked her daughter to introduce herself to the receptionist and to the therapist. Tara's traditional values were further reflected in her self-consciousness when the session first began—she stared at the floor or at the walls while talking. She identified her primary reasons for coming to therapy as wanting to be a better parent and to relate more effectively to her parents and to intimate partners.

Mixed. Alex's behavior and verbalizations during the initial session were indicative of his mixed cultural style, a combination of modern and traditional. He was deferential in his behavior toward the therapist and stated that because he himself was planning to work and do research in mental health, he was hoping that the therapist could be a role model for him. His modern belief system was manifested in his informal dress, his hairstyle, and his use of colloquial English. He reported that his most important therapy goal was to become more independent of others.

Mixed. Like Alex, Raul exhibited a mixed cultural style. His dress was informal, tank top and jogging shorts, but he addressed the therapist in a deferential and formal way. He used a combination of English and Spanish in his speech. He reported that he was active in the Native American Church and that his uncle was a medicine man. He asked the therapist if he would mind talking to his uncle from time to time so that he could combine some of the healing practices of his religion with those of therapy. He appeared comfortable during the initial stage of the session and talked freely and openly about his feelings and past experiences. Toward the end of the session, he asked to use a notepad and pen to make notes about the summary of the session, saying, "I want to take notes on what you are saying so that I can think about it later and make plans for our next session."

Masked Traditional. Rose's initial cultural style was reflective of her "false" self. She admitted during a later session that she tried to deny her preferred style (traditional) and had adopted a modern style because "I was trying to do what I thought others wanted. I was trying to protect myself so I would not be hurt anymore." She was Spanish-dominant, but continued to speak English even after the therapist had indicated that he was bilingual and the session could be conducted in the language of her choice. She gave every indication that she was not interested in establishing a close "working alliance" with the therapist but merely wanted him to give her advice on how to be more assertive and independent. About halfway through the first session when Rose began to feel more trusting and comfortable, she began to manifest her preferred mixed cognitive style—she began to use Spanish along with English, particularly when expressing her emotions. She then began to focus on her primary reasons for coming to therapy—how to accept the change in her role as a parent now that she had impaired vision. She was particularly concerned about how her children were being affected by her loss of vision.

Traditional. Tony preferred to speak in Spanish even though he was a fluent bilingual. He addressed the therapist by using the *usted* (the more formal form of Spanish) even though the therapist was younger than he. Tony also emphasized the traditional value of self-abnegation when it came to his children when indicating what he would like to gain from counseling, He said, *"Lo mas importante para mis es que mis hijos reciban una educacion y que no tengan problemas con la ley"* (The most important thing is that my children receive an education and stay out of trouble).

Initial Match of Preferred Cultural Style

The therapist made an effort to match the preferred cultural style of each of these clients. Based on understandings gained during initial interactions with each client, the therapist sought to avoid mismatch.

Traditional. The therapist addressed Imelda as Ms. and her surname. The therapist also showed respect for her initial shyness and discomfort during the session by using a soothing tone of voice and by projecting acceptance and concern through his body language. The therapist took the cue from Imelda that she would prefer it if he were initially directive, so he began by mentioning the athletic letter on her jacket, opening a discussion about her involvement in basketball and volleyball at school. She gradually approached her problems as she talked about her teammates, teachers, boyfriends, parents, and grandparents.

Modern. The therapist indicated that Harold could use his first name and then proceeded to do the same when addressing the client. Following Harold's lead, the therapist took a notepad and pen and began taking notes as the client spoke. The therapist also followed Harold's focus on self-efficacy and indicated how the therapeutic approach he used might help in understanding and resolving the problems Harold was discussing.

Traditional. The therapist addressed Tara by Ms. and her surname until halfway through the session when the client said, "Please call me Tara." He focused on helping Tara to feel more at ease while she was discussing her problems. He addressed her feelings of inadequacy and guilt directly, "You feel it is difficult for you to balance all the demands you have in your life— being a good mother, employee, and daughter and having intimate relationships that are satisfying and meaningful."

Mixed. The therapist indicated that he was pleased that Alex had chosen him as a potential role model and that he would be glad to serve as a guide. At the same time the therapist addressed Alex's modernism by saying, "You need to focus on feeling good about yourself first, because you feel that most of your life you have been trying to be the kind of person others have wanted you to be. That has not been satisfying for you. You are ready for a change."

Mixed. The therapist responded to Raul's mixture of Spanish and English by combining the languages as well. He reinforced the client for the extensive introspection he had done regarding his problems of adjustment. The therapist indicated that, other than what he had read in the literature, he did not know much about the Native American Church, but that he would be anxious to learn about it from Raul and with Raul's permission would consult with the uncle as the therapy progressed. He was supportive of Raul's interest in taking notes during the time he was summarizing what had transpired at the end of the session.

Masked Traditional. The initial observations of Rose's behavior led the therapist to believe that Rose was employing a cultural style that was uncomfortable for her—the "false" self. He, therefore, focused on establishing an atmosphere of nonjudgmental acceptance by using a soothing tone of voice and body language that gave the message that Rose would be "safe" in the counseling relationship. He said to Rose, "I get the feeling that you are uncomfortable about being here, that you feel that I am not going to accept you as you really are."

Traditional. The therapist spoke Spanish when addressing Tony and used the more formal *usted* form, indicating that he respected Tony as an older person. He said, *"A pesar de que usted esta sufriendo mucho con su salud fisica lo que considera mas importante en la vida es el futuro de sus hijos"* (In spite of the fact that you are experiencing serious physical problems, you feel that the most important thing in life is the future of your children). He went on to say, *"En su terapia voy a concentrarme en ayudarle para que pueda ayudar a sus hijos a tener una vida sana y un buen futuro"* (In therapy I will focus on helping you to help your children have healthy and productive lives and to have good futures).

Categorizing Initial Observations of Preferred Cognitive Styles

Field Sensitive Cognitive Style Preference and Client Behavior. The client whose preferred cognitive style is field sensitive usually communicates using both verbal and nonverbal modes. Facial expression, body posture, and tone of voice are likely to be just as important as what is actually being said. The client who is predominantly field sensitive also tends to give a global, or general, description of problems, and is likely to talk about relationships with others. The preferred field sensitive client gives the therapist the message that direction is welcome: "Where do I begin?"

Field Independent Cognitive Style Preference and Client Behavior. The preferred field independent style client follows a rather strict verbal mode of communication, selecting words carefully. Problems are usually described in detail, with the definitions of problems circumscribed. Further, the client who is preferred field independent views problems as separate from the totality of being: "I just want some help with my lack of patience." The field independent client will usually initiate discussion in therapy and may even discuss hypotheses he has formed about problems: "I've been thinking, and I feel that the reason I don't have much patience is that I can't seem to relax."

Bicognition and Client Behavior. The client who can flex cognitively will use a mixture of behaviors and approaches typical of both field independent and field sensitive clients. For example, a client who can flex cognitively may demonstrate a global view of problems but use an exclusively verbal communication mode.

The Preferred Cognitive Styles Observation Checklist

As with the Preferred Cultural Styles Observation Checklist, the checklist for preferred cognitive styles evolved from research with field sensitive and field independent subjects (Ramirez, 1998). As with the checklist for cultural styles, the therapist can keep the Preferred Cognitive Styles Observation Checklist in view during the course of the initial session in order to make notations or notes based on observations of the client's behavior. Table 7.2 shows samples from the checklist for preferred cognitive styles. The Preferred Cognitive Styles Observations Checklist is provided in Appendix E to facilitate duplication for use by therapists and counselors.

Manifestation of Preferred Cognitive Style in Case Studies

Field Sensitive. Imelda, a preferred field sensitive client, talked about her reasons for attempting suicide in a global way: "I was very lonely." She

TABLE 7.2 Samples from the Preferred Cognitive Styles Observation Checklist

Field Sensitive	Field Independent
____ Is self-disclosing	____ Depersonalizes problems
____ Shows interest in personalizing relationship with therapist	____ Relationship with therapist secondary to focus on problems to be addressed during therapy
____ Indicates that social rewards from therapist will be important to progress	____ Indicates that increase in personal well-being will be important to progress
____ Global focus and deductive (specific-to-global) learning style	____ Detail-focused and inductive learning style

described her adjustment problems in terms of impaired relationships with others: "The people I love just don't seem to understand me the way I am." She asked for direction from the therapist: "Maybe you can tell me how I can get them to understand that I have to be myself."

Field Independent. Harold, who was preferred field independent, was more specific in explaining his reasons for seeking therapy: "I just don't seem to understand what it is that my family and my partners are trying to tell me. It is as if we are speaking different languages, and it is frustrating." He identified what he wanted to get out of therapy with a great deal of self-focus: "I need to regain my self-confidence. I want to feel effective again." Harold made it clear that he wanted the therapist to serve as a consultant for him: "I've been thinking about my problems, and I think it's a matter of improving my ability to communicate with others. This is where I need your help, because I don't know exactly how to go about this. I do know that I have to work on it myself."

Mixed. Tara described her problems of adjustment in a global manner with little emphasis on detail. She made it clear that she wished to personalize her relationship with the therapist: "I choose to come to you because you are Hispanic. I felt that you would understand what it is like to be a minority and to know the importance of my family in my life. I also chose you because you are a man and I have always been able to relate better to men than to women. I have very few female friends." Tara made it clear that she wanted the therapist to serve more as consultant than as a directive guide: "Being a single mother and having to find a partner who is sensitive and understands that I am a mother first and all else second is something I know you cannot help me with, so even though I ask you for advice, those are things I will have to work out by myself."

Mixed.   Alex presented with a mixed cognitive style: He indicated clearly that the relationship with the caregiver was important to him, "Since you are a mental health professional who is also an ethnic minority, I want to be like you. I have never really found a mentor. I assumed that you were probably Catholic so you would be able to understand my religion. It is very important to me." Alex's field independent orientation was reflected in the self-focus on his problems of adjustment: "I need to feel better about myself. If I can learn to solve my own problems, then I can stop lying to others."

Mixed.   Raul showed a mixed cognitive style. He expressed his desire to personalize his relationship with the therapist: "One of my friends, who was in one of your classes at the university, said that you were multiracial and had grown up in the Valley [the U.S.–Mexico border region of South Texas], so that is why I wanted to come see you. I, too, am multiracial and I have family in the Valley." His preference for a field independent style was manifested in his attention to detail; Raul would quote conversations he held with family members and friends in great detail and focused on how he worded his communications with others.

Masked.   Rose initially presented with cultural and cognitive styles that were nonpreferred. She used an extreme field independent style when she described her problems of adjustment; she distanced herself from her feelings and made it clear that she only wanted to use the therapist as a consultant: "I try not to get too close to others so I am having trouble relating to you right now. Is it possible that I can just ask you some questions and only ask for your help when I need it? I can listen to what you have to say and then decide whether I should take your advice or not. I wish we could do this on the telephone."

Approximately two-thirds of the way through her first session, Rose became more relaxed and began to disclose more of herself. She became less defensive and responded to social rewards from the therapist concerning decisions she had already made in her life. She was then able to express her field sensitive cognitive style and recounted the guilt she felt about her fear of not being a good mother because of her vision impairment.

Field Sensitive.   Tony's focus was on his physical symptoms and how these interfered with his relationships with family members and friends, a predominant field sensitive orientation: *"Me pongo muy nervioso cuando no me puedo acordar del nombre de alguien a quien me encuentro en la tienda y llevo mucho tiempo de conocer. Siento mucha tension en el cuello y luego mi cabeza comienza a temblar de lado a lado y no me puedo controlar"* ("I get very nervous when I run into someone I've known for a long time. I feel a great deal of tension in my neck muscles and then my head starts to shake from side to side and I cannot control myself.").

Initial Match of Preferred Cognitive Styles

As he did with cultural styles, the therapist in these cases attempted to match the cognitive styles of the clients.

Field Sensitive.   The therapist matched Imelda's global approach to conceptualizing her problems by focusing on her feelings: "It must have been terrible to feel so alone." He focused on her concerns about problems in relationships with others, indicating that he would be directive in therapy and would attempt to serve as a model for her.

Field Independent.   Harold's focus on specifics, indicating a field independent communication style, was matched by the therapist's reflection of the specific concerns the client had identified as his major problems. The therapist also matched Harold on his self-focus with respect to his reasons for seeking therapy: "Differences in communication styles can cause us to feel ineffective and confused." The therapist encouraged Harold to continue an active role in therapy and indicated that he would work with Harold in a consultant role: "You've made the right choice in seeking therapy, because it can help you to improve your communication style and to understand the communication styles of others."

Masked.   The therapist, sensing that Rose was not initially using her preferred cognitive style, reflected the style she was using but also emphasized an atmosphere of nonjudgmental acceptance during the session so that Rose might eventually feel free to express her true preferred styles. He accomplished this by not overreacting to Rose's abrupt style and her initial defensiveness and, at the same time, talking in a soothing, relaxed tone that communicated acceptance regardless of what she was saying or how she was behaving: "I can sense your reluctance in coming here. I am glad you decided to come, and I will do all I can to make you feel comfortable at the sessions." As Rose began to express more and more of her field sensitive style, the therapist changed his approach to match hers and to support her in her use of this style.

Terminating the Initial Session

Following the observations and discussions during the initial session in multicultural psychotherapy and counseling, the therapist uses the final twenty or thirty minutes of the first session to administer the assessment instruments to clients to help assess their cognitive and cultural styles. These include the Multicultural Experience Inventory (Appendix A), the Traditionalism–Modernism Inventory (Appendix B), the Family Attitude Scale (Appendix C), and the Bicognitive Orientation to Life Scale (Appendix G). While the client is completing the instruments, the therapist reviews the notes and ratings made on the Preferred Cultural and Cognitive Styles Observation Checklists, comparing these to the self-ratings (see Chapter 6) made on the therapist's Preferred Cognitive and Cultural Styles instrument completed during the course of the session.

Through this exercise the therapist is able to determine how effective she is likely to be in matching the client and makes the decision to either schedule the client for another session or to make a referral to another therapist. If the professional is in doubt at this point, it is possible to wait to evaluate the data from the instruments the client completes before reaching a final decision. The therapist either schedules the client for another appointment or agrees to call at a later time to give feedback on the initial session and to inform the client as to whether another appointment should be scheduled or a referral made to another therapist who might be better able to match the client's styles.

In summary, the first session includes the following six techniques and procedures:

1. Establishing of an atmosphere of nonjudgmental acceptance.
2. Observing and categorizing client behavior using the Preferred Cultural and Cognitive Styles Observation Checklists.
3. Matching the client's preferred cultural and cognitive styles.
4. Determining the professional's self-assessment of preferred cultural and cognitive therapeutic styles.
5. Comparing the therapist's and client's preferred styles.
6. Scheduling the client for another session or referring to another therapist.

SESSION 2

Continuation of Match

The matching strategies initiated at the first session are continued during the second. In the opening stages of the second session, the focus of therapy is similar to that of the first session: helping the client to overcome the negative effects of the mismatch syndrome, establishing trust (particularly if the client is presenting with the nonpreferred styles), and continuing to provide a safe atmosphere in which the client can express the unique self. The matching techniques and approaches used for the second session with four of the clients discussed in Chapter 1 are presented next.

Imelda.   The therapist began the session with Imelda by addressing her by Ms. and her surname and by making every effort to be warm and supportive. Imelda seemed much happier and more at ease than she had been at the initial session. To encourage her to feel even more at ease, the therapist asked her about her plans for the spring term. She talked willingly and enthusiastically about her forthcoming games with the basketball team and reported that she was the team captain. She talked about her plans for attending the state university the coming fall.

The therapist's matching behaviors with Imelda included matching both her cultural and cognitive styles; for clarity of presentation, these will be categorized according to the five domains of cognitive style:

1. *Interpersonal relationship style.* The therapist leaned forward in his chair, listening attentively while Imelda talked. He asked questions that allowed her to personalize her accomplishments in sports and in her classes, such as, "You said that you are the captain of your team this year. The other players must think a lot of you" and "You mentioned you had made an A on your term paper for English. What was it about?"

2. *Communication style.* The therapist's facial expressions and tone of voice reflected warmth and support. He maintained eye contact with Imelda while she was talking. The feelings Imelda expressed were reflected through both verbal and nonverbal modes of communication.

3. *Motivational–reward style.* The therapist commented on the fact that Imelda looked happier and seemed more relaxed. He gave verbal and behavioral signs of approval when Imelda talked about her successes. He also showed verbal and nonverbal signs of enthusiasm when Imelda said that she had felt better after the first therapy session.

4. *Problem-solving style.* Whenever the opportunity presented itself, the therapist indicated that he would be glad to serve as a model for Imelda. He showed signs of being directive in his style. When Imelda talked about her problems in her relationship with her parents and teachers, he said, "I know that this is hard for you, but we're going to work on your problems together, as a team. You won't feel like you are all alone anymore."

5. *Therapy–teaching–parenting–supervisory style.* In the latter stages of the second session, when the therapist presented the flex theory to Imelda and gave her feedback on his assessments, he personalized this material by relating it to Imelda's interests and life experiences. He used a global–deductive method of presentation; that is, he presented the overall idea or concept first, and then focused on the details, describing how the theory could be applied to her life. For example: "Value conflicts have been responsible for many of your problems. You and your grandparents used to be very close. When you started getting involved in sports, an activity they felt was not appropriate for girls, they disapproved of you. You felt lonely, rejected, and misunderstood."

Harold. In the case of Harold, the therapist's match behaviors were oriented more toward field independence. Harold entered the office for his second session carrying a portfolio. In it he carried a notepad on which he had analyzed his communication problems with his wife, his children, and his partners. As soon as the session started, he said, "I've been doing some thinking since the last session, and I have made notes on the communication problems I talked about last time. I'd like to read these to you."

1. *Interpersonal relationship style.* The therapist greeted Harold by using his first name, and he allowed Harold to begin the session by reading his notes. As Harold read, the therapist made notes of his own and assumed a formal, businesslike manner.

2. *Communication style.* The therapist used an impersonal tone of voice, making minimal use of nonverbal communication. His statements were short and to the point. He chose his words carefully.

3. *Motivational–reward style.* The therapist focused on encouraging self rewards: "It must feel good that you are finally beginning to deal with your problems rather than just worrying about them."

4. *Problem-solving style.* The therapist functioned as a consultant and made recommendations and suggestions only when Harold asked for help or advice.

5. *Therapy–teaching–parenting–supervisory style.* When the therapist presented the concepts of the flex theory of personality to Harold, he did so by focusing on details and by using a formal–analytic–inductive presentation style: "Communication styles can be classified according to two dimensions: modern–traditional and field sensitive–field independent."

Tara.   The therapist began with a mix of field sensitive and modern styles. He projected warmth and support in both his verbal and nonverbal behaviors, but he also encouraged Tara to begin the session by saying, "What would you like to talk about today?"

1. *Interpersonal relationship style.* Tara seemed to feel more comfortable in her interactions with the therapist as evidenced by increased eye contact. She responded well to his attempts to personalize the relationship as he asked how her daughter liked school.

2. *Communication style.* Tara was able to talk more about her feelings. She used a global style relating her experiences as a mother to the time when she was a child and how she felt about her parents. She also talked about her relationships with her intimate partners and how important it was to her that they be interested in and relate well to her child.

3. *Motivational style.* Tara made it clear that she felt that her principal goal in therapy should be to achieve independence from those whom she felt had dominated her choices in the past, her parents and her ex-boyfriend. The therapist encouraged this: "You need to feel that you are in control of your own destiny and that you can feel free to make your own decisions without feeling that you have to please others or that you have to conform to the way they would like you to be."

4. *Problem-solving style.* Tara needed to think globally—"to see the big picture"—regarding her problems of adjustment. She needed to understand how her past, particularly her relationship to her parents, was related to her present situation as a single mother and as a woman of color who was trying to adjust to the demands of college life and her world of work in a community in which she faced prejudice: "I feel that I have just been pulled by the tide since I was a kid. I need to understand what has happened to me because I usually blame myself and this makes me angry and sad." The therapist responded to her need for making sense of her life by saying, "I will help you to try to understand how your past is related to your present feelings and to your tendency to be too hard on yourself."

Alex. The therapist tried to make Alex feel at ease during the second session. Alex arrived distraught because he had talked to his parents over the phone the previous evening and he had had to lie to them again. The therapist conveyed to Alex, in both verbal and nonverbal behaviors, that he empathized with his feelings and that he was not going to judge him negatively for what he had done. Alex seemed reassured by this approach.

1. *Interpersonal relationship style.* The therapist continued approaching Alex in the "accepting authority figure" role. Alex responded by becoming more relaxed. He noted that the feelings of guilt that he had felt at the beginning of the session began to dissipate.

2. *Communication style.* Alex's field independent style was reflected in his emphasis on the details of what his parents had said over the phone and how he had responded to them. The therapist matched this style by helping Alex to understand the nuances of the messages his parents were giving him and how these affected his feelings.

3. *Motivational style.* Alex continued to emphasize his self-focus with respect to the goals of therapy. He said, "I need to know how to listen to what my parents have to say without personalizing it and feeling like the bad son. I need to understand that I need to be myself without feeling bad about it." The therapist matched this by saying: "You feel that you are in control of your feelings and thoughts until you talk to your parents. Then you feel like a child and start feeling guilty. It is important that you continue to view yourself as an adult who can make his own decisions."

4. *Problem-solving style.* Alex expressed a relational style much like Tara's: "I want to be able to put all the pieces together in my life. I have been getting confused by all the conflicting information I have received from the Vietnamese student group and the gay and lesbian support groups I have been attending on campus." The therapist matched this communication by saying, "I will try to help you sort out all the conflicting information you have been getting so that you can make your own decision about how to approach your friends, parents, and family."

The Life History

An important aspect of the second session of multicultural psychotherapy is the life history. This technique not only identifies the developmental stages of the client's preferred cultural and cognitive styles—the unique self— but also reveals how and why the client suppressed the true personality and developed a false self. Specifically, the life history yields the following information:

1. The client's basic foundation for multicultural development: the degree of client motivation to experience diversity and to learn from it, and the degree of openness of the client's learning–experience filters.
2. The number and types of barriers to multicultural development such as stereotypes (whether negative or positive), ethnocentric behaviors and attitudes, and shyness.
3. The initial manifestations of the unique self in life and values and belief systems as well as intellectual and/or occupational interests that may have been suppressed or rejected later on in life.
4. Those periods or phases in the client's life when maximum cultural and cognitive match and mismatch were experienced.
5. The effects of socialization—attitudes of parents toward diversity; attitudes of other socialization agents and of peers toward diversity; attitudes toward diversity reflected by cultures, communities, and religions in which the client was socialized.
6. The effects of life experiences—how much exposure the client had to diversity over the course of life and the nature and quality of those diversity experiences: the different countries, communities, and neighborhoods in which the client lived; the schools attended; the positive and negative experiences the client had with diversity (e.g., conflicts, experiences with prejudice, and rejection).

The life history also provides information the therapist can use to personalize the next phase of the second session—introducing the client to the flex theory of personality—and to set the goals for multicultural psychotherapy. The life history is an important component of multicultural therapy because it is the initial stage of the process of client empowerment.

Guidelines for Taking the Life History.   The therapist introduces the life history by explaining what it is and why it will be useful: "I would like to do a short life history with you in order to better understand how your personality developed and to determine how your adjustment problems started." A good way to begin a life history is to use what Alfred Adler (1931) called the Earliest Childhood Recollection (ERC). The therapist does this by asking the client to recall the earliest memory of childhood. After the recollection of earliest childhood, the life history is continued by focusing on the following five life periods:

1. *Infancy and early childhood.* This period would include the childhood years prior to beginning school. Some specific questions can be asked in this area:

- How did you get along with your parents and siblings?
- Describe the adults you interacted with.
- Describe the peers you played with most often.
- What were your fantasies and daydreams?

2. *Early school experiences and elementary school years.* This involves asking the client about his or her earliest memories of school and about elementary school experiences. Questions could include:

- How comfortable did you feel with your first teacher or teachers (counselors, coaches, etc.)? With classmates? With the school environment as a whole?
- What languages did you speak?
- What classes did you do best in? Which ones were of most interest to you?
- What awards did you get?
- What failures did you experience?
- What countries, regions, states, communities, and neighborhoods did you live in during these early schooldays?
- Who were your best friends?
- What kinds of families did you visit with?
- Who were you parents' best friends?
- What jobs or careers were you most interested in?
- What were your hobbies?
- When you traveled with your family, where did you go?

3. *Middle school years.* Late childhood and early adolescent experiences can be probed with modified versions of the questions used to explore early educational experiences (item 2), as well as by asking if the middle school was different from the elementary school and how.

4. *High school years.* The adolescent years of the client's life history are investigated through the use of the questions suggested in item 2. When necessary, the questions can be made more age-appropriate. Additional questions about job experiences and more in-depth questioning about socializing with peers include:

- Did you work during high school? What kind of job did you have? Describe your supervisor(s).
- Did you date? Describe the background of the people you dated.

5. *Post–high school period.* Focusing on the period since the client left high school, the therapist asks about:

- College(s) attended and experiences with professors, courses, reading assignments, peers, and decisions involving career choices

- Training program experiences, if any
- Military service experience, if appropriate
- Marriage and/or meaningful intimate relationships
- Jobs or initiation of a career
- Travel and other interests
- Religion

The information collected through the brief life history is invaluable in doing an analysis of match and mismatch experiences and in identifying shifts in cultural and cognitive styles during the client's lifetime.

Imelda's life history, for example, revealed that during her early years she experienced cultural compatibility with her grandparents in terms of their willingness to serve as a support system for her when her mother left home, when her father remarried, and when she experienced conflict with her half-sister and stepmother. Later in her life, however, mismatch developed in the area of gender roles when she developed a strong interest in sports.

Harold's early interest in art and music were a good match to his mother's preferred field sensitive cognitive style. She provided Harold with the nurturing he needed because of the rejection he felt from his father and older brother. After his brother's death, Harold shifted to a preferred field independent style in order to please his father.

Tara's attempts at becoming closer to her father and her brothers in the absence of her mother and her father's rejection of these attempts because he felt that farm work was not appropriate for a girl were critical in Tara's later feelings that people would not accept her. Her first major experience with match was the boyfriend she had in college whom she felt provided a good cultural style match for her, but the euphoria of finally having found someone who matched her led her to have premature sexual relations without having received adequate sex education.

Alex felt well matched to the cultural styles of his grandparents early in life. When the family immigrated to this country, his parents became more active in his childrearing and the influence of his grandparents decreased; Alex felt mismatched to his mother's cognitive style, which was very field independent. She had had to be individually competitive to survive as a businesswoman in the traditional, male-dominated businessworld of South Vietnam.

Introducing the Flex Theory of Personality

Once the life history is completed, the therapist introduces the client to the concept and principles of the flex theory of personality. This phase of the second session of multicultural psychotherapy reinforces the client-empowerment process initiated through the life history. It encourages the client to become an active partner in the therapeutic process. This is done by acquainting the client with the major principles and assumptions of the personality theory on which multicultural therapy is based.

The therapist begins this stage of the session by explaining that multi-cultural psychotherapy is an approach to personal counseling based on the flex theory of personality. The therapist then presents the following six basic principles of flex theory:

1. *The unique self.* Everyone is unique, because every person has a unique arrangement of values, or cultural style, and cognitive style preferences reflected in their personalities.

2. *Cultural styles.* There are two major kinds of cultural styles, each representing a different set of values and belief systems. The traditional style is typical of rural communities, conservative religions, and minority and developing cultures. People who are identified with traditional values have a spiritual orientation toward life, emphasizing spiritual ideas when explaining the mysteries of life. They are strongly identified with their families and communities of origin; they usually believe in separation of gender and age roles; and they usually believe in strict approaches to childrearing. The modern style, on the other hand, is typical of urban communities, liberal religions, and of North American and Western European cultures. People who are identified with a modern value system usually emphasize science when explaining the mysteries of life; they have a strong individualistic orientation; they tend to deemphasize differences in gender and age roles; and they emphasize egalitarianism in childrearing practices. These styles are a continuum and individuals can fall anyplace along that line.

3. *Personality styles.* There are three kinds of personality styles, each representing different types of cognitive styles: The field independent style includes people who tend to be introverted in their orientation to life. They focus on words when communicating with others, and they are usually motivated by material and monetary rewards and by personal achievements. In their thinking and problem-solving styles, field independent people are more likely to be analytical and inductive, paying a great deal of attention to detail. They usually tend to be nondirective in childrearing and in teaching or supervising and counseling others.

Field sensitive style people tend to be extroverted in their general orientation toward life. They tend to focus more on nonverbal than on verbal messages when they are communicating with others. They are usually motivated by the possibility of achieving for others and by social rewards. People with a preferred field sensitive orientation are more global, integrative, and deductive in their thinking and problem-solving styles, and they tend to be directive in childrearing and teaching or when they supervise and counsel others.

People who are bicognitive have the ability to shuttle between the field sensitive and field independent styles. Their choice of style at any particular moment is dependent on the demands of the situation they are in. For example, if the situation calls for individual competition, they behave in a field independent manner; if the demand is for cooperation or group competition, they behave in a field sensitive manner. People with a bicognitive orientation can also use elements of both the field sensitive and field independent styles to develop new composite or combination styles. They can also evolve communication styles that highlight both verbal and nonverbal behaviors.

4. *Components of styles.* Each cognitive and personality style is made up of five components:

- *Communication style.* How people express themselves to others
- *Interpersonal relationship style.* How people go about establishing relationships with others and how they relate to others
- *Motivational style.* What people consider rewarding about life
- *Learning and problem-solving style.* How people learn new things and how they solve the problems they are faced with
- *Teaching–parenting–supervisory–counseling style.* How people impart knowledge or give direction to others, how they guide others, and how they provide emotional support

5. *Personality development.* Cultural and cognitive styles are related to personality development. People who are socialized and have lived in traditional environments—be they cultures, communities, families, and institutions—are more likely to be preferred field sensitive in cognitive style. Those who are socialized or who have lived in modernistic environments are more likely to be preferred field independent in cognitive style. People who have been socialized in both modern and traditional environments and have lived in both modern and traditional settings are likely to be bicognitive in their cognitive style.

6. *Variations.* Cultural and cognitive styles can vary from being flexible and adaptable to being inflexible and specific to certain environments or situations. People with rigid cultural and cognitive styles have multicultural personalities and are well adjusted to a pluralistic society.

The figures presented in Appendix I may make it easier for the client to follow the therapist's presentation about the important features and concepts of the flex theory of personality. Providing the client with copies of these figures will facilitate reference to them as needed during the course of therapy.

The client should be encouraged to ask questions during the presentation. The therapist attempts to match the presentation style to the client's preferred learning and problem-solving style. For example, the therapist can personalize the presentation with field sensitive clients by referring to information obtained from the client's life history. On the other hand, with field independent clients, the therapist can focus more on the details of the charts and diagrams and on the specific research that led to the theory's development (see Chapters 2 and 3).

Feedback on Assessment of Preferred Styles.   The therapist initiates this phase of the session by referring to the questionnaires the client completed during the first session and by explaining their purpose. The therapist is encouraged to use the Feedback Summary Sheet (see Appendix J). The following is an excerpt of the assessment feedback done with Imelda:

> At the conclusion of the last session I asked you to complete some questionnaires. I asked you to do these to help me determine your preferred cultural and cognitive styles. I have also been doing an assessment during our sessions by noticing your behaviors and by noting what you said and how you said it. Let me tell you what my assessments indicate.
>
> Your preferred cultural style seems to be traditional, but you tend to have modern views in the area of gender-role definition. Most indicative of your preferred cultural style is the fact that your score on the Traditionalism–Modernism Inventory was 38. [The version of the TMI given to Imelda was the original pre-revised version.] You indicated strong agreement on those items that were concerned with family identity, spiritualism, and sense of community, all indications of a traditional orientation. Despite an overall traditional cultural orientation, you did indicate that you are modern in the domain of gender roles—you believe that men and women should have equal rights.

The therapist continued by giving feedback on the ratings he had made of Imelda's behaviors in the sessions using the Preferred Cultural Styles Observation Checklist, showing that her global cultural style was indeed traditional. In the process of discussing the behavioral ratings he made, the therapist read excerpts from notes he took during the course of the therapy sessions to give specific examples which helped to clarify the ratings to the client. (See Appendix K for responses given by Imelda to the Traditionalism–Modernism Inventory and for copies of the notes that were made by the therapist as he interacted with Imelda during the initial session.)

Feedback on Cognitive Style Assessment.   This feedback is given in much the same way as it is for cultural style. The following are excerpts from the feedback given to Harold:

> Your preferred cognitive style at the present time is field independent. For example, your score on the Bicognitive Orientation to Life Scale was 31, and you scored in a field independent direction in all five domains. Most revealing of your field independent orientation are the following items: 3, 7, 8, 11, 14, 15, 20, and 21. However, your responses to items 5 and 13 indicate that you also have strong field sensitive interests. My observations of your behaviors during our sessions also

show a strong field independent orientation, but again there are some indications that you are somewhat more balanced in the domains of interpersonal relationships and teaching–parenting–supervisory style. On a scale of 1 (no flexibility) to 5 (maximum flex), your cognitive style balance at the present time appears to be 2.

(See Appendix L for the response given by Harold to the BOLS and for copies of the notes made by the therapist during the first therapy session with Harold.)

The therapist then summarized the findings of Harold's evaluation:

In summary the results of the assessment of your preferred cognitive and cultural styles show that you need to be more flexible in the following domains: cultural; gender roles, time orientation, and child socialization, and cognitive; communication; motivation; and thinking and problem solving.

Establishing the Goals of Therapy

The therapist introduces the final stage of the second session by proposing some tentative goals based on the problems identified by the client during the first session and on the findings of the assessment. The therapist engages the client's help in formulating the goals of therapy. The following is an excerpt from the case notes on Imelda:

One goal of therapy can be to help you develop your modernistic cultural style and your field independent cognitive style in order to get your parents, teachers, coaches, and some of your friends at school to better understand you. You could also develop more of your field sensitive and traditional preferred style in order to get your grandparents to understand you better. Would you like to suggest some goals that you would like us to work on?

Imelda answered, "Well, I need to have more friends. Coming to therapy has made me realize that I have been too lonely. I also need to know how to get my teachers and coaches to listen to my ideas." As Imelda spoke, the therapist listed the goals with a marking pencil on a large pad on an easel.

In summary, the second session includes the following five techniques and procedures:

1. Continuing to match of the client's preferred cultural and cognitive styles.
2. Conducting a life history.
3. Introducing the flex theory of personality.
4. Establishing the goals of therapy.
5. Providing feedback on the findings of the life history, the assessment instruments, and the observation checklists.

SUMMARY

The first two sessions of multicultural psychotherapy have as their principal goal helping the client to overcome the symptoms of mismatch syndrome by matching his preferred cultural and cognitive styles. The initial match strategies facilitate expression of the unique self so that the client can begin the next phase of therapy—the development of cultural and cognitive flex.

8

THE SECOND STAGE
OF MULTICULTURAL THERAPY
AND COUNSELING

Acceptance of the Unique Self
and Development of Cultural
and Cognitive Flex

The previous chapter presented the principal goals of the first and second sessions of multicultural psychotherapy and counseling. This chapter focuses on two major objectives: encouraging clients to accept their unique selves and encouraging them to develop an orientation to life that reflects cultural and cognitive flexibility. Both client and therapist have important roles to play in this phase of multicultural therapy.

SESSIONS 3 THROUGH 5:
ENCOURAGING ACCEPTANCE OF THE UNIQUE SELF

The degree of difficulty of this phase of counseling for both the client and the therapist can vary, depending on the degree to which the client has suppressed and/or denied his or her unique self. Imelda, Harold, Tara, and Alex are representative cases.

Imelda had continued to develop her preferred style with respect to a modern orientation in gender role despite pressures to conform from parents and grandparents, but fear of alienating her grandparents and her boyfriend's parents had caused her to downplay her interest in sports and had kept her from establishing close friendships with her coaches and with other players on her teams. Imelda had not denied her unique self with respect to the other domains of her preferred cultural and cognitive styles.

Harold, on the other hand, had undergone a more extensive suppression of both his preferred cultural and cognitive styles. After the death of his brother, he had abandoned his preferred styles in an attempt to please his father. Nevertheless, he did occasionally make use of his preferred styles in certain domains of life—his traditionalism and field sensitivity were reflected in the fact that he was the charismatic leader of his company, establishing a sense of community for his employees and in his interest in developing an extensive graphics software product line.

Tara had forced herself into a traditional cultural style orientation when she lived with her boyfriend. He believed in strict separation of gender roles, and she found herself in the role she had played when she lived in the home of her parents, something she deeply resented. Since she had broken up with her boyfriend, she had expressed her modern views regarding egalitarian relationships with the men she dated, but this had led to conflict. She still felt she had to conform to her parent's traditional expectations of her when she visited them or talked with them on the telephone. She had begun to exert her field independence at work; an older close friend had encouraged Tara to mimic her approach to problem solving in the workplace. Tara decided to refuse her friend's offer for help by finding her own way to solve work tasks.

Alex had developed a mixed cultural style in changing his major without seeking the permission of his parents, but he still maintained his need for advice from family members by informing his favorite aunt and uncle about his decision. Alex had forced himself to try to adapt to a field independent orientation with respect to personal interests and to his study focus in college. His change in major to sociology and social work allowed him to express his preferred field sensitive style in the learning/problem-solving domain.

The Role of the Client

Clients learn to recognize pressures to conform to which they have been most vulnerable. They also learn to understand how these pressures are related to the development of the false self and the suppression of the unique self. To identify the sources of pressures to conform, clients have to do thorough and careful assessments of their social environments. The sources of pressures to conform can include people and/or institutions with important roles in the clients' life. In the case of Imelda, these include her grandparents, parents, boyfriend's parents, and teachers, as well as the traditional community in which she lives. For Harold, sources of pressure to conform include his father, partners, colleagues, and his company. For Tara the tyranny of the shoulds had its origins in the behavior and expectations of her parents, her ex-boyfriend, and her older coworker. For Alex it was his grandparents (early in his life), his parents (after the family immigrated to the

United States), his heterosexual friends, and the strict views of the Catholic Church regarding homosexuality.

With the direction of the therapist, clients ask themselves where the conformity pressures originate, how these pressures are making themselves felt, what responses these pressures have provoked in the past, and how they can recognize when they are falling back into using the cultural and cognitive styles of their false selves in response to these pressures. Another important task for clients during Sessions 3 through 5 is learning how to come to terms with the discomfort of being different.

The Role of the Therapist

In this phase of multicultural counseling, the therapist focuses on establishing an atmosphere to enable the client to begin exploring and developing the unique self, which may have been suppressed by pressures to conform. The therapist facilitates the process of expression and acceptance of the unique self by projecting respect and acceptance of the client's preferred styles. Additionally the professional gives the client the opportunity to accomplish the matching goals identified in the previous session. These cultural and cognitive match goals have three objectives:

1. To help the client to feel comfortable with the unique self
2. To encourage the client to feel pride in that uniqueness
3. To initiate the process of developing the unique self to its maximum potential

Strategies for Matching Cultural Style Goals

Examples of the strategies used for achieving match goals have been taken from the counseling progress notes and therapeutic plans developed for Imelda, Harold, Tara, and Raul.

Imelda. The therapist asked Imelda to focus on the first of the cultural match goals established in the previous session: those of developing her modernistic orientation vis-à-vis equality in gender roles and developing her traditionalistic behaviors in such a way as to encourage her grandparents and parents to understand that her interest in sports is important to her well-being.

The therapist asked Imelda to think of people in her environment—teachers, coaches, friends of the family, authority figures, peers, or others—who could help her become more modernistic. After discussing a number of people, Imelda and the therapist settled on one of her basketball coaches, a Latina, as the best possibility because, according to Imelda's description, this person seemed to have established a good balance in her identification with modern and traditional values.

The therapist encouraged empathy projection by asking Imelda to answer two questions: What is important to your coach? What does she want out of life? This set the stage for writing a script, based on the coach's preferred cultural and cognitive styles, which Imelda could use when she solicited help from her. While Imelda described what she knew about the coach's interests and personality characteristics, the therapist and Imelda used the concepts from the flex theory of personality to develop hypotheses regarding the coach's preferred cultural and cognitive styles.

The therapist then asked Imelda to outline the script she could use for approaching the coach. The therapist and Imelda discussed the script and developed it to fit the coach's unique style. They decided Imelda would begin as follows: "Some time ago you asked me to come to you if I needed any help with my hook shot. Do you have time to help me now?" If the coach were to agree to help Imelda, the script to be used when Imelda and her coach were alone was as follows: "I need your advice on something personal. My parents and grandparents are opposed to my playing on the team. This has been bothering me. Do you have any advice for me?"

The next step in this stage of therapy is role-playing. The therapist assumed the role of the coach while Imelda tried out the script. Following the role-playing exercise, the therapist and Imelda developed a homework assignment that included a day and a time when Imelda would try out the script with her coach. Following this, Imelda was to do ratings and take notes to evaluate the degree of success she felt she had experienced in implementing the script (see Appendix J).

If necessary, the therapist and Imelda would modify the script and either try again with the same person or select someone else as a possible mentor in Imelda's efforts to achieve her cultural styles match goals. The therapist warned Imelda that she could encounter rejection from the person(s) for whom the script was intended. He also cautioned her that unforeseen circumstances might lead to failure of the script in part or in whole. Imelda was instructed that, should either rejection or failure occur, she should not blame herself, but merely take note of what happened and what was going on at the time. She was also asked to phone the therapist should she need to talk about feelings related to rejection or failure of a script.

As soon as they felt that the first goal of the cultural match series had been achieved, Imelda and the therapist proceeded to the other goals they had identified. They focused on three life domains: the interpersonal domain; the life activities domain; and the information, travel, and media domain.

In the interpersonal domain, Imelda gained enough confidence through her initial contact with the one Hispanic basketball coach to make a greater effort to get to know both her Hispanic and non-Hispanic coaches better. Most of these coaches proved to be good models for arriving at a comfortable mix of traditional and modern values and belief systems.

From the encouragement she received from her coaches, Imelda made gains in the activities domain; she joined a support group of Hispanic women in sports in one of the local churches in her community. Other changes in the activities domain included having one of her Hispanic coaches accompany her as she talked to her grandparents about her commitment to sports. Further, Imelda succeeded in getting her grandparents to go to one of her games. This improved relations between Imelda and her grandparents. As they became proud of her achievements on the court, they began to view Imelda's accomplishments as an achievement for the family.

In the information, travel, and media domain, Imelda started to read books and magazine articles about female athletes such as Nancy Lopez, Babe Zaharias, and some of the tennis players from Spain who had played at Wimbledon. She shared these with her parents and grandparents. Imelda also attended a women's basketball clinic at a state university. At the clinic she met other Hispanic women active in sports who had succeeded in making a good adjustment by combining traditional and modern values.

Harold.   For Harold the first goal on the cultural match goals list was to develop traditional values with a view toward improving his relationship with his wife and children. In the interpersonal domain, the therapist began by asking Harold to think of a script that would increase his opportunities to interact with his wife. This task appealed to Harold's desire to do things on his own; he immediately began taking notes and developing a script. He wrote, "You mentioned some time ago that the Art League is having a reception during an opening at one of the galleries. I would like to go with you, if you wouldn't mind." As with Imelda, the therapist discussed the script with Harold, role-played it, and after the necessary modifications, asked Harold to enact it with his wife.

In the life activities domain, the therapist and Harold examined some possibilities for activities that could match his traditional cultural style. They decided Harold could use his interest in photography to strengthen his bond with his wife and children. The family could go on photography expeditions together on weekends; they would be able to drive out to a scenic spot or historic sections of town and each family member would take photographs. The family would then talk about what they were trying to accomplish with composition of the picture, the subject matter, and the lighting.

To develop changes in the information, travel, and media domain, Harold began visiting museums and galleries in neighboring cities and universities in the Bay Area. He began reading magazines and books on photography and art, discovering a special interest in Leonardo da Vinci and others who had combined art with science and mathematics. He and his wife also planned an art tour of Europe for the coming summer, something she had wanted to do for a long time.

Tara. Tara needed to become more modern in the domain of equality of gender roles in her intimate relationships. In the interpersonal domain the therapist began by asking Tara to think of a couple she knew whom she admired because of the egalitarianism in their relationship. She identified a male cousin and his spouse who had been happily married for twenty years. She visited with this couple and asked about how they had achieved equality in their relationship. She received some useful advise.

Following this, Tara participated in the scriptwriting activity with the therapist. She needed to develop a script to discuss equality in the relationship with the person she was newly dating. One of the things she had learned from her cousin was that equality needed to be established early in a relationship. Tara developed the following script: "I need you to know that there is something that is important to me in a relationship, that it has to be fifty-fifty. We both have to feel that we have equal say-so. What I learned from the previous failed relationships is that I become unhappy when I feel that things are not equal."

In the activities domain, the therapist encouraged Tara to join a local women's center support group which focused on equality in intimate relationships. In the information, travel, and media domain, the therapist encouraged Tara to read several books to help make her relationships more successful, including:

- McMillan, T. (1994). *Waiting to Exhale.*
- Norwood, R. (1991). *Women Who Love Too Muc*
- Gray, J. (1992). *Men Are from Mars, Women Are from Venus*
- Estes, C. P. (1995). *Women Who Run with the Wolves*
- Beck, M. D. (1989). *Love Is Never Enough*

Raul. Raul needed to develop his mixed traditional and modern values reflective of his multicultural/multiracial background and experiences in his artwork. In order to fulfill the interpersonal domain, he joined an international art school in a nearby city and began to take courses there. He was able to meet and work collaboratively with Native American, Mexican American, Mexican, Asian American, and African American artists.

In the information, travel, and media domain, Raul started to take trips to Santa Fe, New Mexico, and San Francisco, California. During these visits he was able to observe the confluence of cultures through art. He also read books about Native American, African American, Asian, and Latino art.

Strategies for Meeting Cognitive Style Goals

In addition to establishing and meeting cultural style goals, clients and therapists also strive to meet cognitive style goals in Sessions 3 through 5. These also include goals in the interpersonal domain; the activities domain; and the information, travel, and media domain.

Imelda. The therapist and Imelda focused on one of the cognitive styles match goals identified in Session 2: the need to further develop Imelda's field sensitive cognitive style in the learning/problem-solving area. The first step was for Imelda to examine her environment and identify a person who might serve as a model for her. After some discussion, she and the therapist identified one of Imelda's peers, a student described by Imelda as being successful as a preferred field sensitive student. This time Imelda was able to develop her script without much help from the therapist. She then role-played the script with the therapist, and together they made some minor modifications. As her homework assignment, Imelda explored the idea of approaching her friend for help on some of her schoolwork. She carried out the assignment, took notes, and reviewed them at the next session with the therapist.

In the activities domain, Imelda approached the therapist with the suggestion of working as a volunteer in a program to tutor children in one of the economically depressed neighborhoods in her community. The therapist helped her to see that this could not only help to further develop her field sensitive learning style by her observation of it in others, but it could help her to develop her field sensitive teaching, counseling, and supervisory style as well. He suggested that she be observant of those children whose cognitive styles may be preferred field independent as well, because this experience could serve as an early introduction to the next phase of multicultural psychotherapy: mismatch.

Discussion of information, travel, and media experiences, which might encourage Imelda to develop her preferred field sensitive style, led to the idea of her visiting relatives in Mexico. There she was able to visit one of her aunts, a teacher in a Mexican school, where field sensitive learning/problem-solving styles are emphasized. During her trip Imelda discussed term papers she was working on with her aunt. The aunt gave Imelda some ideas for using a field sensitive style in her English classes. She also lent Imelda some of the texts and workbooks used in grammar and literature classes in Mexico. Imelda and the therapist reviewed these and identified materials that could be helpful in Imelda's development.

Harold. The cognitive style goal on which Harold decided to focus was his communication style. He and the therapist agreed that Harold would develop his field sensitive communication style to better match those of his wife and children, and also to further develop the preferred style, which he had abandoned after his brother's death.

Within the interpersonal domain, the therapist encouraged Harold to review his social environment and identify a person with the best field sensitive communication style he had known. Harold recalled a professor at his alma mater who was highly developed in terms of field sensitive communication style. When Harold was a student, it was this professor who had encouraged him to take up photography as a hobby. Harold developed a script for approaching the professor and, after trying the script out with the therapist, made some minor changes. Harold then planned for implementing the script and for evaluating its effectiveness.

In an effort to match his field sensitive style within the activities domain, Harold enrolled in advanced photography classes at one of the community colleges near his home. In the information, travel, and media domain, Harold and his wife went on a European tour that included seminars in art and photography. Both the content and the teaching style of classes as described in the travel brochures seemed to be predominantly field sensitive in orientation.

Alex.   Alex was encountering some difficulty in a required statistics and research design course he was taking; thus, his first cognitive style goal was to develop some field independent learning/problem-solving style skills. After a short discussion with the therapist regarding people in his class with whom he related well and who could be good models for learning field independent skills, Alex identified Janet. He described her as being bicognitive and socially sensitive; she had made an A on their last exam. He felt Janet would be receptive to his request that they study together. He developed a script, discussed it with the therapist, and proceeded to role-play it. He then carried it out successfully.

In the activities domain, the therapist asked Alex to modify the content of the practice problems in his statistics book by including some information about people and cultures he had been familiar with. The therapist assisted him initially; Alex then was able to do this on his own. In the information, travel and media domain, the therapist recommended two books on research methods that were written in a bicognitive style.

Tony.   Tony's first goal in the cognitive styles domain concerned his being able to develop a more field sensitive communication style when dealing with his adolescent children. He was concerned about a negative report from school about their behavior. Tony reported his children were "not listening to me and being *cabezudos*" (hardheaded or stubborn). The therapist asked him to consider that the approach he had been using had been too direct and that they might react more positively if he gave them an opportunity to present their side of the story. The therapist suggested that Tony allow his children to explain their feelings at the time the events in question had occurred. Tony and the therapist wrote a script together.

The therapist was aware that clients who are traditional in their value systems, as Tony is, may feel that scriptwriting and role-playing are too much like a game, and they might feel insulted by the activity. The therapist anticipated this reservation and explained that these activities are valuable teaching tools and that he would demonstrate first. He also assured Tony that if he felt uncomfortable, they would discontinue the practice and try something else. Initially Tony was reluctant but once he became engaged in the task he enjoyed it. He used the broad outline of the script, written partly in English and partly in Spanish, the way Tony and his children communicate.

In the activities domain, the therapist asked Tony to identify someone in his life whom he admired and who was field sensitive in communication style with adolescents. Tony identified a *compadre* (close friend) who was the godfather of two of his children and who had a close and warm relationship with his adolescent son and daughter. The therapist asked Tony to observe his *compadre* closely when he interacted with members of his family and to incorporate some of what he learned in his scripts.

In the information, travel, and media domain, the therapist suggested that Tony watch *telenovelas* (TV soap operas in Spanish) that demonstrated field sensitive communication styles between adults and adolescents or younger adults.

Conformity Pressures and the Adoption of a False Self

Recognizing and overcoming pressures to conform are examined in Sessions 4 and 5. The following are the three components to this phase of client empowerment:

1. Becoming aware of conformity pressures both with respect to the source and the type of pressure
2. Becoming aware of the mismatch situations most associated with conformity pressures
3. Avoiding self-criticism and other types of negative thinking that could result in falling back into the styles of the false self

Imelda.   Imelda and the therapist discussed those people and institutions that were the greatest source of pressures to conform. They identified her parents, grandparents, boyfriend, and school. These people—her parents, grandparents, and boyfriend—were the greatest source of conformity pressures for cultural styles. Her school, on the other hand, and more specifically her English teacher, were the greatest source of this type of pressure with respect to cognitive styles.

The therapist and Imelda discussed how these pressures were applied to her and how she experienced them. The focus here was on the negative thinking triggered by these pressures: "I tell myself I'm being too different, too rebellious, that I'm not obedient, that I'm bad."

With the help of the therapist, Imelda became aware of mismatch situations in her daily life. She came to recognize that on the days she was playing in a game, her parents and grandparents applied the strongest pressure to have her conform to the traditional cultural style. This usually led to heated arguments, upsetting Imelda, and affecting her concentration during the game. It was at these times, she realized, that she was most vulnerable to falling back into the styles of her false self.

Harold. An analysis of the sources of pressures to conform for Harold identified his father, his partners, and the professional societies to which he belonged. Harold discovered that he experienced this pressure as guilt: "I feel like I'm letting my partners down; I feel that I cannot be the kind of son my father always wanted, especially since my brother passed away. When I am with my colleagues at professional meetings, I feel that I don't really belong with them, with their interests and ways of doing things—I feel like a misfit."

For Harold the strongest instances of pressures to conform were when he visited his father or they talked on the phone. Harold was especially aware of the pressures when they talked about business or about his new ideas for product development. They got along well when they discussed other topics such as politics or sports. With his partners Harold recognized that the strongest pressures to conform, especially with respect to cognitive styles, were exerted when he made a presentation about his ideas for new product development or when he discussed personnel problems with them.

In the area of avoiding self-blame, self-criticism, and other forms of negative thinking, the therapist worked with both Imelda and Harold to get them to recognize their tendencies toward these forms of thinking. These cognitive distortions, identified by Ellis (1970) and by Beck (1976) in their work with neurotic and depressed clients, often trigger a return to the cognitive style of the false self.

Tara. Conformity pressures for Tara centered in the demands of her parents that she get married and settle down so that her daughter could have a good home. Conformity pressures were also coming from her ex-boyfriend by way of Tamisha. Without Tara's permission, he was going to Tamisha's school and telling her he missed her mother and her, that he would like to live with them again so that he could become her real daddy, and that they could all be a real family like those most of her classmates had. In therapy Tara said, "I usually think that I need to do what is best for Tamisha and me: that I need to give myself time to finish my degree and get settled in my new job and my new home, but I begin to question myself when my parents keep lecturing me about making up with my ex-boyfriend and marrying him, because I need to think about Tamisha's future. I wind up feeling guilty and questioning my decisions."

To exert some control over the ex-boyfriend's conformity pressures, with the therapist's support, Tara talked to the school personnel and informed them that he could no longer see her daughter during school hours. She also confronted her mother and was very clear in letting her know why she had broken up with her ex-boyfriend and asked both of her parents to respect her right to make decisions for Tamisha and herself.

Enhancing Self-Esteem

A necessary accompaniment to the strategies for empowerment is the development of client's self-esteem and sense of mastery. The therapist not only assists clients in facilitating self-discovery, but also helps clients recognize that they should be proud of their unique selves. Further, the therapist helps clients to recognize and enjoy the rewards that result from match experiences. Finally, the therapist assists clients in realizing the positive aspects of feeling that they are gaining control over their own destiny.

Self-Acceptance. Imelda expressed her growth in self-acceptance and pride in the feeling that she did not have to be as dependent on others for support as she had been: "I feel that I can rely on myself more now. I like myself more, and I don't feel that I need others to approve of me as much anymore."

Harold's growing pride in his unique self and his self-acceptance were reflected in his feelings of enthusiasm about his work: "I feel excited about my work and my ideas again. I feel creative for the first time in a long time."

Mastery. For Imelda, gaining more control over her life and feeling less like a victim of circumstances was a result of knowing what to anticipate. The feeling that she could deal with situations more effectively without getting upset and angry added to this realization of mastery: "I know what's coming now, and I feel more prepared for it. I don't lose my temper as much as I used to, because I no longer feel like I have to convince people; I just tell them how I feel and then take it as it is. There are no longer the big conflicts I had with my parents and grandparents."

For Harold, mastery was equated with the loss of the feeling of disorientation and confusion: "I feel at peace with myself. I feel I understand myself and others better." Mastery for Tara meant making her own decisions and feeling comfortable about them. For Tony it meant feeling that he could still be an effective parent to his children in spite of his physical disability. He could still be a good role model to them. For Alex, mastery represented his ability to tell the truth to his parents and to feel comfortable about forging an identity as both Asian American and gay. Rose's sense of mastery involved arriving at the realization that her loss of vision would not interfere with her goal of continuing to be a teacher, a good parent, and leading an independent lifestyle.

Summary of Sessions 3 through 5

Sessions 3, 4, and 5 included the following nine techniques and procedures:

1. Selection of a cultural match goal from the list developed during the second session.
2. Identification of a model.

3. Projection of empathy vis-à-vis the model.
4. Identification of the model's preferred styles.
5. Development of a script for approaching the model.
6. Role-playing.
7. Assignment of homework: enacting the script.
8. Evaluation of homework.
9. Modification of script and reenactment (if necessary).

These procedures and techniques are also used for achieving the following cognitive match goals:

- Awareness of sources of conformity pressures.
- Identification of mismatch situations associated with conformity pressures.
- Avoidance of self-criticism and cognitive distortions.
- Development of feelings of self-acceptance and mastery.

SESSIONS 6 THROUGH 10: ENCOURAGING CULTURAL AND COGNITIVE FLEX

In this phase of therapy, the therapist helps the client to develop unfamiliar, or nonpreferred, cultural and cognitive styles in order to initiate the process of multicultural personality development. The therapist also encourages the development of client mastery and empowerment.

Some clients have used various aspects of these unfamiliar or less-preferred styles in their efforts to conform (i.e., in their false selves) in the face of conformity pressures. For example, Imelda tried to force herself to be field independent in her cognitive style even though she was preferred field sensitive. She did this because she felt pressured to behave like most of her classmates. Harold, on the other hand, tried to adopt a modernistic orientation in his relationships with his wife and children in his effort to be more like his father. This phase of therapy involves the use of mismatch. Mismatch is introduced to the client gradually, in the context of match, and only after the client feels comfortable with his unique self.

As the therapist introduces clients to mismatch, she continues to match client's preferred cognitive and cultural styles to encourage the continued development of the preferred styles while the unfamiliar styles are being developed.

Distribution of the Sessions

As discussed in the match phase of therapy, the therapist makes a decision about the number of sessions necessary for achieving the client's mismatch goals, based on the number of goals to be achieved and the client's rate of progress. Some clients require more time, others less. Since successful accomplishment of homework tasks is a crucial part of this phase of therapy, the number of sessions needed will depend on the difficulty of achieving the goals, the motivation of the client, and the rapidity with which the techniques of the multicultural model can be learned.

Introducing Mismatch. Mismatch is introduced only after the client has overcome most of the negative symptoms of the mismatch syndrome. The client should feel comfortable and self-confident. Feelings of alienation, anger, anxiety, and defensiveness should have subsided before mismatch is introduced.

The therapist should postpone the introduction of mismatch processes until the client begins to feel some pride in the unique self and some sense of mastery over his or her own destiny. To avoid reemergence of the symptoms of the mismatch syndrome, mismatch should always be introduced gradually and with caution.

The processes and techniques of therapy used to achieve mismatch goals are similar to those used to achieve match goals: There is an examination of the client's social environment for the purpose of identifying persons and institutions the client should learn to match. Again, as with match, techniques include empathy projection; scriptwriting; role-playing; homework assignments to try out scripts; assessment; and, if necessary, reworking of the scripts and trying again.

In addition to the step-by-step process summarized previously, the procedures for accomplishing mismatch goals introduce two new therapeutic techniques: awareness of feelings and awareness of diversity challenges. Awareness of feelings is an introspective technique requiring the clients to recognize their feelings at a given moment in time. Clients ask themselves, "How am I feeling right now? Is this the right time for me to attempt match?" Awareness of feelings is important when clients are trying to match people or institutions with whom they have experienced conflicts.

Diversity challenges are similar to the emersion approach used for teaching languages: The person is placed in a situation where only the new language is spoken. In multicultural psychotherapy, clients are encouraged to interact with persons or to adapt to sociocultural environments that can stimulate development of the new values and personality characteristics they will need to achieve flex. Diversity challenges require the person to adopt new styles promoting the development of flex.

Traditional Adopting Modernistic. One of Imelda's mismatch goals was to adopt modernistic values and belief systems in domains other than equality in gender roles. Achieving this goal would make it possible for her to develop a wider and more diverse circle of friends. The process followed in achieving Imelda's first mismatch goal included the therapist's review of the definitions of modern values and belief systems, as well as examples he had presented to her when he introduced the flex theory of personality during the second session (see Chapter 7):

When we discussed values in our second session, I said that modern values are typical of people who live in large cities. They are also typical of those who tend to be members of liberal Protestant religions and whose lives are relatively free of the pressures of tradition and family. People with modern values tend to be individualistic in their orientations to life. Some examples of modern values, which I presented at that time, included individual competition and achievement and independence from the family. Do you think you would be okay trying values like these?

With this question the therapist gave Imelda the opportunity to express any reservations she might have about trying out behaviors reflecting modern values. These reservations could have taken two forms: feeling uncomfortable using nonpreferred styles because these are associated with pressures to conform or feelings of discomfort because they are associated with individuals or with institutions with which the client has had negative experiences in the past. In Imelda's case, she said that she had some trouble accepting modern values because they were associated with the pressures to conform she had experienced from her father and stepmother. She also reported that modern values made her uncomfortable because she associated them with the parents of a Caucasian boy she had once dated and whom she felt had rejected her because she was Hispanic.

At the same time, Imelda said, "I feel as if I'm already learning to use modern values because I am spending more time with my coaches. Getting closer to the Anglo coaches has also helped me to realize that not all Anglos are the same." The therapist reinforced her for this insight.

The therapist and Imelda reviewed her social environment in order to identify people and institutions that could help her to achieve her mismatch goals. They also examined the notes from her life history. The search led to the identification of Betty, one of her Caucasian teammates who was individually competitive and who seemed financially and emotionally independent of her family.

For Imelda, the third step in developing mismatch goals was empathy projection. She and the therapist discussed Betty:

THERAPIST: What do you think Betty wants out of life?

IMELDA: Well, I think she wants to be the best player on the team because she likes to have her name mentioned in assemblies when we win games. There have been times when I have disliked her because of the way she is—so competitive and all; but she has been friendly to me. She has invited me to parties at her house and at her friends' houses.

Awareness of feelings is yet another technique the therapist used with Imelda to encourage her to adopt modernistic values:

THERAPIST: How do you feel right now?

IMELDA: I don't feel so good; I'm upset because my Dad and I got into a big argument about my half-sister again last night.

THERAPIST: So this would not be a good time for you to try to match someone like Betty. You need to try it when you're feeling better about things.

IMELDA: Yes, I see. That makes sense. Otherwise, I'm likely to botch it up, right?

Imelda and the therapist discussed the possible script Imelda could use to approach her teammate for help. Recognizing that Imelda was field sensitive in terms of learning/problem-solving style, the therapist modeled for her and worked cooperatively with her in developing the script. Using a large pad on an easel, the therapist began by making suggestions and then encouraged Imelda to come up with ideas. As the process continued, Imelda did more and more of the work on her own.

After Imelda was satisfied with her script, she and the therapist role-played it, making changes suggested as the roles were tested. Imelda decided when and where to actually try the script with Betty; she decided to approach her during the next practice session and ask her if she could walk home with her since they lived near one another. Immediately after trying out the script with Betty, Imelda evaluated its effectiveness.

A second mismatch goal that Imelda and the therapist identified was to learn to communicate in a field independent style. They felt that this style would be more effective in matching the preferred style of her English teacher, and that a successful match might make the teacher more receptive to becoming more flexible in her teaching style. The process for achieving this goal included the therapist's reviewing the definition and examples of the field independent cognitive style with a focus on communication styles:

THERAPIST: When we talked about cognitive styles, I said that field independent styles were usually the preferred styles of people who are modern in their cultural style. We talked about how preferred field independent people communicate with others in messages that are short and to-the-point. These people usually do not include any personal information or feelings in what they say.

IMELDA: Yes, that describes my English teacher.

THERAPIST: Do you think it would be hard for you to communicate in a field independent style?

IMELDA: I can do it, but I have a negative reaction to it because that's the way my parents talk to me when they are angry with me. Besides, I don't think I have been able to ever get along with teachers who talk that way. Lately, though, I have noticed that some of my coaches talk that way and I do like them, so I guess it's okay.

As Imelda recognized that some of her coaches used the field independent style to communicate, she identified one of them as the person she could try her script with once it was developed. The therapist led Imelda in empathy projection:

THERAPIST: What do you think your English teacher wants out of life?

IMELDA: I think she wants to be voted the best teacher so that she can get the annual teaching award.

THERAPIST: How do you think she is feeling these days?

IMELDA: She was one of three teachers nominated for the award, so I think she feels pretty good right now.

Again, the therapist reminds Imelda to monitor her own feelings and to choose a time to try her script when she is not angry or upset. Imelda and the therapist discussed a possible script, wrote one, and role-played it, making changes as they saw necessary. Imelda tried out the script, evaluated it, and modified it. After trial and evaluation, the therapist and client reworked it as necessary until they were satisfied with it.

Concurrently with scriptwriting and homework assignments for achieving mismatch goals, Imelda, with the help of the therapist, was also identifying diversity challenges she would try:

1. She would go to a party where she was likely to be the only Hispanic. Imelda had turned down Betty's earlier invitations since she had been uncomfortable with the thought of being the only Hispanic in the group. Accepting an invitation now would be a good immersion opportunity for learning how to use modernistic values in interpersonal relationships.
2. Imelda decided to participate in teacher–student get-acquainted sessions sponsored by the student council. This experience would give Imelda an opportunity to interact with teachers who were field independent in communication style. It would also provide an opportunity to try out the field independent communication behaviors she was learning through scriptwriting and role-playing with the therapist.

Throughout this phase of therapy, the therapist gave Imelda social rewards as she progressed. He gave frequent encouragement by saying "I'm very proud of the progress you are making."

Realizing Imelda's preferred styles, the therapist used modeling as a teaching style in developing the scripts and in role-playing them while Imelda watched, saying, for example: "Here is the way I would do it." Then he demonstrated what he would say and do when communicating with someone who was preferred field independent.

Summary of Sessions 6 through 10

In summary, Sessions 6 through 10 focused on the introduction of mismatch using the following seven techniques and procedures:

1. Reviewing the characteristics of unfamiliar cultural and cognitive styles.
2. Allowing the client to express feelings about these values and styles.

3. Reviewing the client's social environment and life history interview notes in order to identify people and institutions that can help the client to achieve mismatch goals.
4. Projecting empathy.
5. Being aware of feelings.
6. Scriptwriting and role-playing.
7. Enacting and evaluating scripts.

SUMMARY

The second stage of multicultural psychotherapy focuses on encouraging clients to accept their unique selves and initiates the process of flex development. The principal strategies and techniques employed are scriptwriting, role-playing, and homework assignments.

9

ASSESSMENT
OF PROGRESS
IN FLEX DEVELOPMENT

Once the mismatch phase of multicultural psychotherapy is well underway, the therapist should reassess the client in order to gage the client's progress in the various areas and domains of cultural and cognitive styles and flex development. The information obtained can be compared with the data obtained from the initial assessment. The comparison helps the therapist determine the need to make changes in the therapeutic plan and should answer two principal questions: How many and which of the goals have been met? Which domains or areas of cultural and cognitive styles will require additional work? For most people this reassessment can be done in Session 11 or 12, depending on the progress made by the client. For others it may be done earlier. The therapist is the best judge of when it is best to assess progress.

The assessment phase of multicultural psychotherapy also is the time for the therapist to conduct a self-evaluation. This evaluation will focus on whether the therapist is matching and mismatching the client effectively, on whether to give additional emphasis to certain strategies, or to certain domains of cultural and cognitive styles; and on whether the therapist's cultural and cognitive style preferences are in any way interfering with the development of client flex.

Client and therapist assessment is multimodal. It involves the use of personality and value inventories, behavioral (verbal and nonverbal) ratings, and the evaluation of the degree of progress made in homework assignments. This chapter reviews both the assessment procedures for clients and therapists and the feedback procedures used with the client after the assessment results have been evaluated.

ASSESSING CLIENT PROGRESS

The therapist introduces the assessing progress phase of therapy by emphasizing the need to review the degree of change made with regard to the therapeutic plan established in Session 2 or 3. The therapist then readministers the instruments used during the initial session.

To evaluate cultural style, the therapist again uses the Family Attitude Scale (FAS), the Traditionalism–Modernism Inventory (TMI), the Preferred Cultural Styles Observation Checklist, and the Multicultural Experience Inventory (MEI). After readministering the FAS and the Traditionalism–Modernism Inventory, the therapist focuses on each of the three scores: the total traditionalism score, the total modernism score, and the traditionalism–modernism balance score. The new total traditionalism and the total modernism scores are compared to the scores from the initial administration of the instruments.

The changes in scores are considered in light of the client's goals with respect to the need to be more traditional, or more modern, in cultural style. The traditionalism–modernism balance score is a crucial indicator of progress toward the development of cultural flex, because it is arrived at by adding the total traditionalism score and the total modernism score. The balance score is also compared to the balance score obtained after the first administration of the TMI. Ratings made by the therapist on the Cultural Styles Observation Checklist during the session prior to the assessment session are compared to those made during the first session. The following are the main areas of focus:

- Behaviors (verbal and nonverbal) associated with traditional values
- Behaviors (verbal and nonverbal) associated with modern values
- The degree of balance between traditional and modern behaviors
- Behaviors that are reflective of a combination of traditional and modern values

The therapist directs the client to complete the Multicultural Experience Inventory again. The total score is compared to that obtained during its previous administration. Comparison of scores on individual items, such as being involved in more activities with people of other ethnic groups (from the Contemporary Multicultural Identity items), is also important.

The total score on the MEI may be more important as an indicator of progress for some clients than it is for others. With respect to four of the case studies presented in this book, the total score was more important to Imelda, Tara, and Raul than it was to Harold. For Harold, the more important goal of multiculturalism, at least at that point in time, involved being more flexible in cultural and cognitive styles within his own cultural group, while it was less important for him to relate more effectively to members of other sociocultural groups.

To evaluate the client's progress in cognitive flex, ratings on the Preferred Cognitive Styles Observation Checklist made during Sessions 1 and 2 are compared with ratings made during the sessions prior to the assessment session. The therapist evaluates specific domains of cognitive style such as communication and learning/problem-solving. He rates behaviors, both verbal and nonverbal, associated with field sensitivity and with field independence. Using the checklist, the therapist also examines the degree of balance between field independent and field sensitive behaviors as well as the development of behaviors reflecting a combination of the two cognitive styles. The therapist also readministers the Bicognitive Orientation to Life Scale to compare with responses given to those items during the initial administration.

In addition to progress indicated by the Preferred Cultural and Cognitive Styles Observation Checklists and the different assessment instruments, the therapist examines the progress made on homework assignments and diversity challenges. Still another indicator of progress in multicultural therapy is the development of more positive attitudes toward people and groups whom the client considers to be different from himself. One gage of success on the homework assignments is the ratings and notes made by the client after completion of implementation of scripts.

The degree of progress made in diversity challenges is also useful in assessing overall progress. At this time, the therapist evaluates the number of challenges undertaken and the degree of success, as judged by the client, achieved on each. The therapist also reviews progress on homework assignments, on diversity challenges, and on the client's change in attitudes and stereotypes regarding people and groups different from himself.

FEEDBACK TO THE CLIENT

Feedback to the client should be done during the session following the readministration of the assessment instruments. Before sharing the results of the reevaluation with the client, the therapist must ensure that a good rapport has been established. In all cases, the positive feedback should be given before any barriers to growth are discussed.

With preferred field sensitive and traditional clients, such as Imelda, the therapist is advised to start with the global picture and then proceed to specifics, and to use personal examples from therapy notes to personalize the feedback as much as possible. For the preferred field independent and modern client, such as Harold, however, the therapist should start with details and work up to the global, emphasizing concepts rather than personalizing communications. With clients of mixed style, such as Alex and Raul, the therapist should begin with the global picture and then proceed to specifics. With Rose, also a mixed client but one who is a preferred field independent, the initial approach is on self-efficacy goals then it moves to the big picture and finally focuses in on goals relating to improvement of relationships with others.

The client must be encouraged to understand the importance of active participation in those situations necessary to change the therapeutic plan and/or to develop strategies for goals that have not yet been achieved. Excerpts from the feedback given to two of the case study clients, Imelda and Harold, illustrate the procedures and strategies implemented to modify the therapeutic plan and/or to work more effectively on those goals on which little or no progress has been made.

Case Studies

Note that the feedback is individualized to match the unique personality style of each client; in these examples, descriptions of efforts to match are set off by italics in brackets.

Imelda.   Imelda's preferred cultural and cognitive styles are traditional and field sensitive, respectively. Therefore, the therapist is directive in his approach and personalizes feedback. He also emphasizes social rewards and improvement of sense of community with respect to therapy goals achieved. Here is an excerpt from some of the feedback the therapist gave Imelda:

> The assessment I have done shows that you are making excellent progress in developing modern cultural styles. You're also making good progress in developing the field independent cognitive style. You have continued to develop in the traditional cultural style and in the field sensitive cognitive style as well. You seem to be getting along better with others—parents, grandparents, teachers, coaches, and friends. I'm very proud of your progress *[personalizing and giving social rewards]*.
>
> The results of the Traditionalism–Modernism Inventory [the pre-revised version of the TMI is presented in Appendix M] show that your modernism score is now 42 compared with 38 when you first took the inventory about ten weeks ago. What impresses me most is your balance, or flex, score: When you first took the Traditionalism–Modernism Inventory, your score was lopsided in the direction of traditionalism, but this time your score indicated that you are more balanced in your cultural styles.
>
> On the ratings I have made in our sessions, I notice that you are tending to use both traditional and modern behaviors; in the first few sessions, most of your behaviors were traditional. I'm also impressed by how well you've done on your homework assignments and on diversity challenges. I looked through the ratings you made after your homework and diversity challenges; they indicate that you were successful in what you did.

Your attitude toward Caucasian peers and teachers at your school has also improved a great deal. You started out making angry and negative comments about Caucasians in the first few sessions, but these have been replaced by more positive statements in the last four sessions. The results of the Multiculturalism Experience Inventory also show that you are now doing more things with Caucasian friends and with your Caucasian coaches and teachers.

The results of the assessment show that you have made good progress in learning how to use field independent cognitive styles. The results of the Bicognitive Orientation to Life Scale show that your field independent score has risen from 12 to 32. At the same time your field sensitive score and bicognitive flex, or balance, scores have also improved.

The ratings on the Preferred Cognitive Styles Observation Checklist show that you still need to make progress in field independent learning/problem-solving and in teaching, counseling, and supervisory styles. The homework assignment and diversity-challenge ratings you made show that you are still uncomfortable in these two domains.

These are the two areas, or domains, we need to concentrate on in the next few sessions. Here is what I would suggest: Let's do some scripts together that will concentrate on using some of the field independent behaviors and strategies in learning/problem-solving and in teaching, counseling, and supervisory styles.

I will play roles in which I will use field independent learning/problem-solving or teaching, counseling, and supervisory styles, and you will match my behaviors and strategies. I would also suggest that you do more diversity challenges in which you have to use field independent styles for learning and teaching. Here is a suggestion: Volunteer to help coach some of the junior varsity teams with some of your coaches who use field independent approaches.

Harold.   Harold's preferred styles are modern and field independent, so the therapist's style for giving feedback is data-centered, much like that of a scientist reporting research findings. He even prepared bar graphs on a large tablet resting on an easel. The therapist encouraged Harold to participate actively in the session. Improvement in therapy focuses on increased self-efficacy and individual achievement. Excerpts from the therapist's feedback to Harold follow:

I prepared these charts [matching Harold's field independent preferred learning style] to show the degree of progress you have made [emphasis on modernistic style of individual achievement] between the first time you completed instruments and those done more recently. As you can see, you have made great progress in all of the domains of the traditional cultural styles. You made a higher traditionalism score on the Traditionalism–Modernism Inventory, and the ratings made on the Preferred Cultural Styles Observation Checklist show growth in all areas, particularly in communication.

In your most recent sessions, you also have been expressing more positive attitudes toward people who have traditional orientations. Your self-ratings on homework and diversity-challenge assignments are quite good.

However, there is one area in which you still need progress—you still look somewhat uncomfortable when you interact with traditionally oriented people, and you still have a tendency to interrupt them while they are talking. You need to work on these areas [emphasis on individual effort]. These same problems show up in the communication domain of the cognitive styles chart.

My ratings, as well as yours on homework and diversity-challenge assignments, show that your messages still tend to be too short and that you are not very self-disclosing when you converse with others. Here are some of the evaluation feedback sheets you completed after doing your homework assignments and diversity challenges. As you can see, they show that you often rate yourself as being too abrupt and self-conscious; you often behaved as if you were in too much of a hurry to complete the assignment.

I have some suggestions for improvements in this area. I would like your input on these [independent orientation of the modernistic–field independent preferred client]. How about writing some more scripts that focus on a traditional communication style and use traditional behaviors in communication? For some ideas I'd recommend that you read the communication chapter in Beck's book, Love Is Never Enough. I would also suggest role-playing in which I use field sensitive and traditional communication behaviors and you try to match me.

A few sessions back you showed me some literature on marriage-encounter weekend workshops for couples. Some of the exercises described in the brochure were oriented toward the traditional cultural style—writing letters to spouses and open discussions of feelings in small groups. I think that this experience would help to develop your field sensitive and traditional modes of communication and of interacting with others.

ASSESSING THE THERAPIST

The assessment phase of multicultural psychotherapy examines the therapist as well as the client. Ratings of cultural and cognitive therapeutic styles made in Sessions 1 and 2 are compared with those made in the two sessions prior to the assessment session. There are two questions on which assessment of the therapist is focused:

1. How effectively is the therapist matching and mismatching the client?
2. Is the client's false self or preferred style negatively affecting the therapist's ability to flex in therapy and achieve the goals of the therapeutic plan?

For example, while he was doing therapy with Imelda and Harold, the therapist discovered that the clients' dominant styles had a pull effect in the mismatch phase of therapy. With Imelda, the therapist tended to start the sessions of the mismatch phase in a modern mode, but Imelda's strong traditional orientation resulted in pulling the therapist to match her. With Harold, on the other hand, the pull was in the direction of field independent therapeutic behaviors, especially in the domain of communication and interpersonal relationship styles. In this case, the therapist started the sessions of the mismatch phase in a field sensitive mode, but after a few minutes found himself shifting to field independent behavior to match Harold's style. These findings gave the therapist valuable insight into his own preferred styles and how he was failing to encourage the development of client flex.

The therapist took the following four steps to address his concerns:

1. Consulting with a colleague to discuss possible counter transference issues with Imelda and Harold.
2. Remaining cognizant of those client behaviors (both verbal and nonverbal) that elicited the triggering or pull effects, using these as warning signs in his attempt to prevent the tendency to be pulled into match behaviors.
3. Calling these problems to the attention of the clients so that they could assist in the therapist's attempt to resist pull by recognizing and discussing it with him when it happened.
4. Developing scriptwriting exercises and role-playing the scripts using a modified version of the empty chair technique (Levitsky & Perls, 1970) in front of a video camera, playing the roles of both client and therapist, moving from one chair to the other. In this way he tried out response strategies to client behaviors that had a pull effect on therapeutic style. He then watched the video tape and rated his therapeutic behaviors using the two observation checklists.

SUMMARY

In summary, the following techniques and procedures were included in the assessment sessions: (1) making a decision as to the session in which it is most appropriate to assess progress—for some clients it may be as early as Session 5 or 6, for others it may be later; (2) preparing the client for re-administration of the instruments used in the first session; (3) readministering the instruments; (4) scoring and comparing new scores to those obtained previously, comparing ratings on the Preferred Cognitive and Cultural Styles Observation Checklists, evaluating progress on homework assignments, diversity challenges, and in the development of positive attitudes toward the "different." The assessment sessions were followed by giving feedback to the client; making changes in the therapeutic plan, and giving additional assignments to the client, if necessary; self-assessing by the therapist; and eliminating therapist behaviors that interfere with the development of client flex.

10

THE CLIENT AS CHANGE AGENT AND MULTICULTURAL AMBASSADOR

The principal goal of the fourth and final phase of multicultural therapy is to complete the task of client empowerment. The specific objective of this stage of therapy is to encourage the client to become an active participant in the development of a multicultural society.

FINAL PHASE OF THERAPY

This final phase of therapy addresses an issue of major concern to the "different"—the fear that psychotherapy will be used as a tool to encourage client conformity and assimilation to the values and lifestyles of the power structure. The African Martiniquean psychiatrist Franz Fanon (see Bulhan, 1985) exposed this perspective in traditional psychoanalytic personality theories and therapies. Bulhan, in his book *Franz Fanon and the Psychology of Oppression,* wrote:

> How can an intervention liberate the patient from social oppression when the "therapist–patient" relationship itself is suffused with the inequities, nonreciprocity, elitism, and sadomasochism of the oppressive social order? Can there be realistic grounds for changing self-defeating behaviors and a negative self-concept in a context in which only the "doctor" initiates and the "patient" accommodates, where one is powerful and the other powerless? (p. 272)

Ryan (1971) has also criticized the "blame the victim" orientation of many of the traditional personality theories and psychotherapies. The client-as-activist phase of multicultural therapy, then, represents a radical departure from traditional forms of psychotherapy and counseling.

Role of Client

Multicultural psychotherapy encourages the client to play four roles:

1. *Change agent.* In this role the client helps to create changes in the institutions and agencies that have had a significant impact on him. For Imelda, the focus was on the school she attends; while for Harold, it was on his workplace.
2. *Educator.* In this capacity the client introduces people who have the power to influence the policies and practices of institutions and agencies to the concepts of the flex theory of personality and to the multicultural model of psychotherapy. The objective is to encourage "power holders" to better understand and to attempt to resolve problems of mismatch.
3. *Peer counselor.* The client provides emotional support and facilitates change and empowerment in those of his peers who are victims of mismatch shock.
4. *Multicultural ambassador.* As an ambassador, the client promotes the development of multicultural environments that encourage understanding and cooperation among different people and groups.

As the therapist encourages clients to learn concepts, techniques, and procedures by which they can change the environment and influence others, he also warns against using these as tools to manipulate others. The therapist points out that the knowledge possessed by the client is potentially damaging and carries responsibilities. The client is encouraged to keep the principal goal of environmental change in mind and to help make society sensitive to the cultural and individual differences of all its citizens.

Imelda as Change Agent.   Gender roles are usually separated in traditional societies, resulting in pressures for female athletes to conform, because athletics are usually seen as the exclusive domain of men. Imelda faced this problem. Having experienced the disapproval of parents, grandparents, and other authority figures in her traditional community and having realized that other players and coaches faced similar conflicts, Imelda became interested in doing something about this problem. She proposed a program that the athletic and counseling departments of her school could develop to help women athletes with the value conflicts they experienced as a consequence of these pressures.

Imelda's goal was to encourage the coaches and counselors to help female athletes experiencing value conflicts in a traditional community to conceptualize these conflicts. In addition, Imelda proposed that coaches and counselors develop plans to intervene with parents and other members of the athletes' families to lessen value conflicts.

The therapist asked Imelda to identify someone in her social environment who might be interested in working on the problem with her. Imelda decided on one of the Latina coaches whom she had gotten to know well during the match homework assignment. Imelda remembered the coach telling her that she had also faced opposition from parents and grandparents when she first showed interest in sports.

The therapist asked Imelda to consider what the majority of those coaches and counselors who could play an important role in intervention with women athletes in conflict wanted out of life. Imelda could speculate about her coaches' goals, but since she only knew two of the four counselors, she was limited in her knowledge about their life objectives. She said:

> I know most of the coaches want us to concentrate and keep our minds on the game. They always talk about how being distracted hurts our game plan. I know all of the assistant coaches would like to become head coach in a school; some of them would even like to be coaches in college some day. The two counselors are great fans of the women's teams; they always come to our games. I know one of them is working on her doctorate degree; the other one likes to read a lot about sports sociology and psychology and stuff like that, because she helped me out with a term paper that I did on women in sports.

Imelda thought of ways to encourage the coaches and counselors to work together to develop a program of lectures and workshops addressing value conflicts often faced by female athletes in a traditional community and of intervention with the athletes and their families. She decided to approach the coach she had chosen as her ally to see if she would be willing to work on this with her.

Imelda would prepare a script that she would use to enlist the support of her coach. The therapist and Imelda discussed the content of the script and the broad outline of the presentation to be made to the coaching staff and to the head counselor. Because Imelda was working on developing her field independent learning/problem-solving and communication styles, Imelda and the therapist decided that she would prepare the script on her own and bring it to the next therapy session, when they would discuss and role-play it. After the role-playing exercise, she would modify the script as necessary. She followed the details for the implementation of her homework assignment, empathy projection, and feeling awareness-exercises as discussed in the chapters beginning with Chapter 5.

Once she gained the support of her coach, Imelda and the coach developed a plan for approaching the coaching staff. The head coach, in turn, approached the head of the counseling department for the final development and implementation of the intervention program.

Harold as Educator. A source of great frustration for Harold and his partners was the employee turnover problems at their branch plant in Southern California. This was one of the reasons Harold had not felt confident that his company was on solid financial footing. After gaining familiarity with the cultural styles component of the flex theory, Harold concluded that the on-site observations he had made, along with the reports from managers at the plant, could be explained in terms of cultural and cognitive styles conflicts between a predominantly Anglo supervisory staff and employees who were mainly Hispanic in origin.

Harold's goal was to help his partners conceptualize the turnover problem at this plant as a result of cultural and cognitive conflicts between the managers, the supervisory staff, and the employees. Harold identified a friend from college who was a professor in the business school of an East Coast university. When Harold asked him for advice, his friend suggested a number of references in the management literature addressing employee satisfaction problems relating to mismatch of supervisor and worker styles.

The therapist asked Harold to consider what his partners wanted out of life. Harold said, "Right now it's stabilizing things in the Southern California plant. We can't move on to decide on new product development until things settle down there. They are all upset because they don't understand what is happening over there."

Harold suggested developing a presentation for a directors' meeting at which he could discuss the issues described in the references his friend had recommended. He would try to get his partners' backing to hire a consultant who could assist them in resolving the problem. Because Harold was learning how to use a field sensitive approach to learning and problem-solving, he and the therapist worked on the script together. The script they developed used a field independent approach to communication and teaching to match the preferred cognitive style of Harold's partners. The script included identifying and defining the problem and reviewing the literature Harold had read at his friend's suggestion. Further, the script called for Harold to share copies of some of the references he had read.

Harold then presented a plan for training supervisors to be aware of preferred cultural and cognitive styles in those they supervise, and he volunteered to direct the training efforts. Assuming the role of educator includes the following ten techniques and procedures:

1. Identifying an individual or institutional change goal.
2. Identifying an ally.
3. Presenting the idea to the ally.
4. Changing the idea as suggested by the ally and discussed with the therapist.
5. Projecting empathy.
6. Developing a script.
7. Role-playing the script with the therapist.
8. Enacting the script.
9. Implementing and evaluating the script.
10. Discussing the results of assessment with the therapist.

Rose as Multicultural Peer Counselor.   In the process of going through multicultural counseling, Rose became very conscious of the problems facing

Latinas who have impaired vision. With the encouragement and help of friends she had met through an interfaith community group, she started a support group for women who had lost their vision as adults. The group concentrated on the following issues:

1. *How the vision-impaired woman is treated by the extended family.* Is she, in particular, an object of pity and overprotection? They entitled this set of issues *"pobrecita esta ciega"* (I feel so sorry for her because she is blind)—a phrase often used by members of the traditional Latino community to describe an adult woman who is vision impaired. Rose recalled that her siblings and parents had become so overprotective of her that they were opposed to her attending a state rehabilitation center for the vision impaired where she would receive training in mobility, in independent living skills, and vocational skills.

2. *How children perceive a vision-impaired parent.* Rose felt that her children resented her inability to do as many things with them. Now she also felt that they resented the drop in income because she had been unable to continue her work as a teacher. Some of her children refused to accept her blindness. They would say, "You could see if you really wanted to, but you just don't want to take care of us anymore." The women also felt that some of the issues in their changing relationship with their children concerned the fact that they were embarrassed to be seen in public with a blind mother. In Rose's case, her children had helped her before she learned mobility skills, only to leave her side and forget about her when they saw someone they knew.

3. *How spouses change, particularly with respect to sexual relationships.* Many visually impaired women in the group believed their husbands were resentful that they were unable to do the many things they had done around the house before. Rose's husband would even say to her, *"Ya no sirves para nada"* (You are no longer useful). Rose was sensitive to the fact that while they had enjoyed a good sexual relationship before she became blind, her husband avoided intimacy now.

In addition to providing support to each other about these issues, the members made themselves available for discussions and presentations to community groups. The clergy of different churches agreed to tell their congregations about the support groups and to discuss some of the issues of concern to them in their sermons and church bulletins.

Harold as Multicultural Peer Counselor. Harold's involvement in area professional societies led him to realize that many of his colleagues were in crisis because they felt burned out and bored with their jobs. These were professionals in their late twenties and early thirties who, despite the fact that they had achieved success in their professions, had become increasingly disillusioned with their work. Most were experiencing stress and confusion, and several of them were considering returning to college to pursue career interests they had abandoned earlier in their lives.

This struck a familiar chord in Harold, and he decided he wanted to do something about it. His preliminary conversations with some of these colleagues indicated that most of them did not want to go into psychotherapy or counseling, partly because of the stigmas of seeking help and partly because they felt this was something they should do on their own.

When Harold discussed his observations with the therapist, they arrived at the idea of having Harold look into the possibility of forming a support group of technical professionals suffering from burnout. Specifically, the goal was to form such a group for professionals who were considering career changes because of burnout or because of a perceived lack of meaning in their lives.

The therapist suggested that Harold contact a local medical school professor who had developed such a support group for his colleagues. After talking to the professor, Harold refined his ideas and enlisted the support of two of his closest friends in one of the professional organizations in which he was a member. Together they approached the governing board of the organization for sponsorship and financial support for their ideas.

The next step was for Harold to develop a script for presenting the idea to the officers of the organization. Since Harold was developing a field sensitive learning/problem-solving style, the therapist encouraged him to develop the script in cooperation with his friends in the organization. Through discussions with his collaborators, Harold learned that the preferred styles of the officers of the organization were modern with respect to culture, but mixed with respect to cognitive styles. Harold and the therapist decided to modify the script to reflect this knowledge.

The therapist alternated between playing an officer who was field independent and one who was field sensitive in order to allow Harold to prepare answers to questions emanating from either perspective. Harold's homework assignment was completed in cooperation with his two friends. A final step was to implement and evaluate the script.

Encouraging the client to assume the role of multicultural peer counselor includes the following nine techniques and procedures:

1. Identifying the individual change goal.
2. Developing a preliminary plan with therapist.
3. Identifying resource people or institutions.
4. Identifying allies, discussing the plan with them, and making changes they suggested.
5. Developing a script for presentation of the plan to "power holders."
6. Role-playing the script with the therapist.
7. Making plans for enacting the script.

8. Enacting the script and assessing its effectiveness.
9. Discussing the results of assessment with the therapist.

Alex as Peer Counselor and Change Agent.   Because one of the homework activities related to multicultural therapy, Alex began to do volunteer work with a community agency that offered support services for adolescents and young adults who are homosexual. Alex became aware that few members of traditional cultural ethnic/racial groups and multiracial people would take advantage of the services offered by this agency because they felt these were not relevant to their traditional values. With the support of the director and associate director of the agency, Alex was given a small budget to begin a hot line for lesbians and gays who were members of traditional cultures. The contacts he made through this effort led him to initiate support groups for homosexuals from traditional cultures, addressing the following issues:

- *The unique needs of traditional homosexuals related to coming out.* Homosexuality in traditional cultures is often a greater stigma than it is in modern cultures.
- *Issues related to the family.* Many traditional families feel as if they are losing face in the community—getting married and having children to carry on family traditions are so important in traditional families.
- *Issues related to rejection by members of the traditional culture-of-origin.* These people may tend to see the homosexual as disloyal to the group because they tend to view the lesbian/gay movement as dominated by whites.

Tara as Multicultural Ambassador.   As she identified allies who could help her become more flexible, Tara thought about some of her teammates in her city basketball league—some were African American, some Latina, and others Native American and Asian. They realized that the concept of "midnight basketball," which was being implemented with adolescent males in poor ethnic neighborhoods, was not being extended to females. They applied for and received a grant from a community development agency to begin a multicultural basketball league. They ensured that the members of the teams would be of different ethnic/racial groups, and they combined cultural celebrations such as Juneteeth (date of implementation of the Emancipation Proclamation in Texas), Cinco de Mayo, and powwows. Through movies, videos, music, and art, as well as informational shows, they were able to involve different generations—grandparents, parents, and other members of the extended family—and the community in their activities.

SUMMARY

The final phase of multicultural therapy completes the task of the client's empowerment begun during the initial phase of counseling. In this phase of therapy, the client has a role in changing institutions, in helping others, and in educating people in the concepts of personality flex and in the strategies of multicultural psychotherapy. Most important, this phase introduces clients to the role of ambassador for a multicultural society of peace and cooperation.

11

COUPLES COUNSELING

When the multicultural model of psychotherapy is used in couples counseling, the focus of therapy is on individual differences in cultural and cognitive styles—the root source of many conflicts and misunderstandings occurring between partners. Therapy is directed at helping the clients to understand mismatch in communication; interpersonal relationships; motivation; and learning/problem-solving, teaching, parenting, supervisory, and counseling styles. Each partner then learns to match the other's preferred styles and to help one another develop the flexibility in values and cognitive styles that can improve their level of satisfaction within the relationship.

The multicultural model is also sensitive to the fact that environmental forces and demands play a major role in the degree of satisfaction experienced by the partners in a relationship. Demands of jobs or careers, people, and institutions can produce strains in a relationship that are often manifested as rigidity in cultural and cognitive styles, and/or as the triggering of developmental trends in cognitive and cultural styles, which can lead to mismatch between partners who were previously well matched.

The cultural component of the multicultural model focuses on values match and mismatch. As such, it is useful for working with ethnically or racially mixed couples, or with partners who may be of the same culture and race but whose backgrounds are different in terms of socioeconomic, religious, regional, or family variables. Specifically there are four major goals:

1. To make partners aware of match and mismatch domains in their relationship.
2. To teach partners how to use the flex theory of personality and the multicultural model of psychotherapy and counseling to analyze conflicts associated with mismatch.
3. To teach both partners to match each other's preferred styles and to develop the flexibility they will need to negotiate effectively with each other.

4. To teach the partners to change environmental demands that are affecting the relationship and causing disharmony.

CASE HISTORY

This chapter describes how the multicultural model of personality change was used in conducting couples counseling with a couple whose members were from different ethnic groups. Wanda, whose case is one of those highlighted in this book, participated in counseling with her husband, Javier.

Wanda and Javier: A History of the Relationship

Wanda and Javier had been married for eight years when they sought counseling. They met after graduation from college when they were working for the same state agency. Although Wanda had grown up in a more modernistic sociocultural environment, she was attracted to the emotional closeness in Javier's extended family and by Javier's strong familial orientation.

For Javier, who had grown up in an urban–traditional Hispanic cultural environment, Wanda represented independence and assertiveness with a strong familial orientation, characteristics he had always wanted in a partner. The couple remembered that the initial years of their marriage were characterized by harmony and happiness: Wanda had left her full-time job and assumed the role of the traditional mother, taking primary responsibility for the home and the couple's two children, born in the third and fourth years of the marriage. In those early years of their marriage, Wanda had accepted small consulting contracts, working from an office at home.

Things changed drastically for the family in the sixth year of marriage when Wanda began working full-time as a mid-level manager in a large company. The couple's conflicts centered on the fact that Wanda did not feel supported in her career by Javier. Both Javier and the children felt that Wanda was devoting too much time to her work.

Wanda initially approached the therapist requesting individual counseling. In the first session with Wanda, it became obvious to the therapist and to Wanda that the problems in her marriage and family were critical to her psychological adjustment. When Wanda and the therapist began to identify her therapy goals during the second session of individual counseling, they decided that she would approach Javier about the possibility of his participating in couples counseling with her. The following sections describe the process used for the couples-counseling sessions with Javier and Wanda.

Session 1. The therapist greeted Javier and Wanda in the waiting room. Wanda introduced her husband to the therapist. Javier addressed the therapist by his title and surname, and the therapist responded by addressing

Javier formally, using his surname. After Javier and Wanda were seated, the therapist explained that during Wanda's individual therapy sessions it became clear that couples counseling might be appropriate. The therapist asked Javier for his feelings or thoughts on the idea.

JAVIER (RESPONSE TO THERAPIST): I thought it was a good idea myself, because I've felt for a long time that our relationship has been getting worse. I didn't know what to do about it.

THERAPIST (TO JAVIER): Do you have any concerns about the fact that Wanda will be in individual therapy with me while your couples counseling is in progress?

JAVIER (TO THERAPIST): No, not as long as our marriage problems are discussed in our sessions so that I can take part in them.

WANDA (TO THERAPIST AND JAVIER): I think that's the major reason why we are doing the couples counseling—to discuss our problems together and to work them out.

THERAPIST (TO JAVIER): I would like you to know that if at any time you feel that you would like to be in individual counseling I would be very happy to discuss this with you.

JAVIER (TO THERAPIST): I'm fine with that.

The brief introduction and explanation were followed by the administration of the Dyadic Adjustment Scale. This scale was developed by Spanier (1976) to assess the quality of marital and other dyads by having both members rate their degree of agreement and disagreement in several areas such as handling family finances, household tasks, and demonstrations of affection. It also asks for ratings of frequency of those times the couple have stimulating exchanges of ideas and laugh together, as well as for the degree of happiness about their relationship, from perfect to extremely unhappy.

The therapist attempted to establish an atmosphere of acceptance in which the clients could feel free to report the problems they perceived in their relationship. As soon as Wanda and Javier completed the questionnaires, the therapist proceeded to develop an atmosphere of nonjudgmental acceptance and rapport with them. He gave each of them the opportunity to talk about the problems in the marriage from their individual perspectives. He also laid some ground rules, making it clear that he would not permit interruptions or arguments during the course of each person's presentation.

The next step of the first session was a short discussion of the partners' perspectives on the relationship and of the feedback on the results of the Dyadic Adjustment Scale based on preliminary observations made by comparing the ratings made by each of the partners.

While the discussion between the partners was in progress, the therapist observed, made notes, and rated the behaviors each member used when interacting with the other, using the Preferred Cultural and Cognitive Styles

Observation Checklists. He remained cognizant of the fact that, in disordered relationships involving mismatch, the individual partners tend to adopt a false self in their interactions with each other. Thus, during the first two sessions, the partners are likely to use their false selves as they interact with each other. However, as the clients respond to the nonjudgmental, safe atmosphere of multicultural couples counseling, they usually adopt their preferred cultural and cognitive styles when they relate to each other.

Following the discussion about the individual perceptions of problems in the relationship, the therapist asked Javier to complete the BOLS and FAS. (Wanda had already completed these at her initial session—see Appendices C and G) to assess his preferred cultural and cognitive styles. The therapist used the time in which Javier completed these pencil-and-paper instruments to do a more thorough comparison of responses given by the partners on the Dyadic Adjustment Scale, noting both areas of agreement and of disagreement in their relationship.

After Javier completed his questionnaires, the therapist introduced the couple to the principal concepts of the flex theory of personality and of the multicultural model of psychotherapy. In making the presentation, he used the same approach employed with individual clients discussed in Chapter 7.

The therapist used some of the results of his preliminary observations and those from the Dyadic Adjustment Scale to personalize some of the concepts for Javier, whose preferred cognitive style in the learning/problem-solving domain—based on initial observations of his interactions with Wanda and the therapist—appeared to be field sensitive. The therapist also discussed some of the background research on the concepts to best match Wanda's more field independent style in the learning/problem-solving domain.

For example, to match Javier, the therapist said, "What the two of you have described with respect to the different ways in which you relate to your children indicates that you have different parenting values. You, Mr. M____, tend to be more traditional, wanting your children to respect you and to see you as an authority figure. On the other hand, Wanda is more modernistic, allowing the children to make their own decisions and to learn from experience rather than from direct teaching."

The therapist concluded the session by telling the clients that he would give them feedback during the second session about the findings of the behavioral ratings he had made and on the findings of the instruments they had completed. He asked each of them to think of one domain in the relationship in which they would like their partner to match them during the coming week. Javier chose the recreation domain; he asked Wanda to play a board game with him and the children after dinner on two nights. Javier agreed to allow Wanda one hour after coming home from work each evening to unwind and to shift from her work mode to her family mode.

The therapist asked each partner to keep records of the dates, times, and situations in which they experienced match and mismatch. Each was given several copies of a record form on which to describe the matches and mismatches they experienced. They were asked to complete these without consulting each other to see if there would be differences in perception of the experiences (a sample record form appears in Appendix N). In summary, the first session included the following seven techniques and procedures:

1. Initial match and introduction to the goals of couples counseling.
2. Administration of the Dyadic Adjustment Scale.
3. Establishment of an atmosphere of acceptance in which the clients could feel free to report the problems they perceive in their relationship and in which they would feel free to express their preferred cultural and cognitive styles.
4. Short discussion of each partner's perception of the relationship and of preliminary findings of the Dyadic Adjustment Scale, and observation of cognitive and cultural styles used when interacting with the partner and therapist.
5. Administration of the BOLS and FAS.
6. Introduction of the flex theory of personality and of the multicultural model of psychotherapy.
7. Closure of the session and assignment of homework for the coming week.

Session 2. During the second session, the therapist continued to build an atmosphere in which each partner could feel free to express concerns about the relationship as well as one in which each could assume the cultural and cognitive styles most reflective of their unique selves.

The therapist asked each of the clients to give him the forms on which they had recorded the experiences of match and mismatch for the week. He read these aloud, asking the clients to comment or to supply details. During the examination of the match and mismatch experiences each had perceived as being most important, the therapist included an explanation using the concepts of the flex theory of personality and of the multicultural model of psychotherapy.

In those situations in which conflict had occurred, the therapist pointed out how attempts at match by either or both partners might have prevented conflict. For example, both Javier and Wanda agreed that the major mismatch experience of the week had occurred when they disagreed about whether one of the children should be allowed to visit a neighborhood friend before completing his homework. Wanda is preferred modern cultural orientation; her preferred field independent orientation in parenting style was reflected in her position that children should be allowed to develop their own sense of responsibility. Javier's traditional and field sensitive orientation, however, stressed the need to be firm and directive with the children. They argued over their different orientations, with Wanda accusing Javier of being too controlling and Javier accusing her of not caring enough about the children. Application of concepts from the flex theory and the multicultural model led to negotiation between Wanda and Javier and to a better understanding of how conflict could have been avoided.

Each member of the couple reported on how well matched they had felt with respect to the match assignments for the week. The therapist helped the clients to understand how cultural and cognitive match had contributed to harmony in their interactions.

The therapist reported on the findings from the different instruments the clients had completed during the earlier session. He also shared the following findings of his observations regarding preferred cultural and cognitive styles:

> The ratings on your Dyadic Adjustment Scale indicate that you have good agreement on many domains of your relationship: religion, family, finances, philosophy of life, decision making, and household tasks. There are a number of areas in which you seem to have disagreement: demonstration of affection; ways of dealing with parents, in-laws, and friends; amount of time spent together; and career decisions.
>
> On the Bicognitive Orientation to Life Scale, Wanda scored as a preferred field independent with partial development of the field sensitive style in interpersonal relationships and communication style domains. Javier's scores indicated a strong preference for field sensitivity in all domains, although he did show some development of field independence in the learning/problem-solving styles domain.
>
> With respect to preferred cultural styles, you are well matched on religion and time orientation but mismatched on definition of gender roles. Javier tends to be more traditional in this area, whereas Wanda tends to be more modernistic. The same is true for childrearing orientation.

After a short discussion relating to these findings, the therapist asked the clients to focus on the identification of their goals for couples counseling. Wanda and Javier agreed on three:

1. Understanding how value and cognitive style differences are related to the areas of greatest disagreement between them.
2. Attempting to achieve a better cognitive styles match in learning/problem-solving and in parenting styles.
3. Attempting to match cultural styles in gender roles and in childrearing orientations.

The therapist focused on parenting styles and on values related to parenting. He concentrated on the major mismatch conflict situations reported by the clients during the initial stages of the session as he role-played with each of the clients, showing them how match and negotiation could have been accomplished. He followed these five steps:

1. *Values conflict analysis for understanding cultural styles mismatch.* First the therapist interpreted the differences in values reflected by the incident previously mentioned: "Wanda values independence; she feels that children should make their own decisions and be responsible for the consequences of those decisions. Javier, on the other hand, values discipline and feels that parents should be models for their children."

2. *Arriving at values negotiation.* The therapist led a discussion of these differences in values, asking the clients to attempt to negotiate. They both agreed that the other's values had some merit, concluding that their children needed to be independent and that they needed to learn that their decisions had consequences. They also agreed that discipline and guidance were important as a stage preceding the development of independence. Wanda and Javier decided that conflict between them could have been avoided had they been able to respect each other's values. They decided, for example, that their family rule is that the children can either complete their homework before dinner and then watch an hour of television after dinner or play for an hour before dinner and then do their homework during the time they would have watched television.

3. *Cognitive styles conflict analysis for understanding mismatch.* The therapist asked the clients to focus on cognitive styles in communication, showing them how they could have matched each other more closely in this domain to avoid conflict.

4. *Cognitive styles negotiation.* As an example, the therapist pointed out that Javier could have been more to-the-point in his explanation to Wanda as to why he objected to her decision to allow the children to play before they completed their homework. Wanda, by the same token, could have been more expressive in her explanation for making the decision she had made.

5. *Empathy projection.* Finally the therapist asked the clients to practice empathy projection (see Chapter 6) so that they could experience what it was like to be in their partner's shoes.

Under the direction of the therapist, the couple discussed another major mismatch situation that had occurred during the week. They used the same procedure as they had used with the discussion of the first incidence of mismatch. Taking into consideration the areas of cultural and cognitive styles in which the clients need to effect a better match, the therapist led the clients in an examination of their social environments (see Chapter 8) so that they could identify diversity challenges in which they could engage for the coming week.

Javier recalled that one of their son's Little League coaches seemed to be modernistic and field independent in his orientation as he worked with the children. Javier decided to watch him while he worked with the members of the team during practice. Wanda remembered that one of Javier's older sisters was traditional and field sensitive in her childrearing, and she decided to visit with her and closely observe her while she interacted with her children. During the coming week, Wanda agreed to use a field sensitive style while communicating with Javier. Javier agreed to try to use a field independent style. The therapist suggested that they should both read Beck's *Love Is Never Enough* for ideas about communication match.

Session 2, in summary, included the following six techniques and procedures:

1. Continued development of an atmosphere permitting expression of the true self.
2. Clients' reports of match and mismatch experiences for the past week.
3. Clients'reports of the degree of success with match assignments for the week.
4. The therapist's feedback on the results of assessment.
5. An analysis of cultural and cognitive match and role-playing to achieve match goals.
6. Homework match assignments for the coming week.

Session 3.   The therapist began the third session by asking the couple to report on the degree of success they had achieved in their match assignments for the previous week. This was followed by reports on each partner's perceptions of the most significant mismatch incident of the week.

The therapist noted that both Wanda and Javier followed the steps for analysis and match he had introduced during the previous session. He congratulated them on their efforts. The therapist also observed that both were interacting in a way that showed growth in cultural and cognitive match.

The major techniques introduced during Session 3 were scriptwriting and role-playing for both match and negotiation. The match script was developed with the therapist selecting one of the areas of conflict identified by each of the clients in their discussions—Javier's belief that since Wanda had returned to work outside the home, she had become cold and distant, and Wanda's belief that Javier had become too emotionally demanding and was not supportive of her career goals.

The therapist presented a scenario and asked each member of the couple to predict how the other would react in the following hypothetical situation:

THERAPIST: After Wanda has had her hour to unwind, Javier approaches her to tell her he would like to discuss a conflict he has experienced with one of his coworkers.

The therapist gave Wanda and Javier each a pad and asked them to predict what the other would say and do in this situation. When each had completed the task, the therapist asked them to take turns in reading their predictions out loud.

JAVIER: I wouldn't get much emotional support from Wanda. Instead of focusing on my hurt feelings, she would be objective and want me to give a lot of detail about what happened. Then she would interpret the incident as a misunderstanding between my colleague and me.

WANDA: Javier would get very emotional and would wind up confusing me with his description of the incident. Whenever he is angry or upset, he is not clear in what he communicates. He has a hard time getting to the point. Basically, I wouldn't know what he expected from me, and we would end up arguing.

THERAPIST: From a traditional cultural styles perspective, the one major thing Javier seems to want is for Wanda to focus on his feelings. At least for the moment, he wants her to ignore the details of the incident. From a cognitive styles point of view, the communication, human relations, and problem-solving style domains seem to be involved. When he is upset, Javier becomes field sensitive in his communication style and this mismatches your (*looking at Wanda*) preferred field independent style. From the perspective of human relations style, Javier would like you to focus on his nonverbal communications and from the learning/problem-solving styles perspective, he would like for you to show sympathy and caring, to let him know that you support him, and that you want to help him to find a solution. This is a field sensitive approach. A field independent approach would be to analyze the situation in order to help him to understand why the conflict occurred.

The therapist then role-played the script (taking the role of the opposite partner) with each client. When the role-playing was in progress, the partner whose role the therapist had taken observed and rated the behavior with the Preferred Cognitive and Cultural Styles Observation Checklists.

The next step involved discussing the observations made by the clients, making changes, and repeating the role-playing with the changes incorporated. Both clients role-played the final script while the therapist observed and rated. Following this exercise, the therapist reintroduced the same incident and asked the clients to write a negotiation script—a script in which each one of them was partially but not completely matched in their preferred styles. Each partner read the negotiation scripts out loud.

WANDA: Culturally, I would be more traditional in listening and observing Javier's expression of feeling. I should tell him right away that I support him and stand behind him. Once he has settled down, I can use my field independent problem-solving style to help him analyze what happened.

JAVIER: I need to calm down before telling my troubles to Wanda. I could develop a little exercise for myself based on what I've learned from writing scripts. I could write down what happened and organize what I want to say so that I can use a field independent communication style when I actually communicate with her. However, I would still make it clear that I need and want her support.

The therapist and the couple discussed the negotiation scripts. Wanda and Javier then role-played them while the therapist observed and evaluated them using the observation instruments. Finally the three discussed the role-playing and made changes in the scripts and behaviors as necessary.

The session ended with homework assignments of match and diversity challenges for the coming week.

In summary, Session 3 included the following four techniques and procedures:

1. Reports of client's match and mismatch experiences for the past week.
2. Introduction of scriptwriting and role-playing activities for match and negotiation.
3. Writing a match script for one of the major conflicts and role-playing that script.
4. Writing a negotiation script and role-playing it.

Sessions 4 and 5.   During these sessions, the therapist and clients continued with the development and role-playing of match and negotiation scripts.

Session 6.   This session focused on environmental demands and forces that cause strain on the relationship. The first step was to identify these demands. The therapist began the discussion by reminding this couple about three areas that appeared to be most affected by environmental forces as indicated by their responses on the Dyadic Adjustment Scale: friends; aims, goals, and things believed to be important; and relating to parents and in-laws.

The therapist led Wanda and Javier in a discussion directed at identifying the exact nature of the demands and forces causing conflict. In the area of work and career, both partners expressed dissatisfaction: Javier was unhappy when Wanda's unit managers called her at home to discuss problems in their unit, while Wanda resented Javier's supervisor's attempts to pressure him into playing golf on weekends.

Another environmental force identified as affecting the couple was exerted by their friends: Javier's friends wanted him to meet them after work on Fridays for happy hour. Wanda was angered by this because she felt that it cut into the time she and Javier could spend together. Javier did not like to socialize with Wanda's friends because, at times, they made ethnic or racial jokes, which made him uneasy.

Parents and in-laws were also identified as a source of pressures for Wanda and Javier: Javier's parents pressured them to teach their children Spanish, and Wanda felt that they were too demanding on this subject. Wanda's parents accused Javier of encouraging the children to be too dependent on him.

Their children's demands also affected the couple's relationship. They complained to Javier that Wanda wasn't spending enough time with them anymore while they complained to Wanda that Javier was too strict with them.

After identifying these environmental forces, the therapist asked the couple to negotiate on their solutions. They agreed on compromises for a number of the problems. The negotiations included Wanda's asking her coworkers not to call her on weekends or after 9 P.M. on weekdays; Javier agreed to tell his supervisor that he needed to spend more time with his family, so he would only be available for golf every other weekend. Wanda agreed to confront her friends about their racial jokes, while Javier agreed to limit happy hour with his friends to every other Friday.

The next step during the sixth session of couples counseling involved an analysis of cultural and cognitive styles mismatch related to environmental pressures and demands. The therapist asked each partner to write the answers to three questions:

1. In your opinion how are the demands and pressures of work and career changing the cultural styles of your partner?
2. How are these pressures changing his or her cognitive styles?
3. How are you reacting to these changes?

After completion, each partner read their answers aloud and discussed them.

WANDA: Ever since Javier took the job with the Hispanic firm he works for now, I feel he has become more traditional in his values and more rigid in his definition of gender roles. He has also become more field sensitive in his cognitive style in the parenting area. He wants the children to do things exactly the way he wants; he has become more autocratic in his manner as a father and as a husband.

JAVIER: Since Wanda got her job as manager, I feel she has lost interest in us as a family. She has become more self-centered. Her cognitive style has become very field independent—she lets the children make too many decisions on their own; they are too young and not ready for that.

Hearing the opinions of their partner regarding the changes resulting from their jobs and careers was enlightening for both Javier and Wanda. The discussion facilitated negotiation. They agreed that they would each make an attempt to be more flexible culturally and cognitively. They agreed that their relationship was more important than their careers; they decided to be more conscious of how job and career demands were causing mismatch.

The sixth session ended after match and diversity challenge assignments were made for the coming week. Session 6, in summary, included the following five techniques and procedures:

1. Identification of environmental demands and forces.
2. Discussion to discover the exact nature and impact of environmental forces and demands on the relationship.
3. Negotiation, discussion, and decisions.

4. Identification of specific cultural and cognitive developmental trends triggered by environmental forces and demands.
5. Negotiation decisions.

Sessions 7, 8, and 9.   During these three sessions, the couple continued to
practice techniques and procedures introduced in earlier sessions: analysis
of mismatch experiences of the previous week, development of match and
negotiation scripts, role-playing the scripts, development of strategies for
controlling environmental pressures, and negotiating to keep those pressures and demands from leading to extreme cultural and cognitive styles
mismatch. During Session 9, they retook the Dyadic Adjustment Scale, and
the therapist completed observational ratings throughout the course of the
session.

Session 10.   During Session 10, the therapist gave the couple feedback on
the findings obtained from the readministered Dyadic Adjustment Scale,
comparing these to the findings from the first administration. He reported
the following to Wanda and Javier:

> I am happy to report that your recent ratings on the Dyadic Adjustment Scale show
> that there has been a substantial reduction in areas of disagreement in your rela-
> tionship. Most impressive is the fact that you now show good agreement in sev-
> eral areas: demonstration of affection, philosophy of life, major decision making,
> and career decisions. The ratings indicate that you are now communicating more
> effectively.
>
> Certain areas of disagreement remain—for example, the amount of time you
> spend together. You still need to identify more things you can do together and you
> need to make more time to be together. You both reported that you occasionally
> disagree about this.
>
> The ratings I made of your behaviors during the last session indicate that you
> are matching each other better on cultural styles: You are both flexing well in
> terms of traditional and modern values. Javier, however, is still showing a prefer-
> ence for traditional values, while Wanda seems to have a preference for modern
> values. Nevertheless, you are now much more sensitive to these differences, and
> I noticed several attempts to negotiate.
>
> I've also noticed that you are negotiating well on cognitive styles, even though
> Javier is still preferred field sensitive and Wanda is still preferred field indepen-
> dent. You have learned to match each other and to negotiate bicognitive orienta-
> tions in the teaching and parenting, and learning/problem-solving domains.

This was followed by a long discussion, but no major unresolved problems emerged. The therapist proceeded to wrap up counseling, making an
appointment for one month hence for a follow-up session. He made it clear
that he would be available for an earlier appointment should they feel it
necessary.

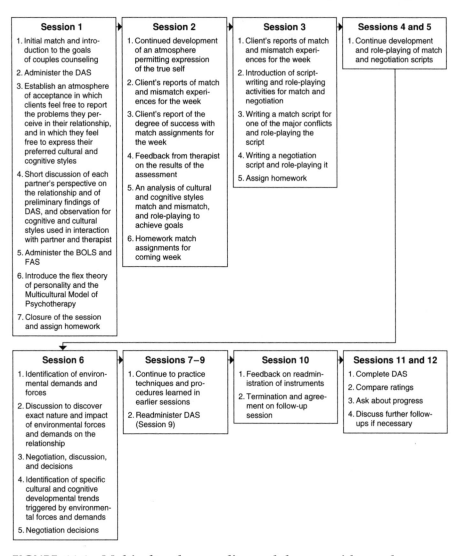

FIGURE 11.1   Multicultural counseling and therapy with couples

Session 10, in summary, included the following two techniques and procedures:

1. Feedback on readministration instruments.
2. Termination and agreeing on follow-up sessions.

Session 11.   During the first follow-up session, Wanda and Javier completed the Dyadic Adjustment Scale again. The therapist compared their ratings, noting that there were now no areas of major disagreement. The therapist asked each of them for their perceptions of the progress being made in their relationship. Although they did report some major mismatch situations since their last session, they agreed that they had been successful in negotiating them. The therapist scheduled another follow-up session in six months and ended the session.

Session 12.   The second follow-up proceeded along the same lines as the first. When Javier and Wanda agreed that no problems had surfaced since Session 11, the therapist indicated that he saw no need for continued sessions. Wanda and Javier concurred. The therapist assured them that he was available should they need additional counseling.

A graphic summary of the different sessions of multicultural counseling with couples is presented in Figure 11.1 on the preceding page.

SUMMARY

When the multicultural model is applied during couples counseling, the primary focus is on mismatch in values and in cognitive styles—the root source of many conflicts in relationships. In addition to teaching techniques and procedures that can lead to match and negotiation, the therapist also helps the clients to identify external, or environmental, forces and demands. Environmental demands can cause dissatisfaction in the relationship and can trigger the development of trends in values and cognitive styles that are also related to mismatch. The partners learn to identify and negotiate with respect to the disrupting forces.

12

FAMILY COUNSELING

Innovative approaches to family therapy that have been developed for use with people who are culturally different have focused on matching the values, worldviews, and unique family structures and roles as well as special needs and personality variables such as biculturalism and/or multiculturalism. Carolyn Atteneave (1969) was a pioneer in the development of culture match approaches. Her work with Native American families living in urban settings combined the "Medicine Man" role and the strategies of Network Therapy (Speck and Atteneave, 1974). Atteneave referred to her approach as retribalization.

Minuchin and his colleagues (1967) introduced the structural approach to family therapy, which had been developed with inner-city poor families, some of whom were African American and Latino. Aponte (1974) introduced the ecostructural model of family therapy, which had been developed in his treatment approaches with African American and Puerto Rican families. He was influenced by Auerswald's (1968) ecological therapy. The ecostructural approach seeks to empower families by helping them to "navigate the system." That is, the goal of therapy is to help families interact with institutions and agencies—schools, courts, child welfare, and housing offices, as well as health and mental health providers—that impact their lives.

The work of both Minuchin and Aponte influenced Szapocznik, Scopetta, Aranalde, and Kurtines (1978), who adapted the ecostructural approach to the values and special needs of Cuban American families at the Spanish Family Guidance Clinic in the Department of Psychiatry at the University of Miami School of Medicine. Ho (1987) introduced an ecological systemic approach for doing therapy with families of different ethnic groups. The focus of Ho's strategies emphasized sensitivity toward traditional family values of different ethnic groups and attention to acculturation processes, which are related to bicultural orientations to life. Ho postulated that his emic approach offered promise for enhancing the understanding of ethnic families and for enlarging the intervention repertoires available to the family therapist.

Boyd-Franklin (1987) argued for the use of a structural/ecostructural approach with African American families, citing the importance of unique family structures, roles, and the degree to which poor families are impacted by institutions outside themselves. She also argued for the use of Bowen's (1976) *genograms* (a family tree to help the family map its family organization and intergenerational emotional issues) in doing therapy with African American families.

McGill (1992) introduced the concept of the cultural story in his work with ethnic minority families. The cultural story assumes that a family brings to therapy not only a story of its idiosyncratic problems, but that this story also reflects society's stories about gender, life cycle, ethnicity, class, and race. To use the cultural story in therapy, therapists need to be acquainted with the value systems and worldviews of various cultures. McGill recommended the use of diversity genograms to record the family's story, including the stories of generation, gender, ethnicity, race, class, and migration. A diversity genogram expands standard genogram methods used in family therapy.

In their work with Latino families, Cervantes and Ramirez (1995) have evolved a model of family therapy based on the *Mestizo* (multicultural/multiracial) worldview and the cultural value of spiritualism. Emphasizing the mestizo psychology perspective (M. Ramirez, 1983), mestizo spirituality, and the philosophy of *curanderismo* (Mexican faith healing), they evolved strategies for family therapy used effectively with Latino families in Texas. In the first edition of this book, M. Ramirez (1991) introduced an approach to couples counseling based on a values and cognitive styles match and mismatch. His focus on the cultural and personality styles of couples experiencing conflict led to expansion of this multicultural perspective for doing psychotherapy with families. The rest of this chapter describes the multicultural model of family therapy.

THE CASE OF THE ROSALES

Presenting Problems

The initial contact was with Anna, a mother who had been referred to the therapist by her church. Anna and her husband, Jesse, had been having conflicts for approximately two years, and it had gotten to the point where they were threatening to divorce. Anna felt that their marital problems were having a strong negative influence on their two children, Tati and Nancy. Tati, an eight-year-old boy, was having academic problems; Nancy, fourteen, wanted to date a student in high school; she had taken the family car without permission and had gotten into an accident.

Jesse had been experiencing symptoms of panic disorder without agoraphobia. He was also experiencing some symptoms of somatization disorder, having had several false alarms thinking that he was having symptoms of a ruptured ulcer. He was rushed to the hospital where medical tests showed that the symptoms were related to anxiety. Anna, too, was experiencing symptoms of anxiety, but she tended to be stoic about them. One incident shocked her and the rest of the family: She was driving the children to an evening school event when, without warning, she lost control of the car and drove from the parking lot into one of the playgrounds of the school. Fortunately, no one was hurt. This incident scared Anna because she suffered from some of the symptoms of amnesia; she could not remember losing control of the car or the kids screaming from the backseat warning her that that she was driving at high speed into the playground.

General Clinical Considerations

Anna needed to be assessed for a dissociative disorder and for generalized anxiety disorder. She also needed to learn stress-reduction techniques. Jesse was assessed for panic disorder without agoraphobia. He also needed to learn stress-reduction techniques and be evaluated for any need for medication. Tati was evaluated for learning disorders to see if he needed special services such as placement in resource classes at school. Nancy was evaluated for oppositional defiant disorder.

History of the Rosales Family

A family history done with Mr. and Mrs. Rosales during the second session revealed that Anna and Jesse were likely to differ in their preferred cultural and cognitive styles and that these differences were likely related to exposure to different socialization and life experiences. Although their Latino cultural background was the same, differences in their personality styles reflected a difference in values.

Anna had been born and reared in an urban environment in Central Texas, which was predominantly Caucasian (about seventy percent) with some African Americans and Latinos (approximately twenty and ten percent, respectively). The predominant Caucasian cultural influence in her community exposed Anna to modern values; Caucasian values in the schools and in other community institutions had the greatest influence on the development of her personality. Most of Anna's close friends in school were Caucasian, and she had also felt the influence of Caucasian culture because of her involvement in Girl Scouts. Further, her family socialization experiences had been very different from those of Jesse. She had grown up with three brothers; and her parents had encouraged her to be as independent as her brothers, encouraging the entire family to adopt flexible gender roles; Anna had been encouraged to be active in sports and was given the same freedom to date that her brothers had.

The schools Anna attended valued field independent thinking, learning/problem-solving styles, and emphasized field independent teaching styles. Anna's father was an engineer and had been the informal math tutor for all the children in the family. He encouraged all his children to excel in math and science. Anna had also been encouraged in individual competition, both at home and at school. She had participated in Interscholastic League competitions and had won several ribbons.

Jesse's socialization and life experiences had been different from Anna's. He had grown up in semi-urban small South Texas city, which was predominantly Latino (eighty-five percent) with Caucasian and African Americans making up the other ten and five percent of the population, respectively. Almost all Jesse's close friends during childhood, adolescence, and young adulthood were Latino; others had been African American and very few had been Caucasian. In fact, Jesse had not had Caucasian close friends until he was in the service.

Jesse's family had encouraged traditional gender roles. He had only sisters, so when their father passed away when Jesse was in high school, he adopted several aspects of the father's role as principal breadwinner and authority figure in the home. Jesse dropped out of high school and took a full-time job to help support the family. He obtained his GED while in the service, but he had not pursued a college education.

Most of the institutions (principally the schools and the churches) in Jesse's community encouraged a field sensitive approach to learning/problem-solving. His participation in school sports was oriented toward identity with the team and the community and encouraged group rather than individual competition. His mother had been interested in history and in reading autobiographies, so she encouraged Jesse's good performance in social sciences courses at school. One of Jesse's uncles, a mural painter, encouraged Jesse to assist him with several murals he had painted as community projects.

Anna and Jesse met at a church dance held in Anna's hometown. At the time, Jesse had been in the service and stationed at a nearby army base. Both said something to the effect that it had been love at first sight and that they had felt they were right for each other from the first moment they met. A history of the courtship, which had been two years long, indicated there had been little conflict or differences of opinion between them. Both recalled that their only areas of disagreement had been about handling money and dealing with extended family. In the area of money, Anna would become upset because of Jesse's spending habits, particularly his tendency to buy watches for a collection he had.

Jesse had objected to Anna's continued closeness to her brothers and her seeming need to please them. Discussion of this topic led to revelation of a wider problem—neither's family had approved of their relationship and marriage. Acceptance had only occurred after they adopted their children. Jesse's sisters and his mother had felt that Anna was too modern and *agabachada* (Anglicized) for Jesse. While Anna's siblings and her parents felt that Jesse was too traditional *muy rancho* (member of a small, rural Latino community) and not ambitious enough because he had not gone to college.

Anna envied her brothers who were already married, had children, and had their own homes. She had hoped that marriage would lead to these same things for Jesse and her. Jesse's first goal had been to have children so that he could pass on family history and traditions to them and so that his mother could be a grandmother before she passed away.

The first major problem the couple encountered was economics. Without the resources to buy a house, they were forced to live with Anna's parents. This put a lot of strain on the relationship and furthered Anna's brothers opinion that Jesse lacked ambition. Anna began to share this opinion. The couple's failure to have children early in their marriage was the basis of additional problems. After numerous medical tests and approaches, they were finally told conclusively that it was medically impossible for them to have their own children. Jesse perceived that it was Anna's fault. His mother and sister supported his traditional views of the woman's role— somehow Anna was less than a "complete" woman because she could not have children.

After much agonizing and discussions with their pastor, Anna and Jesse decided to adopt Nancy. Both members of the couple agreed that because of Jesse's traditional views regarding gender role, he had been minimally involved in childrearing and parental care early in Nancy's life. This resulted in a very close bond between Anna and Nancy with Jesse being an outsider. A year after this adoption, Anna was promoted to a supervisory position with a much higher salary. The couple was able to purchase their own home and decided to adopt a second child, a boy. Since Anna had established such a close bond with Nancy, it was an unspoken agreement between the couple that the next child would "belong" to Jesse. Tati was adopted and indeed he and Jesse developed a strong bond. Jesse had been very involved in Tati's early care and socialization. The alliances were formed.

The Initial Sessions of Multicultural Counseling and Therapy with the Rosales

The Initial Session.   The goals of the initial session of family therapy are similar to those of the first session in individual therapy: to establish an atmosphere of nonjudgmental or uncritical acceptance, to attempt to match the preferred cultural and cognitive styles of the clients, and to make behavioral observations to determine if the styles with which the family members present are their preferred or nonpreferred styles. The additional goal of family counseling is to observe interactions between family members in order to assess family alliances, which may be contributing to conflict.

At the first session with the Rosales family, the therapist began by welcoming them and asking them to introduce themselves. The therapist observed family dynamics immediately, determining who talked first and the degree of identification with traditional values by seeing if the clients used their first or both first and last names. He also had a chance to observe the seating patterns, and he determined that Jesse and Tati had sat next to each other while Nancy and Anna sat side by side. He observed that Anna talked first followed by Jesse, then Nancy and finally Tati. Jesse, Nancy, and Anna seemed to be expressing their preferred cultural and cognitive styles, but Tati seemed to be uncomfortable, looking to the other members of his family for direction.

The therapist asked each family member to think of one thing that was a strength in the family and one thing that was a problem. Anna began: "The way I see it our family problem is that we have a lot of disagreements, in particular Jesse and me. The strength I see is that when we do things together as a family we seem to forget our differences and enjoy what we do." Jesse spoke next, "The problem I see is that Anna criticizes Tati and me too much. Our strength is going to church on Sundays and doing activities through the church." Nancy's response was, "Most of the time there seems to be a lot of tension, but it is fun when we go visit our cousins in the Rio Grande Valley. We seem to be a different family when we visit there." Tati finished with, "Most of the time I feel it is my fault that Mom and Dad fight; it makes me feel bad. The time I like too is when we visit with our relatives and have fun." During this exercise the therapist observed that, when Nancy talked, she looked at Anna and not at the others, while Tati looked only at Jesse when he was talking.

More intensive discussion of the problems and strengths of the family followed. After approximately one hour the therapist said, "Before I ask you to fill out some forms, I would like for each of you to think of something that is fairly simple and straightforward, something that can easily be done by your family in the next two weeks, that would make things better for the entire family." After a short discussion and agreement on a family activity, the therapist asked each of them to complete the FAS (Appendix C), TMI (Appendix M), BOLS (Appendix G), and MEI (Appendix A). Because of Tati's problems with reading, the therapist asked him if he would like help with the forms. Tati agreed, and they went to the empty waiting room while the others completed their forms individually in the therapist's office.

While Tati was alone with the therapist and as he was responding to the items of the instruments he was taking, he became more talkative and self-disclosing, sharing that he was worried that his parents might separate. The therapist listened empathetically and indicated to Tati that the decision to come to family counseling was a good sign. Tati seemed reassured.

The therapist then met with all the family members again and said, "I will be calling you in a few days to let you know if I think I am the right therapist for you and to see if you think I m right for you. I would like you to discuss this as a family in the next two days. If I do not feel I am the right therapist or if you feel I am not right for you, I can refer you to some therapists who might be a better fit. If we all agree that we should work together, I would like to see only Mr. and Mrs. Rosales for the next session. After that I will usually see all of you together. However, there may be times when I have to meet individually with Mr. and Mrs. Rosales again."

The initial and all subsequent sessions were one and one-half to two hours in length. The initial session, in summary, included the following:

- Observing family interactions through seating pattern, verbal and nonverbal behaviors, and the communication patterns suggesting alliances based on match and mismatch.
- Having each member give a family strength and a family problem.
- Observing for preferred cultural and cognitive styles of individual members using the Preferred Cultural and Cognitive Styles Checklists (Appendices E and F).
- Establishing one change the family members would like to see in the family during the next two weeks.
- Administering the FAS, TMI, BOLS and MEI instruments.

Session 2. The therapist opened the session by asking Anna and Jesse to complete the Dyadic Adjustment Scale (DAS). After they completed this instrument, the therapist asked the Rosales to relate the history of their relationship and their family as they saw it, beginning with how they met. As they told the early history of their relationship, the therapist asked how things went when they were dating; how they felt from the start about their fit with one another; when they decided to marry; what hopes they each had for the marriage. He then asked about their history of sexual intimacy and whether it had changed from early in their relationship. He finally explored how their families had felt about the marriage and early problems.

From the Rosales' responses to these questions and from their responses to the DAS, the therapist determined that their expectations for marriage were similar, but did show some differences in what they considered problem areas in the relationship, particularly with finances, dealing with relatives, and household chores. The couple and therapist discussed these.

At the conclusion of the session, the therapist summarized by saying, "You have agreed to spend more quality time together as a couple—a date night during the week. You both agreed to discuss your concerns about your adjustment to the sexual relationship more openly." The second session (parents only), in summary, included the following:

- Introducing the goal of session—to learn about the relationship and its history.
- Administering the DAS.
- Learning the history of the relationship and of the family.

- Providing feedback on findings of the DAS and the history.
- Offering suggestions for improving the relationship between partners.

Session 3. The therapist began the session by asking all the family members to report on how they had perceived progress toward attaining the one goal they had jointly selected for improving the well-being of the family. He started with Tati's and Nancy's goals and then moved to those of Jesse and Anna. All in all, the members felt that there had been significant improvement in their feelings toward each other and that Anna and Jesse had done less arguing during the two weeks since the last session with the entire family.

The therapist introduced the cultural and cognitive flex model to the Rosales, using the approach described in Chapter 7. This included a discussion of the importance of values and cognitive styles, match and mismatch, and how these can lead to family conflict. He gave the family feedback on the findings of the assessment instruments they had taken. He began with values indicating how similar Tati and Jesse were, contrasting this with the similarities between Anna and Nancy. The discussion that followed centered on selecting a cultural styles goal that the family would focus on during the next session. They all decided they wanted to work on the definition of gender roles and division of labor in household chores.

The therapist asked Anna and Tati and Nancy and Jesse to work together as pairs in scriptwriting. Mother and son moved to a different part of the room so that they could concentrate on their scripts. The specific goal of the scripts was how to encourage Jesse and Tati to help with the vacuuming and the laundry and how to get Nancy and Anna to help with washing the cars.

An important issue surfaced during this session: Jesse's reluctance to participate in role-playing. He said he felt embarrassed to participate in something that seemed like a game for an adult (a traditional value) and that he feared his children might lose respect for him if he participated (also a traditional value in Latino culture). A discussion with the family about the values related to Jesse's reluctance ensued and in the process he agreed to serve as Nancy's coach during role-playing; the other family members felt it might be good to have an outside observer in addition to the therapist when they were role-playing. About two-thirds of the way through the session, Jesse became so involved in giving direction to all the family members that essentially he became involved in the role-playing himself.

The therapist moved back and forth between the two pairs as consultant. From suggestions given by Tati as to how best to approach Jesse on the housecleaning chores, Anna realized that she had usually compared Jesse negatively to her brothers when she had asked him to help out with the housework. She realized that this usually led to Jesse becoming defensive and resulted in an argument between them. Jesse, on the other hand, with

Nancy's help, arrived at the realization that he usually assigned the menial tasks of cleaning the hubcaps and the tires to Anna and Nancy, never allowing them to do what they really enjoyed—waxing the cars. He had always reserved this task for Tati and himself, usually saying, "They are not very good at this because they don't have the arm and hand strength it takes to do it right." This would alienate Nancy and Anna.

Gender Roles and Division of Labor on Household Chores, Scripts

JESSE AND NANCY'S SCRIPT: At least one day before he planned to wash the cars, Jesse was to say to Nancy, Anna, and Tati, "I would like for us to wash the cars tomorrow afternoon. Who would like to help and what jobs do you want to do?" It was agreed that if Anna, Nancy, and Tati wanted to participate in the activity, Anna and Tati would wax one of the cars while Nancy and Jesse concentrated on the hubcaps and tires; the roles for the pairs would be reversed for the other car.

TATI AND ANNA'S SCRIPT: A day before she planned to do housecleaning, Anna would say to the family, "I would like for us to clean the house tomorrow. Can we all do it together?" She agreed not to compare Jesse unfavorably with her brothers. Following housecleaning, they all agreed to do something that Tati wanted—for the family to see a movie together.

The scripts were role-played, with all members participating, with the assistance of the therapist. This was followed by a family discussion as to how they had benefited from the exercise.

Homework Assignment – The therapist gave a homework assignment. Anna and Jesse would both ask the family to participate in housecleaning and car-washing chores. The entire family was to discuss how the assignments had gone and to report back to the therapist at the next session.

The third session, in summary, included the following:

- Obtaining individual family members' perceptions of degree of success in accomplishing change goals identified at the end of the initial session.
- Introducing the cultural and cognitive flex model.
- Obtaining feedback on the findings of the assessment instruments administered during initial session.
- Selecting a cultural styles goal.
- Assigning scriptwriting in pairs.
- Writing scripts.
- Role-playing.
- Discussing role-play and, if necessary, making script changes and role-playing again.
- Assigning homework.

Session 4. The therapist began the session by asking the family members about the outcome of the homework assignment and improvements and problems they had noticed in their family during the past week. They made necessary changes to the script and replayed the roles, focusing on the cultural goal. The therapist then reviewed the major concepts of the flex model, indicating that the primary goal for this session would be to identify a common cognitive styles goal and to again proceed to write a script and to do role-playing. The cognitive styles goal on which members of the family agreed was communication style.

They decided to work on this in the context of the basis of the majority of the arguments between Jesse and Anna—his spending habits and her frequent business trips. Again, assignment for scriptwriting was made to the pairs. They were asked to focus on both goals, writing scripts for both. Again, Anna and Jesse were surprised by the insights provided by their children. Jesse realized that his frustration over arguments with Anna concerning one of her trips led him to start shopping for an addition to his watch collection.

Jesse also came to realize that his stated reasons about why he did not like Anna to travel so much were very broad: "It's not good for the family for you to be gone so much." Nancy helped him to identify some of the specific reasons for his opposition to the frequency of her business trips: He felt Anna valued her job and career advancement opportunities more than she valued the family and his jealousy about the male coworkers who went on the trips with her. On the other hand, Anna's criticisms of Jesse's spending habits were always focused on too much detail and usually included dire predictions about family finances, which made Jesse resentful. When the scripts were completed, role-playing was done with discussion following.

TATI AND ANNA'S SCRIPT: First Anna was to be very specific about the reasons for her trip and about which coworkers would be going on the trip. The family discussed when Anna would call while she was gone and how long she would be gone. When she returned and learned that Jesse bought a new watch for his collection, she would say: "Can I see your new watch? How does it fit into your collection?"

The role-playing was followed by an extensive discussion concerning communication style conflicts in the family; some of these concerned arguments between Nancy and Tati, particularly when Tati relayed phone messages to Nancy. She was always upset that he failed to give her enough specific information. The family agreed to buy a message pad to use for this purpose.

JESSE AND NANCY'S SCRIPT: Jesse would be more explicit about his concerns about her trips. He explained, "In movies and on TV I see people who work together and travel on business trips falling in love. I get jealous." Tati would say, "I miss having you around because Dad and Nancy get into more arguments when you are away." They then allowed Anna to respond.

During the role-playing, Anna was surprised to learn that Jesse was jealous. She had never considered this and had seen his opposition to her business trips as an attempt to curtail her freedom. She was even more surprised by Tati's observation that Jesse and Nancy would argue more while she was away. A long discussion ensued about communication style conflicts that led to disagreements and arguing between Nancy and Jesse.

Homework Assignments – The therapist made a homework assignment. Both pairs would try out what they had learned at least once in their teaching–learning efforts during the week. Again, they would discuss the successes and the problems of their efforts.

The fourth session, in summary, included the following:

- Assessing the outcome of the Session 3 homework assignment and giving suggestions, if necessary.
- Identifying a cognitive styles goal.
- Writing scripts.
- Role-playing.
- Discussing the efforts and making any necessary changes in scripts and replaying them.
- Assigning homework.

Session 5. Again the therapist started the session by asking how each member of the family perceived things had gone the previous week and asking them if they had any questions. They then worked on another cognitive style goal that the family had identified as very important. This one focused on learning–teaching style—this time on the need for Anna to tutor Tati on math without losing her patience with him and the need for her to match her teaching style to his preferred learning style. The therapist had Anna and Tati focus on the characteristics of field sensitive learning/problem-solving on a Child Behavior Observation Checklist (Cox, Macaulay, and Ramirez, 1983).

TATI AND ANNA'S SCRIPT: After reviewing and discussing the Child Behavior Observation Checklist, Tati and Anna worked on the teaching styles script. Anna would say, "How would you like me to help with your homework?" She also agreed to give more social rewards when Tati succeeded and to use more modeling and less of the discovery approach when teaching. She would say, "Would you like me to show you how I learned to solve that type of problem?" Tati agreed to be less passive and to take more initiative in what he was doing.

Jesse and Nancy focused on the techniques used to teach Nancy to drive. The therapist had them focus on the learning behaviors of a field independent style and on the field sensitive teaching styles. He assisted them in writing a script in which there would be a better match between learning and teaching styles.

JESSE AND NANCY'S SCRIPT: Jesse agreed to be more responsive to the way Nancy preferred to be given driving lessons. She would say, "I would like for you to have more confidence in me and let me try it my own way. When you are going to show me how to do something new, tell me about it and then just let me try it. If I have any questions, I can ask you." Jesse also agreed to be more explicit and attentive to detail in his explanations. For example, in teaching Nancy to parallel park, he would say, "The idea is to use the car that will be in front of you for alignment when you are backing into the parking spot. You turn the wheel so that the rear end of the car goes toward the curb. Once you are far enough in, turn the wheel the other way to get the front end of the car close to the curb."

Homework Assignments – Both pairs would try out what they had learned at least once in their teaching–learning efforts during the week. Again, they would discuss the successes and the problems of their efforts.

Assessment of Progress – All four family members again completed the FAS, TMI, and BOLS. Jesse and Anna took the DAS again. To identify areas in which progress had been made, as well as areas that still required work, these scores were compared with those from the first administration.

The fifth session, in summary, included the following:

- Assessing outcome of homework and giving suggestions, if necessary.
- Identifying a second cultural or cognitive styles goal.
- Writing scripts.
- Role-playing.
- Discussing scripts and role-playing, making changes, if necessary.
- Assigning homework.
- Assessing progress by readministering the assessment instruments.

Session 6.   The therapist started the session by asking about the outcome of the homework assignment. Family members then identified a second cultural goal they wanted to work on. After a short discussion, the Rosales settled on the goal of how relationships with members of the extended family had an influence on their family. In particular, Tati and Nancy felt that Jesse and Anna were influenced by their aunts, uncles, and parents with respect to childrearing behaviors. This frequently led to conflict between Jesse and Anna and to Nancy and Tati feeling they were being treated unfairly, particularly by the parent to which they were mismatched in terms of cultural and cognitive styles. More specifically, Jesse would be criticized by his mother and sisters as too *moderno* or *agabachado,* because he and Anna were considering allowing Nancy to date at age fourteen. Anna, on the other hand, was being criticized by her parents and brothers for what they referred to as "Jesse's macho influence" on Tati. They felt this would make it impossible for Tati to become a "good American" and to be able to compete in high school and college. The family members perceived this problem differently. What follows is what they had to say.

NANCY: A lot of arguments at home start when we visit my grandparents and aunts and uncles. Dad becomes stricter and Mother wants to give us more freedom. We become confused.

TATI: I think that our family is different, but our parents want us to be like my cousins.

ANNA: It is embarrassing to me that my brothers, my sisters-in-law, and parents think that we are not being good parents.

JESSE: Every time we visit with my family, I come away thinking that my mother and my sisters know the best way to bring up children. After all, my sisters and I came out okay and my nieces and nephews are all doing well in school.

The therapist asked the family to break up into two scriptwriting pairs, but this time he asked if they were ready to change partners—Tati and Nancy together and Jesse and Anna together. The family members were enthusiastic about this idea. The pairs went to different areas of the room with the therapist again circulating between them serving as a consultant. Once the scripts were ready, the therapist encouraged the pairs to reassemble as a family; at this time the script for what Jesse and Anna would say when their family was criticized by members of the extended family began.

In the past Nancy and Tati overheard many of the conversations between their parents, grandparents, aunts, and uncles, so they were effective in playing these roles. Now they enacted the scripts they wrote regarding their behavior should their parents be influenced by the members of the extended family. The role-playing led to an extensive and animated discussion. Toward the end of the session, the therapist asked each of the family members to share their views regarding what they had learned and what they felt the exercise had done for the family.

All the family members felt that what they were learning during the sessions had extensive carryover to their daily interactions. They all reported that their relationships with each other had improved dramatically. They also reported that the role-playing and scriptwriting had helped them to understand the family member who was most mismatched to them and had helped them achieve an empathy for that member that they had never had.

The sixth session, in summary, included the following:

- Assessing the outcome of homework.
- Identifying a second cultural or cognitive styles goal.
- Reassigning pairs—exchanging partners and writing new scripts.
- Role-playing.
- Discussing and changing scripts, if necessary, with the therapist assuming a nondirective role.
- Reporting by family members about what they have learned from therapy thus far, with their individual assessment of progress made to this point.

Sessions 7 through 10.   The following is a summary of four procedures and activities used for the Rosales's multicultural family therapy sessions:

1. Identifying additional cognitive (types of rewards given by the parents to the children) and cultural styles (achieving a better balance between career and family goals for Anna and between spirituality and family for Jesse) goals with accompanying scriptwriting, role-playing, discussions, and changes, as necessary.
2. Assigning homework after each session and assessing degree of success at the next session.
3. Wrapping up and terminating at the end of Session 10.
4. Following up six weeks after termination of therapy.

A graphic summary of the different sessions of multicultural family therapy is presented in Figure 12.1.

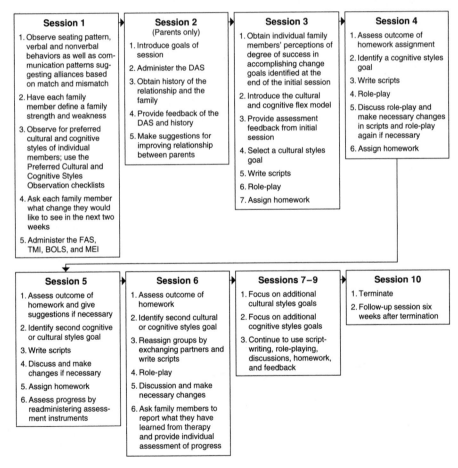

FIGURE 12.1   Multicultural therapy with families

MULTICULTURAL THERAPY WITH
THE SINGLE-PARENT FAMILY

Practitioners and researchers have long recognized that single-parent families have needs and problems of adjustment that differ from those of intact families. As early as 1974, Minuchin observed that the absence of the father from the family requires renegotiation and restructuring of family system boundaries. Ho (1987), focusing on culturally different families, concluded that immigration and acculturation stressors, increasing separation and divorce, and decisions to have children outside of marriage were all related to the rise of single-parent families. He further observed that the traditional closeness of the mother–child relationship within ethnic minority families could contribute to enmeshment and parent–child structural relationships.

The clinical and research experiences of this author in his work with culturally different, single-parent families has led to identification of the following five problems, which need to be addressed in therapy (Ho, 1996, p. 14):

1. The influence of the nonresident parent and that partner's extended family on interactions between the members of single-parent families.
2. The effects of continuing conflict between the parents and involvement of the children in their cultural and cognitive styles mismatch struggles.
3. The influence of the nonresident parent's remarriage and, in particular, the positive and negative impact of stepparents on the single-parent family.
4. The effects of economic pressures on the single-parent family when there is a decline in family income following separation and/or divorce.
5. The influence of differences in cultural and cognitive styles between the estranged parents, as well as between extended family members, on the degree to which children are encouraged or discouraged from identifying with the culture of the nonresident parent.

Johnson (1994) has found that identification with the culture of the nonresident parent is a central issue in the development of mixed-race children.

The Case of Camilla and Her Two Daughters

Initial Contact and Presenting Problems.   Camilla is a Latina who married Robert, a Caucasian. They have two biracial daughters, Tracy and Lavis. Robert and Camilla have been divorced for two years; Camilla has custody and Robert has visitation rights. It had been an acrimonious divorce with many unresolved issues related to the breakup of the marriage.

Camilla contacted the therapist because of conflict with her older daughter. She felt these conflicts were exacerbated whenever the children visited with their father. Camilla also reported that her younger daughter,

Lavis, complained of feeling left out whenever the two girls were with their father. Lavis was also uncomfortable during these visits when Tracy and her father would criticize Camilla. A pattern had developed: Following the visits, Camilla would call Robert to complain and end up in an angry confrontation characterized by accusations, insults, and discussion of unresolved issues related to the failed marriage. Camilla had discussed the possibility of family therapy with Robert, and he had agreed to participate if the therapist felt it was necessary.

Camilla and Robert had met at the community college they were both attending. They were introduced by Camilla's sister, who was married to Robert's best friend. Camilla had dated only one other person before Robert and was quite sheltered. Their dating had gone well, but Camilla admitted that, because of her lack of experience in relationships, she had mainly done whatever Robert had wanted to do and failed to assert herself, even to the point of agreeing to marriage before she completed her college degree. This went against a promise Camilla had made to her parents—that she would complete her education before marrying. Neither Camilla's nor Robert's extended families approved of the marriage; both sets of parents' reasons for opposing the union had been the same: "You are too different. You should marry someone whose background and experiences are more similar to yours."

Robert wanted a stay-at-home wife who would take care of the children and support him in his career. He felt that Latino culture encouraged this type of behavior and his sister-in-law, Camilla's sister, had supposedly adopted that role. Robert's cultural expectations of the marriage were reflected in his responses to the FAS and TMI.

Camilla decided to continue her college education once her children were old enough to go to a day-care facility. She wanted to work with adolescents who were having problems of adjustment. She married Robert because she believed that, unlike Latinos, Caucasian men would be more egalitarian in their relationships and more likely to help with housework and with rearing the children. Camilla's expectations were confirmed in what she perceived to be the role of her brother-in-law in his relationship with her sister.

History of Marital Problems.   Both Camilla and Robert agreed that the first four years of the marriage had been good. Camilla fulfilled Robert's expectations of the stay-at-home wife and mother. Robert was advancing in his career and providing well for the family. Camilla, however, started to become resentful when Robert did not help on household chores and with childrearing. Robert became unhappy when Camilla returned to college and started to do volunteer work. The conflicts between them became more frequent. As she became more involved in her college work and volunteer efforts, Robert felt that Camilla had changed too much.

Robert felt uncomfortable attending social activities in the Latino community: "They look at me as if I don't belong—like I am the white male enemy they hate." Camilla felt she did not have much in common with Robert's work friends or with their wives. She also felt that they were insensitive to social problems and were materialistic. Camilla's values and cultural expectations of her marriage were revealed in her responses to the FAS and TMI given during Session 2.

Session-by-Session Presentation.   The first session included Camilla, Tracy, and Lavis. The therapist greeted the family in the waiting room, introduced himself and escorted them to his office. The office offered a variety of possible seating patterns, so the therapist had an opportunity to observe: Lavis and Camilla sat next to each other while Tracy sat next to Lavis but at a distance from her. The therapist also observed the interactions of the three—who was talking and what facial expressions and eye contact were taking place. He saw that Camilla did most of the talking and that Tracy contradicted her mother frequently and took what she perceived was her father's side on issues. Lavis was silent until addressed by the therapist. The therapist used the observation instruments discussed in Chapter 7 to observe cultural and cognitive styles.

Before the session was over, the therapist asked if all three would agree to have the father involved in a session; they did. The therapist agreed to contact Robert about this. He let the mother and daughters know that for the next session he would like to meet with Camilla and Robert only to ask about the history of their relationship: how they met, why they had decided to marry (including cultural expectations), and how problems had developed in the relationship and the family. He ended by assigning homework like that given during the initial session with the intact Rosales family.

The initial session, in summary, included the following:

- Looking for possible alliances by observing seating patterns, verbal and nonverbal behaviors, and communication patterns based on match and mismatch.
- Assessing the preferred cognitive and cultural styles of individual members by using the Preferred Cultural and Cognitive Styles Checklists.
- Deciding whether to include a nonresident parent in sessions.
- Assigning homework.

Session 2.   The second session for this family included only Camilla and Robert and lasted between an hour and a half and two hours. During this session, the therapist introduced himself to Robert and outlined the rules of the session to both Camilla and Robert: No interruptions, no raised voices, and no personal insults.

The therapist asked the clients to give the history of their relationship. He realized that they would each have different perspectives but that listening should be valuable because it might contain keys as to why they cannot communicate without conflict. "I would like you to start with the time you met and go to the time you broke up. Who would like to go first?" After the history, prior to end of the session, the therapist administered the same instruments used for intact families: first the Dyadic Adjustment Scale to reflect how they each felt prior to their separation and divorce, followed by the FAS, the TMI for cultural styles, and the BOLS for cognitive styles preferences and assessment of degree of flex.

At this time the therapist also discussed expectations based on cultural stereotypes, proposing how these could have contributed to conflict and disappointment in the marriage. Before the end of the session, the therapist asked Robert if he would be willing to participate in the next session, which would also include the children. Robert agreed.

The second session, in summary, included the following:

- Outlining the rules for the sessions.
- Learning the history of the relationship and the family from each parent's point of view.
- Completing the DAS and other assessment instruments.
- Providing feedback about the findings of the DAS and the histories.

Session 3.   This session included Camilla, Tracy, Robert, and Lavis. Once again, the therapist observed the seating pattern. As expected, Lavis and Camilla sat next to each other while Robert and Tracy sat together. The therapist continued to observe the interaction of family members.

The therapist identified goals for therapy—first a cognitive style goal (communication styles when discussing problems the children were having in school): Camilla was too global and Robert too detailed-oriented. The second goal addressed cultural styles—Robert's suspicions that Camilla's extended family was turning the girls against him, and Camilla's belief that Robert was too self-centered and spent money on himself that he should be giving to the children. The therapist assigned the scriptwriting pairs: Camilla and Tracy, Robert and Lavis. The scriptwriting, role-playing, feedback, and discussion were conducted as with the intact family.

The third session, in summary, included the following:

- Observing communication patterns, as suggested by seating, verbal and non-verbal behaviors, and alliances based on match and mismatch.
- Identifying the most important cultural and cognitive styles goals.
- Scriptwriting.
- Role-playing.
- Leading feedback and discussion.
- Making changes in scripts and role-playing again, if necessary.
- Assigning homework.

Sessions 4 and 5.   Scriptwriting and role-playing for additional cultural and cognitive styles goals continued in Sessions 4 and 5 also. By the conclusion of Session 5, the family members were familiar with the procedure and with the cultural and cognitive flex model. They selected one additional goal and worked on it.

The fourth and fifth sessions, in summary, included the following:

- Assessing outcome of the homework assignments.
- Using the same procedures used during previous sessions for addressing a goal selected by the family members.

Session 6.   The clients were sufficiently familiar with the procedure. They no longer needed to consult with the therapist. The therapist merely directed discussion following the role-plays. Toward the end of the session, the therapist assessed progress by readministering the various instruments. Camilla, Tracy, and Lavis requested two more sessions. Robert agreed that these sessions should be done without him, although he was willing to return to the family sessions should it become necessary in the future.

The sixth session, in summary, included the following:

- Additional scriptwriting and role-playing, as needed, with the therapist assuming a nondirective role.
- Assessing progress.
- Scheduling additional sessions for resident family members, if necessary.
- Following up six weeks after termination.
- Working on problems related to homework: spending time with friends, housekeeping assignments, and dealing with the girls' feelings that Camilla does not give them enough quality time at home.

Termination at End of Session 9.   Six weeks later the therapist conducted a follow-up session with all the family members present. The clients reported that they were well satisfied with the progress that had been made. Robert and Camilla were able to communicate without conflict. Tracy and Lavis were getting along well, and they had established closer relationships with Camilla and Robert, respectively. At the close of this session, the therapist agreed to check the family's ongoing progress by phoning Camilla and Robert periodically.

Figure 12.2 is a graphic summary of multicultural therapy for single-parent families.

Nonparticipation by Nonresident Parent

In some situations nonresident parents may be unable or unwilling to attend the sessions. In other cases the resident parent may object to the inclusion of the nonresident parent. In those instances, the initial session is conducted the same as for single-parent families and held with the resident

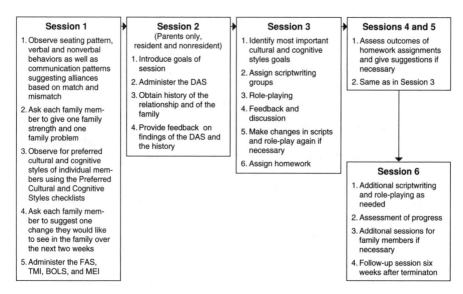

FIGURE 12.2   Multicultural therapy with single-parent families

parent and the children. The session's goals are the same but it is critically important for the therapist to determine the impact of cultural and cognitive styles differences, expectations based on stereotypes, and continuing conflict between the parents on the dynamics of the single-parent family. Also critical here is determination of potential alliances between children and the nonresident parent and his or her extended family members. This is particularly difficult in situations where the resident parent will not allow the therapist to contact the nonresident parent or in those situations where the nonresident parent is unavailable or unwilling to participate.

The sessions mirror those with the single-parent family with a participating nonresident parent. However, during the second session, the therapist meets with the resident parent only. In those cases where the resident parent refuses to allow the nonresident parent to participate and when alliances with the nonresident parent are contributing to significant family conflict, the therapist should attempt to explain the potential implications of this decision on the likely success of the family therapy sessions. During this session, the therapist learns the parent's perspectives on the history of the relationship and, if appropriate, of the marriage. If the resident parent has not allowed the other parent to participate in the history-taking, then the therapist has the difficult task of attempting to obtain a balanced historical picture from what is said by the children during family sessions.

Procedures and strategies of the remaining sessions are the same as for Camilla's family but, if the family agrees, the therapist might play the role of the nonresident parent in the role-playing situations.

SUMMARY

Family therapy models and strategies developed for use with culturally different families have focused on matching values, worldviews, family structures, and roles, as well as addressing special needs and personality variables such as biculturalism/multiculturalism. The multicultural model of family therapy is an extension of the model used for doing therapy with couples. The focus is on cultural and cognitive styles match and mismatch and how these are related to family alliances and misunderstandings that contribute to conflict. In addition, the model also encourages identification of false expectations of parents based on cultural stereotypes.

Scriptwriting, role-playing, and homework are the important therapeutic strategies employed, along with preferred cultural and cognitive styles assessment instruments. The multicultural model of therapy has also been used to address the special needs and dynamics of single-parent families.

13

THE MULTICULTURAL MODEL AND MANAGED CARE

In recent years managed care has transformed the mental health field. In particular, intervention orientations and strategies used by mental health professionals have changed dramatically because of the requirements and guidelines of managed care. Mahoney (1995) defined managed care as a tightly controlled and regulated system in which clients are given access to limited forms of psychotherapy, only if the diagnosis warrants, only for a limited number of sessions, and with substantial demands on psychotherapists for paperwork and justifications. These stringent treatment requirements have led to research focusing on what the future of psychotherapy might be.

Norcross, Alford, and DeMichele (1992) surveyed psychotherapy experts to determine which intervention strategies and approaches are likely to be most commonly employed in the future. Respondents to the survey indicated that they believed several techniques would be most frequently used by therapists: self-change techniques, problem-solving techniques, audiovisual feedback, homework assignments, communication skills training, self-control procedures, imagery and fantasy techniques, behavioral contracting, computerized therapies, didactic (teaching/advising) techniques, supportive techniques, and bibliotherapy.

Another indirect product of the managed-care revolution in the mental health field is the focus on cultural sensitivity and cultural competence in intervention. In response to concerns expressed by members of minority groups that the growth of managed care might lead to a monolithic approach to health care, the state of California established cultural competency guidelines for Medi-Cal health plan contractors. Cultural competency, or the level of knowledge-based skills required to provide effective clinical care to patients from a particular racial or ethnic group, is distinguished from cultural sensitivity, which is psychological propensity to adjust practice styles to the needs of different groups.

The multicultural model of psychotherapy and counseling has much to offer when it comes to meeting the requirements of diagnosis and intervention imposed by managed care. The model also offers many of the strategies and approaches that psychotherapy experts have identified as those most likely to be used with clients in the future. In addition, the model provides concepts and strategies, such as cultural and cognitive styles matching and therapist self-evaluation approaches, for development of cultural competence.

This chapter highlights the contributions that the multicultural model can make to the general as well as the client-specific requirements of managed care in completing outpatient request and authorization forms as well as in formulating treatment plans. The chapter focuses on the case of Raul, who was introduced in Chapter 1 and followed in subsequent chapters.

GENERAL CONTRIBUTIONS OF COMPLETING REQUEST-FOR-TREATMENT AND AUTHORIZATION FORMS ON THE MULTICULTURAL MODEL

Assessment

A central concern in the assessment of multicultural clients living in diverse environments is acculturation level. As discussed in Chapter 3, the Traditionalism–Modernism Inventory (TMI) and the Family Attitude Scale (FAS) can be used to assess the acculturation level of clients along different dimensions: gender-role definition; family identity; sense of community; time orientation; age status; deference to authority; spirituality and religion; and attitudes toward abortion, capital punishment, and aid to immigrants (Ramirez, 1998). Clients can be *bicultural* (balanced in traditional and modern orientations) while others have preferred traditional or modern orientations to life.

The Contemporary Multicultural Identity items of the Multicultural Experience Inventory (MEI, see Appendix A) also reflect degree of acculturation as indicated by friendship patterns and extent of participation in the cultures of different ethnic/racial groups. For example, in the case of Harold, he was very traditional in the domain of gender equality when he first came to therapy. Raul, on the other hand, had developed a mixed-traditional and modern cultural style orientation in most areas of his life.

Diagnosis

The *Diagnostic and Statistical Manual of Mental Disorders* (DSM-IV; APA 1994) provides five categories to consider when assessing the client's cultural and social reference group: (1) cultural identity, (2) cultural explanation of the client's illness, (3) cultural factors related to psychosocial environments and level of functioning, (4) cultural elements of the relationship between the individual and the therapist, and (5) overall cultural assessment for diagnosis and care. In addition, DSM-IV provides the diagnostic category for an acculturation problem (v62.4), defined as a problem involving adjustment to a different culture. Also included in DSM-IV is identity problem (313.82), which is used when the focus is on uncertainty about multiple issues relating to identity such as friendship patterns, moral values, and group loyalties. Use of the cultural and cognitive styles match and mismatch analyses of the multicultural model as well as the responses given by the client to the FAS, the TMI, and the MEI, provide information for meeting appropriate diagnostic requirements.

Clinical Implications

Relevant History.   This information can be obtained by using the life history interview (socialization history, exposure to different cultures and psychosocial environments within the same culture, and similarities and differences between the values and cognitive styles of the client and therapist) and the Historical Development Pattern items of the MEI.

Client Strengths and/or Obstacles to Progress.   This information can be obtained from the life history interview and the subsequent match and mismatch analyses (see Chapter 4). The availability of allies (models) as sources for learning how to use nonpreferred styles or for further development of preferred styles. Information in this area is also related to the degree of familial, community, group, or cultural support or pressure to conform that the client is experiencing. Information concerning familial, cultural, and community support systems is also obtained through the life history interview. In Raul's case, for example, his participation in powwows and spiritual practices on the reservation, as well as consultation and discussions with his uncle and other tribal elders, served as excellent sources of familial, cultural, and community support. Raul's participation in the international art community, which was supportive of his efforts to resolve adjustment problems related to identity confusion by pursuing multicultural/multiracial art themes, was also important to him. Obstacles to Raul's progress included his abuse of marijuana, his poor decision making in intimate relationships, and his tendency to isolate himself from family and friends when he encountered problems in his relationships.

Treatment Plan

Problem.   Adjustment of multicultural clients can be identified by doing cultural and cognitive styles mismatch analyses following the life history interview. In the case of Imelda, it was mismatch to the values of her grandparents and to the cognitive styles of her father as well as those of some of her teachers and coaches that contributed to depressive symptoms and a poor self-image.

Behavioral Goals.   The cultural and cognitive styles flex goals are generated by both client and therapist following the presentation of the flex model and feedback on the findings of the assessment instruments done during the second session. Flex goals are also generated from the observations made by the therapist using the Preferred Cultural and Cognitive Styles Observation Checklists during the initial session. The goals of increased cultural and cognitive flex are achieved through increased self-efficacy and coping accomplished through diversity challenges, scriptwriting, role-playing, and homework.

Time Line.   The multicultural model helps clients to achieve their treatment goals in four or five sessions, with the complete treatment plan for most clients being fifteen to seventeen sessions. Periodic assessment of progress using the assessment instruments provided by the multicultural model and evaluation of the degree of success achieved through homework assignments is recommended (see Chapter 9).

Raul's Treatment Plan: Specific Contributions of the Multicultural Model.
Exhibit 13.1 is representative of the Request-for-Treatment and Authorization Form the therapist completed for Raul's presenting problems.

EXHIBIT 13.1   Example of a Request-for-Treatment and Authorization Form

DSM-IV Multi-Axial Diagnosis
AXIS I: (Primary) 300.4 Dysthymic Disorder, Early Onset.
AXIS I: (Substance-related) 305.20 Cannabis abuse.
AXIS I: (Additional) 309.81 Posttraumatic stress disorder.
AXIS II: 301.9 Personality disorder not otherwise specified (with depressive and avoidant features).
AXIS III: None.
AXIS IV: Problems with primary support, occupation, social environment.
AXIS V: GAF—Current 60 (Moderate symptoms at start of treatment).
　　　　　Highest: Past Year—GAF 80 (If symptoms are present, they are transient and expectable reactions to psychosocial stressors).
Clinical Information—Relevant History
Medical–None.
Family–Alienated from most family members, particularly parents. Has a moderately good relationship with his sister, but his relationships with his brothers are strained and distant.
Vocational–During the past four months the client has been unable to have consistent work attendance at his permanent job and has been unable to work consistently on his artwork (part-time job).

Continued

EXHIBIT 13.1   *Continued*

Social–Has isolated himself from friends and is spending most of his time alone at his home when he is not at his place of employment. His only consistent contact is with his sister and members of her family.

Legal–None.

Marital–Single, never married.

Past Treatment–The client was in individual therapy about four years ago. From information provided by the client and his former therapist, it was determined that an eclectic psychodynamic approach had been used. The client terminated therapy with the approval of his therapist after six months.

Outcome–The client reports that most of his depressive symptoms have gone into remission. However, he also indicates he has remained confused regarding his identity and that his relationships with his parents and brothers have not improved. Furthermore, he states that he has continued to experience failure in his intimate relationships.

Clinical Synopsis

Current Symptoms–Insomnia, low energy, low self-esteem, poor concentration, feelings of hopelessness, recurrent and intrusive distressing recollections of traumatic events (experiences in Vietnam), and recurrent substance use resulting in failure to meet major obligations at work.

Client Strengths and Obstacles to Progress

Client Strengths–The client's skills are highly valued at the print shop where he works. He receives good emotional support from his sister, her husband, and their children. His artwork has given him a good outlet for frustrations in the past and has also provided him with a good source of self-esteem and self-efficacy because he has been able to sell some of his work and because his work has been praised by accomplished artists.

Obstacles to Progress–The client's parents and his brothers are very critical of him, contributing to self-criticism and guilt. He is abusing marijuana, contributing to feelings of depression and to increased isolation from others. Cannabis abuse is also related to decreased church attendance and attendance at prayer groups as well as to decreased participation in Native American spiritual practices, which had served as good sources of support for him in the past. He has also discontinued discussions with elders on the reservation. In the past these people have contributed to good self-esteem and development of a stable identity. His involvement in reservation activities, such as powwows, chants, and sweat lodge meetings, have also given him ideas for his artwork in the past. The client has stopped regular visits to his uncle, who is a medicine man living on the reservation, because of shame related to substance abuse.

Clinical Coordination

With the permission of the client, the therapist agreed to coordinate with the client's uncle, a medicine man. In the past the client's uncle has helped him to overcome some of the symptoms of posttraumatic stress disorder and acculturation problems. The client agrees to contact his uncle; the therapist will be in touch with the uncle upon the client's approval.

Medications

At the time of therapy, the client was not taking medication. Should the depressive symptoms become more serious, particularly if the client experiences longer work absences or begins to suffer from suicidal ideas, the therapist will encourage him to consult with a psychiatrist. The therapist made a suicide contract with the client.

Substance Abuse

Substance Abused–Cannabis.

Date Last Used–A week prior to the client's initial session.

Frequency–The client reported that he smoked five marijuana cigarettes in a week.

Current Use–Client has not used in ten days.

Number of Years Used–Client used cannabis on a daily basis for two years when he was in the service; he used it for six months following discharge from the armed services while he was unemployed.

OD or Withdrawal Symptoms–Client has never overdosed and/or experienced withdrawal symptoms.

Family History of Substance Abuse–Client's father was dependent on alcohol; one of his brothers abused methamphetamines in the past while another abused cocaine and marijuana. No one in his family besides his father appeared to meet the criteria for dependence.

Previous Treatment for Substance Abuse–The client had been active in Narcotics Anonymous (NA) several years ago. He had a sponsor with whom he had not been in contact for two years. His participation in NA led to a successful outcome, and the client has been in sustained full remission for six years.

Mental Status and Risk Assessment

Mental Status–All within normal limits.

Risk–No suicidal, homicidal or domestic violence risk. The client does not have access to firearms.

Treatment Plan

Problem–Abuse of marijuana.

Goal(s)–Discontinue marijuana use and renew attendance at NA meetings as well as regular contact with sponsor, with uncle, and with other tribal elders. Renewed participation in powwows and spiritual discussions with uncle and other elders of his tribe.

Interventions–Scriptwriting and role-playing for renewing contact with uncle and NA sponsor. Identification of allies that can help to reintegrate the client into the international artistic community he was involved with in the past. Teach stress-reduction techniques to substitute for marijuana use.

Problem–Self-blame and low self-esteem related to end of intimate relationship.

Goal(s)–Arrive at realistic assessment as to causes of failure of relationship, renew use of cultural and spiritual support systems, and insight into needs in intimate relationships. Develop coping techniques for meeting potential intimacy partners and for making better choices in intimate relationships through scriptwriting, role-playing, and homework assignments for diversity challenges.

Interventions–Analysis of areas of cultural and cognitive styles mismatch to make a more realistic assessment of why relationship failed. Encourage church attendance and prayer as well as participation with uncle in treatment program to renew involvement in tribal community and spiritual life. Use of life history technique to arrive at insight concerning insecurities in intimate relationships (envy of other men) as well as needs that may be contributing to failure of his relationships.

Problem–Identity confusion.

Goal(s)–Establish a multicultural/multiracial identity.

Encourage renewed active participation in identification of models or allies who are multicultural and multiracial, including scriptwriting and role-playing to facilitate contacts, use of bibliotherapy (*The Autobiography of Malcom X*, *The Original Sin*, and *Ceremony*), and encourage use of multicultural and/or multiracial themes in his artwork.

**EXHIBIT 13.2 Second Phase of a Request-for-Treatment
and Authorization Form**

DSM-IV Multi-Axial Diagnosis
AXIS I: (Primary) 309.28 Adjustment Disorder with Mixed Anxiety and Depressed
Mood.
AXIS I: (Substance) 305.30 Cannabis Abuse, in Sustained Full Remission
305.10 Nicotine Abuse.
AXIS I: (Additional) features of 300.4 Dysthymic Disorder, early onset.
AXIS II: v71.09 No diagnosis.
AXIS III: None
AXIS IV: Primary support group–death of brother.
Other–grief
AXIS V: GAF 60 Highest past year GAF 70.
Clinical Information
Medical–None.
Family–Death of brother.
Vocational–Decreased attendance and productivity at work, again since death of
brother.
Clinical Synopsis–Increased use of tobacco (nicotine), low energy, self-blame.
Current Symptoms and Obstacles to Progress
Client's Strengths–Continued contacts with siblings, parents, uncle, and elders on
reservation and continues to date. Is also continuing to teach at international art
institute.
Obstacles to Progress–Has discontinued a regular schedule of exercise (jogging
and bike riding) which he was following.
Clinical Coordination–With uncle on reservation and with NA sponsor.
Treatment Plan
Problem–Self-blame for brother's death.
Goal(s)–Realistic assessment of causes of brother's illness and death with diminu-
tion of symptoms of anxiety and depression. Discontinue use of tobacco and resume exercise schedule. Resume regular attendance at his job and increase productivity in artwork.
Interventions–Reconstruct life history on brother to understand possible causes of
illness and death, cultural and cognitive styles mismatch analysis, become mentor for brother's children, participate in tribal mourning ritual for brother.

Termination of Treatment – Following implementation of the fifteen-
session therapy plan outlined above here, Raul improved and returned to
familial, community, and cultural support systems. He discontinued use of
marijuana and became active in the powwows and spiritual activities of his
tribe. He met intimacy partners on the reservation and in a singles group he
joined through the Christian church he attends and began dating again. He
continued to be active in the international art community and eventually
began to teach at an international art institute. Raul made amends to his
brothers and his relationships with them improved dramatically. His relationships with his parents also improved.

Raul Returns for Therapy Two Years Later. Following the death of one of his brothers, Raul began to experience symptoms of anxiety and depression once again. The symptoms were more severe than those of bereavement. He remained in recovery from the abuse of marijuana and posttraumatic stress disorder symptoms did not recur. Guilt over his brother's death concerned the feeling that his harsh treatment of his brother during childhood had led to his brother's increased risk for cancer (his brother had died of lung cancer). The information provided on Raul's Request-for-Treatment and Authorization Form for the second phase of treatment is shown in Exhibit 13.2.

Termination of second phase of treatment – After five sessions, Raul improved and returned to family, community, and cultural support systems.

SUMMARY

The requirements imposed by managed care on the mental health field have produced major changes in philosophies and strategies used for interventions with clients. In addition, cultural sensitivity and cultural competence have become central issues in psychotherapy and counseling. The multicultural model of psychotherapy and counseling has much to offer in meeting the requirements of managed care, both with respect to general and client-specific information requested in treatment request and authorization forms. The model also offers cultural and cognitive match and mismatch strategies allowing practitioners to meet the requirements of cultural competence and sensitivity.

14

CONCLUSIONS

Everyone has the potential to have a multicultural orientation to life. However, sociocultural environments can impose barriers that make it difficult if not impossible to achieve the cognitive and cultural flexibility essential to such an orientation.

The barriers to multicultural development fall into three major categories: pressures to conform, prejudice, and oppression. In general, these barriers are reflected in the dynamics of families, of institutions, and of societies. They reflect the messages, whether direct or indirect, passed on to individuals about the desirability of diversity versus ethnocentrism. Through these, the individual learns to view diversity as either positive or negative.

Different individuals are subjected to different barriers to multicultural development and to varying degrees of permeability of these barriers. The cases of Imelda and Harold best exemplify pressures to conform as barriers to multicultural development. Both were subjected to strong pressures to adopt cultural and cognitive styles that were different from those they preferred. They were encouraged by parents or parental figures to reject their unique selves and to conform to an imposed ideal.

The prevalence of certain mythical ideals imposed by all societies, institutions, and families on their members (Brink, 1984) pressures most individuals to conform. These ideals vary from society to society; the following are examples of mainstream American mythical ideals:

- Blonde, blue-eyed, white-skinned people are smarter than those who have darker complexions.
- Men are better at business, science, and math than are women.
- Engineers, physicians, and lawyers are smarter than those who work in the social sciences or the arts.
- Tall and thin is better than short and stocky.

Everyone has had some type of mythical ideal imposed on them. The result has been feelings of inferiority, because it is impossible to fit these ideals perfectly. Beyond limiting the individual, these mythical ideals prevent members of society from recognizing the value of the diversity around them and from benefiting from it.

Prejudice was the most important barrier in the experiences of Tara and Raul. Because Tara is a woman and an African American and because Raul is multiracial and suffers from a learning disability, they were made to feel unwanted and were given the message that they did not belong. Rose experienced prejudice because of her impaired vision.

Those who hold the power in society and in institutions deny equality of status to people who are different from themselves through prejudicial practices. The message is: "You can only achieve the 'goodies' of society if you are like us. You can't be like us if your phenotype, gender, values, or sexual orientation are not the same as ours."

Prejudice is destructive to the development of a positive politics of diversity (Castaneda, 1984), because it keeps members of different groups separated from each other and because it promotes the idea that certain groups and cultures are superior to others.

Oppression is more destructive than the other two barriers. Not only are people pressured to be what they are not and kept from fully participating in society, but they are also exploited for being who they are as individuals (A. Ramirez, 1972).

In Harold's case the barrier was his father's refusal to accept his interest in the arts and his preferred personality style. His father's attempt to force him to be like his older brother was oppressive to Harold. For Imelda, the barrier was her school peers who would cheer her exploits on the basketball court but refuse to include her in their circle of friends, because they felt she did not meet their definition of femininity.

A society that hopes to understand, to nurture, and to value its diversity has to be able to identify and eliminate the barriers preventing multicultural development in its institutions and in its members. How can social scientists and educators encourage the development of positive politics of diversity in families, institutions, and societies? Three approaches may move toward that direction.

First is the development of social science paradigms and research and intervention techniques that are truly based on individual and cultural differences. For example, Ramirez (1998) proposed a theory, along with a set of research strategies and intervention approaches, which is based on the principles of multiculturalism.

In addition, the rise of a positive politics of diversity is reflected in the development of community psychology intervention programs in developing countries. These programs focus on the empowerment of heretofore disenfranchised peoples. During the 1970s and 1980s, the writings, as well as the research and development work, of psychologists in Latin America and the Caribbean showed a trend toward empowerment programs.

For example, Almeida and Sanchez (1985) describe how an interdisciplinary team of social scientists worked in three rural communities in the state of Puebla in Mexico. The team's objective was to provide assistance in community development without producing radical changes in the native culture of the region. Part of the program involved the development of a marketing program whereby local artisans and farmers could sell their products without losing profits to middlemen. Other members of the team worked with school personnel to upgrade curriculum and instruction techniques. The programs actively encouraged parental participation in the education of their children.

Venezuelan psychologist José Miguel Salazar (1981) advocated the development of a social psychology reflecting the historical and political realities of the cultures of Latin America. Another Venezuelan psychologist, Maritza Montero (1979), called for the development of a community psychology with its primary goal of assisting people in the development of their communities.

An overview of social psychology in Latin America (Marin, 1975) indicated that developments there at that time represented a good amalgamation of scientific objectivity with a definite commitment to the solution of social problems. He concluded that applied social psychology was the most important area of concentration in Latin American psychology.

The third approach is the development of multicultural educational programs. These programs address the goal of teaching children and adolescents to recognize, to respect, and to learn from individual and cultural differences in order to prevent the development of negative stereotypes and vulnerability to coercion by the mythical ideals of society.

Ramirez and Castaneda (1974) and Cox, Macaulay, and Ramirez (1982) described a cognitive flex multicultural program that evolved from the perspective of Latinos, based on the philosophy of cultural democracy. Hale-Benson (1986) described a multicultural educational program specifically relevant to African Americans. Darder (1991) advocated combining cultural democracy with the ideas of Paulo Freire (1970) and Henry Giroux (1981) to develop a critical bicultural framework for bicultural education.

The challenge for social scientists and educators in encouraging the evolution of a positive politics of diversity is great. It will be difficult to eradicate notions of superiority and inferiority in the perception of individuals, groups, cultures, and nations. Equally challenging is overcoming negative stereotypes and suspicions peoples hold regarding others. However, the rewards of a positive politics of diversity are high. It is multicultural orientations to life that can lead to the fullest development of the personality, and to peace and cooperation in the world.

For the people whose lives we have followed in this book, a multicultural perspective and a flexible orientation toward life were the keys to self-acceptance, to harmony in interpersonal relationships, to greater awareness of how the environment was affecting their lives, and to the further development of their potential. A multicultural orientation to life gave Imelda, Harold, Raul, Tara, Alex, Rose, and Tony the empowerment they needed to increase control over their own destinies. It also furnished the tools they needed to help the people and societal institutions in their environments to achieve greater multicultural awareness. For Wanda and Javier, as well as for members of the Rosales family, and for Camila, Robert, Tracy, and Lavis, multicultural perspectives reduced conflict and contributed to increased awareness and understanding of individual and cultural differences.

Imelda became more assertive and outgoing. Because of this she was able to develop a circle of friends and mentors who served as a support system to her and who were models and sources of increased knowledge as she strove to develop flexibility in her values and cognitive styles. As she began to work closely with the student council at her school, her efforts in that organization gave students a greater voice in making changes in the curriculum and teaching approaches, as well as in counseling services offered to female athletes. Her relationships with her parents and grandparents improved as she learned to recognize and match their values and behaviors more effectively. They, in turn, became more supportive of her interests and more responsive to her requests for treatment equal to that given to her half sister.

Harold's relationship with his family improved dramatically. He and his wife developed a satisfying and productive partnership in the art gallery they had opened. The family's mutual interests in photography and travel brought them together as they had never been before. After Harold recognized that he had been relating to his own children in much the same way as his father had related to him, he became more involved in their interests and activities while at the same time giving them the opportunity to develop their own styles.

Harold was also successful in convincing his business partners of the need to develop a new graphic-art software product line. This revitalized his interest in the firm. He felt more enthusiastic about playing the role of charismatic leader and about developing a sense of community in the firm. For the first time since he was a student in middle school, Harold returned to the piano. This renewed interest in music helped him to reestablish his relationship with his mother. His efforts at initiating the Silicon Valley support groups for technical professionals who were experiencing symptoms of burnout was also a source of great satisfaction for him.

Harold was happy to have been able to make peace with his father and to establish a meaningful relationship with him. His ability to match his father's style eventually led his father to empathize with him and to apologize for trying to transform him into the image of his older brother.

Raul was able to establish healthier intimate relationships. In these relationships he focused more on match and mismatch in cultural and cognitive styles and less on physical appearance. He made amends to his siblings and became more accepting of his parents, resenting them less for the past. He renewed his visits to his uncle who lived on the reservation and increased his participation in the reservation's tribal and spiritual life.

Tara, after scriptwriting and role-playing with the therapist, confronted her parents and brothers regarding their pressures for her to reunite with her former boyfriend and to marry. Her family eventually came to respect her decision to remain a single parent for the time being. She developed a good adjustment in her new job and continued participating in sports with her coworkers. Eventually she gained financial independence from her parents. She felt that, because of this independence, her family came to accept her as an adult who could make her own decisions and be a responsible parent to Tamisha.

Alex enlisted the help of his favorite aunt and uncle, and, after scriptwriting and role-playing exercises, they were able to tell his parents about Alex's sexual orientation and about his new academic goal. He was accepted for a master's program in social work at a university in another state and completed the program successfully. When Alex last contacted the therapist, he was enrolled in a Ph.D. program and had been awarded a four-year fellowship.

After careful consideration and after repeatedly being turned down in requests to her spouse that they participate in either family or couples counseling, Rose decided to file for divorce. She and her children moved to a city three hundred miles from her hometown. She found a part-time job and enrolled in a bilingual special education college program, planning to earn a bachelor's degree and teaching credentials so that she could teach blind and visually impaired children.

Tony learned to be more assertive and tenacious in his dealings with public service agencies and institutions. He became less embarrassed and more self-disclosing about his memory impairments; whenever he would encounter a longtime acquaintance in the community, he would say that he was sorry but, although he recognized the person's face, his memory loss kept him from remembering names and past events. His communication with his children improved, and he became less authoritative in his relationship with them. When Tony was last in contact with the therapist, he reported a good relationship with a woman with whom he was living.

These individuals and families were able to develop the flexibility of personality and worldview they needed to function effectively in a diverse society. They were able to effect changes in their environments and to assist others who, like themselves, felt mismatched to situations and to people around them.

These clients had a profound effect on me as the therapist: Through them I learned that the definition of pluralism and culture I had been using when I first began my work in multicultural therapy was too limiting and static. I learned that the "differentness" experience is not limited to members of cultural, ethnic, and gender minority groups. Most important, I learned to look beyond the superficial, the external characteristics of differentness, to look for the internal expressions and signs of uniqueness. As a therapist, I learned to examine my value system and my preferred cognitive style and to understand how these affect the clients with whom I work.

As a researcher, I rediscovered the value of intensive study of the individual case. I came to understand that the life history is the path to arriving at understandings about the meaning of life in individuals and families.

The experiences with my clients reminded me of the words of my colleague and mentor, Al Castaneda: "You can learn something from everyone because every person has, through their life experiences, discovered some truths about the meaning of life." These words are an effective statement of the principal mission of multicultural counseling and psychotherapy.

It is my fervent hope that through this book readers will arrive at a greater appreciation of their uniqueness as well as the uniqueness of others. I hope they will appreciate the diversity in themselves and in society as an opportunity for greater self-knowledge and growth.

Appendix A

MEI Inventory – Revised

The Multicultural/Multiracial Experience Inventory (MEI) was developed to assess an individual's type of historical development pattern and contemporary multicultural identity. Originally designed for people of color, it has been modified so that it can be used to inventory the multicultural/multiracial experiences of whites. Both the original and the modified instruments share a common survey of demographic information (Part I). The response choices and scoring procedures and the two instruments (for people of color and for whites) are presented here.

RELIABILITY

The scale, revised in 1996, has two versions—one for people of color and one for whites. The instruments were administered to 115 Mexican American, white, Asian American (Vietnamese and Korean), and African American male and female university students. Split-half reliability for the total group for Type A items was $r = .87$. The content of Type B items makes it impossible to obtain split-half reliability.

VALIDITY

The total Type A and Type B scores of Mexican American university students in Texas and California were correlated with effective leadership behaviors in ethnically diverse groups under conditions of conflict (mediation, ensuring that all members of the group were able to express their opinions, seek compromise, and so on). Correlation coefficients for Type A items ranged from .65 to .71 and for Type B items from .69 to .73.

SCORING

Part II is composed of two types of items. For people of color, Type A items are scored so that a response of "almost entirely my ethnic group" or "almost entirely whites" (alternatives 1 and 5, respectively) receive 1 point; responses of either "mostly my ethnic group with a few people of color from other groups" or "mostly whites with a few people of color" (alternatives 2 and 4) receive 2 points; responses of "mixed" (whites, my ethnic group, and people of color about equally—alternative 3) receive 3 points. Hence, higher scores are indicative of a greater degree of multiculturalism. Some Type A items are historical (reflect Historical Development Pattern, HDP) and others assess contemporary functioning and identity (reflect Contemporary Multicultural Identity, CMI).

All type B items are CMI. Type B items are answered using a Likert-type format ranging from "Extensively" to "Never." Responses of "Extensively" and "Frequently" are assigned 2 points. All other responses are assigned 1 point. Items 1–8 are HDP items and items 9–26 are CMI items. A total Multicultural Score (MC) is obtained by summing the HDP and CMI total scores.

HDP score — 33 maximum
CMI score — 45 maximum
Total MC — 87 maximum

For whites, Type A items are scored so that a response of "almost entirely my ethnic group" or "almost entirely people of color" (alternatives 1 and 5, respectively) receives 1 point; responses of either "mostly my ethnic group with a few people of color" or "mostly people of color with a few people of my ethnic group" (alternatives 2 and 4) receives 2 points; responses of "mixed" (my ethnic group and people of color about equally) receive 3 points. Hence, higher scores are indicative of a greater degree of multiculturalism.

CMI and Total MC scores are different for whites because there are fewer Type B items.

HDP score — 33 maximum
CMI score — 45 maximum
Total MC — 78 maximum

MEI PART I

1. Name _____

2. Address _____
   City, State, Zip _____

3. Gender ____

4. Age _____ Date of Birth ____/____/____

5. Place of Birth (city/state/country) _____

6. Father's Place of Birth (city/state/country) _____

7. Mother's Place of Birth (city/state/country) _____

8. Ethnic background of the following persons (if applicable):

	Yourself	Father	Mother	Step-father	Step-mother
Mexican American/Latino					
African American					
White/Anglo					
Asian American					
Native American					
Multiracial (specify)					

9. In what country were each of the following family members born?

	United States	Other/Specify
You		
Your father		
Your father's father		
Your father's mother		
Your mother		
Your mother's father		
Your mother's mother		

10. What is your religious background?_____

11. How active are you in your religion?

    ____ Very ____ Moderately ____ Somewhat ____ Minimally

    ____ Not active

12. How many years have you lived in the United States? _____

13. Have you lived in a country other than the United States? _____

    ____ Yes. Which country(ies)? _____

              For how many years? _____

    ____ No

14. Have you lived in a state other than the one in which you attend school?

    ____ Yes. Which state(s)? _____

              For how many years? _____

    ____ No

15. Where did you spend the first 15 years of your life (list all the places)?

    _____

    _____

16. Where do you consider "home" (community/state/country)?

    _____

    Would you describe this community as

    ____ rural ____ semi-rural ____ semi-urban ____ urban

17. What language(s) does (did) your father speak? _____

18. What language(s) does (did) your mother speak? _____

19. What language(s) do (did) your parents speak at home? _____

20. What language(s) do you speak? _____

21. What is your marital status? _____

22. If you have had a committed relationship, what is (was) the ethnic background of your partner? _____

MEI PART II

For People of Color

HDP score — 33 maximum
CMI score — 54 maximum
Total MC — 87 maximum

Type A Items: Next to each item, circle the number of the response that best describes your past and present behavior.

1 = almost entirely my ethnic group

2 = mostly my ethnic group with a few people of color from other groups

3 = mixed (my ethnic group, whites, and other minorities, about equally)

4 = mostly whites with a few people of color

5 = almost entirely whites

1 2 3 4 5   1. The ethnic composition of the neighborhoods in which I lived

1 2 3 4 5   (a) before I started attending school

1 2 3 4 5   (b) while I attended elementary school

1 2 3 4 5   (c) while I attended middle school

1 2 3 4 5   (d) while I attended high school

1 2 3 4 5   2. My childhood friends who visited my home and related well to my parents were of . . .

1 2 3 4 5   3. The teachers and counselors with whom I have had the closest relationships have been of . . .

1 2 3 4 5   4. The people who have most influenced me in my education have been of . . .

1 2 3 4 5   5. In high school, my close friends were of . . .

1 2 3 4 5   6. The ethnic backgrounds of the people I have dated have been of . . .

1 2 3 4 5   7. In the job(s) I have had, my close friends have been of . . .

1 2 3 4 5   8. The people with whom I have established close, meaningful relationships have been of . . .

1 2 3 4 5   9. At present, my close friends are of . . .

1 2 3 4 5   10. My close friends at work were (are) of . . .

1 2 3 4 5   11. I enjoy going to gatherings at which the people are of . . .

1 2 3 4 5   12. When I study or work on a project with others, I am usually with persons of . . .

1 2 3 4 5   13. When I am involved in group discussions where I am expected to participate, I prefer a group of people of . . .

1 2 3 4 5   14. I am active in organizations or social groups in which the majority of the members are of . . .

1 2 3 4 5   15. When I am with my friends, I usually attend functions where the people are of . . .

1 2 3 4 5   16. When I discuss personal problems or issues, I discuss them with people of . . .

1 2 3 4 5   17. I most often spend time with people who are of . . .

Type B Items: Next to each item below, circle the number that bests describes you.

  1 = Extensively
  2 = Frequently
  3 = Occasionally
  4 = Seldom
  5 = Never

1 2 3 4 5   18. I attend functions which are predominantly white in nature.

1 2 3 4 5   19. I attend functions which are predominantly of minority groups other than my own.

1 2 3 4 5   20. I attend functions which are predominantly of my own ethnic group in nature.

1 2 3 4 5   21. I visit the homes of whites.

1 2 3 4 5   22. I invite whites to my home.

1 2 3 4 5   23. I visit the homes of persons of my ethnic group (other than relatives).

1 2 3 4 5   24. I invite persons of my ethnic group (other than relatives) to my home.

1 2 3 4 5   25. I visit the homes of minorities other than of my own ethnic group.

1 2 3 4 5   26. I invite persons of minorities other than those of my own ethnic group to my home.

HDP   _____

CMI   _____

Total MC _____

MEI PART II

Modified for Whites

HDP score — 33 maximum
CMI score — 45 maximum
Total MC — 78 maximum

Type A Items: Next to each item, circle the number of the response that best describes your past and present behavior.

1 = almost entirely my ethnic group

2 = mostly my ethnic group with a few people of color

3 = mixed (my ethnic group and people of color about equally)

4 = mostly people of color with a few people of my ethnic group

5 = almost entirely people of color

1 2 3 4 5   1. The ethnic composition of the neighborhoods in which I lived

1 2 3 4 5   (a) before I started attending school

1 2 3 4 5   (b) while I attended elementary school

1 2 3 4 5   (c) while I attended middle school

1 2 3 4 5   (d) while I attended high school

1 2 3 4 5   2. My childhood friends who visited my home and related well to my parents were of . . .

1 2 3 4 5   3. The teachers and counselors with whom I have had the closest relationships have been of . . .

1 2 3 4 5   4. The people who have most influenced me in my education have been of . . .

1 2 3 4 5   5. In high school, my close friends were of . . .

1 2 3 4 5   6. The ethnic backgrounds of the people I have dated have been of . . .

1 2 3 4 5   7. In the job(s) I have had, my close friends have been of . . .

1 2 3 4 5   8. The people with whom I have established close, meaningful relationships have been of . . .

1 2 3 4 5   9. At present, my close friends are of . . .

1 2 3 4 5   10. My close friends at work were (are) of . . .

1 2 3 4 5   11. I enjoy going to gatherings at which the people are of . . .

1 2 3 4 5   12. When I study or work on a project with others, I am usually with persons of . . .

1 2 3 4 5   13. When I am involved in group discussions where I am expected to participate, I prefer a group of people of . . .

1 2 3 4 5   14. I am active in organizations or social groups in which the majority of the members are of . . .

1 2 3 4 5   15. When I am with my friends, I usually attend functions where the people are of . . .

1 2 3 4 5   16. When I discuss personal problems or issues, I discuss them with people of . . .

1 2 3 4 5   17. I most often spend time with people who are of . . .

Type B Items: Next to each item below, circle the number that bests describes you.

   1 = Extensively

   2 = Frequently

   3 = Occasionally

   4 = Seldom

   5 = Never

1 2 3 4 5   18. I attend functions which are predominantly of my ethnic group in nature.

1 2 3 4 5   19. I attend functions which are predominantly of minority groups in nature.

1 2 3 4 5   20. I visit the homes of my ethnic group (other than relatives).

1 2 3 4 5   21. I visit the homes of people of color.

1 2 3 4 5   22. I invite persons of my ethnic group (other than relatives) to my home.

1 2 3 4 5   23. I invite people of color to my home.

HDP   _____

CMI   _____

Total MC _____

Appendix B

Traditionalism–Modernism Inventory – Revised

INSTRUCTIONS FOR SCORING

The traditional (T) items of the Traditionalism–Modernism Inventory (TMI) are the following: 3, 4, 5, 8, 9, 11, 12, 13, 19, 20, 21, 22, 23, 28, 30, 31, 34, 36, 37, 39, 42, 44, 45, 47, 49, and 51. The remainder are modern (M) items. Add the scores for T items and the scores for M items. Then, subtract M from T to obtain the total score. A positive score indicates a traditional orientation, a negative score indicates a modern orientation, and a score of zero indicates a perfect traditional–modern balance.

Reliability and validity data for this revised instrument were not available at the time of publication.

Source: Developed by M. Ramirez, S. Doell, and N. Rodriguez.

TRADTIONALISM–MODERNISM INVENTORY

After each statement, indicate whether you: Strongly Agree (SA), Agree (A), Disagree (D), or Strongly Disagree (SD). Please circle your choice.

1. Husbands and wives should share equally in housework.

   SA   A   D   SD

2. All institutions should follow a democratic decision-making process.

   SA   A   D   SD

3. I prefer to live in a small town or a friendly neighborhood where everyone knows each other.

   SA   A   D   SD

4. Women with children at home should not have a full-time career or job outside of the home.

   SA   A   D   SD

5. Students should not question the teachings of their teachers or professors.

   SA   A   D   SD

6. I prefer to live in a large city.

   SA   A   D   SD

7. Husbands and wives should share equally in child-rearing and child care.

   SA   A   D   SD

8. In industry or government, when two persons are equally qualified, the older person should get the job.

   SA   A   D   SD

9. It's hard to meet and get to know people in cities.

   SA   A   D   SD

10. Women should assume their rightful place in business and in the professions along with men.

    SA   A   D   SD

11. Laws should be obeyed without question.

    SA   A   D   SD

12. You should know your family history so you can pass it on to your children.

    SA   A   D   SD

13. In general, the father should have greater authority than the mother in bringing up children.

    SA   A   D   SD

14. Students should have decision-making power in schools and universities.

    SA   A   D   SD

15. It does not matter to me if my job requires me to move far away from the place where I have my roots.

    SA   A   D   SD

16. Husbands and wives should participate equally in making important family decisions.

    SA   A   D   SD

17. With institutions, the amount of power a person has should not be determined by either age or gender.

    SA   A   D   SD

18. I prefer the excitement of a large city to the relaxed living in a small town.

    SA   A   D   SD

19. Children should always be respectful of their parents and older relatives.

    SA   A   D   SD

20. Traditional observances, such as church services or graduation ceremonies, add meaning to life.

    SA   A   D   SD

21. Adult children should visit their parents regularly.

    SA   A   D   SD

22. We should not let concerns about time interfere with our friendships and inter-actions with others.

    SA   A   D   SD

23. Children should be taught to be loyal to their families.

    SA   A   D   SD

24. Creationism, the Biblical version of the universe, should not be taught in schools.

    SA   A   D   SD

25. Children should be encouraged to be independent of their families at an early age.

    SA   A   D   SD

26. If you are not careful, people can cause you to waste your time and you will never get anything accomplished.

    SA   A   D   SD

27. Most traditional ceremonies are outmoded and wasteful of time and money.

    SA   A   D   SD

28. There is no doubt that the universe was created by a supreme being.

    SA   A   D   SD

29. Children should be taught to always feel close to their families.

    SA   A   D   SD

30. We get into such a hurry sometimes that we fail to enjoy life.

    SA   A   D   SD

31. Everything a person does reflects on his or her family.

    SA   A   D   SD

32. Eventually, science will explain all the mysteries of life.

    SA   A   D   SD

33. A person should only be responsible to himself or herself.

    SA   A   D   SD

34. No matter how many advances we make through science, we will never be able to understand many important things in life.

    SA   A   D   SD

35. Most religions are primarily folklore and superstition.

    SA   A   D   SD

36. When making important decisions about my life, I always like to consult members of my family.

    SA   A   D   SD

37. Religion adds meaning to our mechanized and impersonal lives.

    SA   A   D   SD

38. If my family does not agree with one of my major life decisions, I go ahead and do what I think is right anyway.

    SA   A   D   SD

39. Tradition and ritual serve to remind us of the rich history of our institutions and our society.

    SA   A   D   SD

40. Traditions limit our freedom.

    SA   A   D   SD

41. A woman should have the right to decide whether or not to get an abortion.

    SA   A   D   SD

42. The right to life is more important than a woman's right to decide what she can do with her own body.

    SA   A   D   SD

43. Gays and lesbians should not be considered to be living in sin, but rather as having a right to their lifestyle.

    SA   A   D   SD

44. If the Bible says that homosexuality is wrong, then it should be considered sinful.

    SA   A   D   SD

45. Some criminals deserve to die.

    SA   A   D   SD

46. Criminals should be rehabilitated, not put to death.

    SA   A   D   SD

47. Local communities should run schools without having to put up with federal government mandates and regulations.

    SA   A   D   SD

48. The federal government should ensure that local schools meet national goals and regulations for all students.

    SA   A   D   SD

49. Mothers who have children out of wedlock should not receive welfare payments.

    SA   A   D   SD

50. Unwed mothers and their children should not be penalized by being denied welfare assistance.

    SA   A   D   SD

51. Children who are not U.S. citizens should not be allowed to attend our public schools.

    SA   A   D   SD

52. Children should not be denied an education because they are not U.S. citizens.

    SA   A   D   SD

Appendix C

Family Attitude Scale – Revised

The Family Attitude Scale (FAS) was developed by Ramirez (1969) to assess the degree of identification with traditional Mexican American values. Some items were designed by the author and others were adapted from items in three existing scales: Traditional Family Ideology Scale (Levinson and Huffman, 1955), the Historico Sociocultural Premises Scale (Diaz-Guerrero, 1955), and the Parent Attitude Research Instrument (Schafer and Bell, 1958). The FAS was designed to tap six dimensions of traditional values: loyalty to the family, strictness in childrearing, respect for adults, separation of gender roles, male superiority, and time orientation.

In 1995, Ramirez and Carrasco revised the FAS for use in a cross-national study (Rodriguez, Ramirez, and Korman, in press) with parents and their adolescent children in three cultures: Mexican, Mexican American, and white.

Participants can respond to each item on a Likert scale ranging from Agree Strongly (AS) to Disagree Strongly (DS). Scoring is done as follows: AS = 1, A = 2, D = 3, and DS = 4. Nine items (2, 6, 9, 11, 12, 20, 25, 27, and 28) require "reversed" scoring. The scores for reversed (atraditional) items and nonreversed (traditional) items are added to obtain a total score.

RELIABILITY

SPSS subprogram RELIABILITY was used. Data from 564 participants in a cross-national study collected in Mexico and the United States yielded an alpha coefficient of .75 for the entire sample. For the different cultural groups, the alpha levels were .68 for Mexican adults ($N = 200$), .69 for Mexican American adults ($N = 177$), and .75 for white adults ($N = 187$).

Source: Developed by Manuel Ramirez and N. Carrasco, 1996.

VALIDITY

The FAS was administered to 45 Mexican, 39 Mexican American, and 43 white two-parent families with an adolescent child. All the families were intact and middle class. To test for significant cultural and gender differences on the total FAS score, a 2 (gender) X 3 (culture) ANOVA was performed separately for adolescents and parents. Results for both adolescents and parents yielded a significant main effect for culture. To determine which cultural groups differed on the FAS, a Tukey's Honestly Significant Differences (THSD) test was performed. Results showed that Mexicans reported more traditional family values than whites and Mexican Americans, with whites reporting the most modern family orientations.

FAMILY ATTITUDE SCALE – REVISED

After each statement, indicate whether you: Agree Strongly (AS), Agree (A), Disagree (D), or Disagree Strongly (DS). Please circle your choice.

1. Parents always know what's best for a child.
   AS   A   D   DS

2. A husband should do some of the cooking and house cleaning.
   AS   A   D   DS

3. For a child, the mother should be the most-loved person in existence.
   AS   A   D   DS

4. People who are older tend to be wiser than young people.
   AS   A   D   DS

5. Girls should not be allowed to play with toys such as soldiers and footballs.
   AS   A   D   DS

6. Children should be taught to question the orders of parents and other authority figures.
   AS   A   D   DS

7. It is more important to respect the father than to love him.
   AS   A   D   DS

8. Boys should not be allowed to play with toys such as dolls and tea sets.
   AS   A   D   DS

9. Men tend to be just as emotional as women.
   AS   A   D   DS

10. It doesn't do any good to try to change the future, because the future is in the hands of God.
    AS   A   D   DS

11. It is all right for a girl to date a boy even if her parents disapprove of him.
    AS   A   D   DS

12. It's all right for a wife to have a job outside the home.
    AS   A   D   DS

13. Uncles, aunts, cousins, and other relatives should always be considered to be more important than friends.
    AS   A   D   DS

14. We must live for today; who knows what tomorrow may bring?
    AS   A   D   DS

15. Young people get rebellious ideas, but as they grow older and wiser, they give them up.

    AS   A   D   DS

16. A person should take care of his or her parents when they are old.

    AS   A   D   DS

17. Parents should recognize that a teenage girl needs to be protected more than a teenage boy.

    AS   A   D   DS

18. All adults should be respected.

    AS   A   D   DS

19. The father should be considered to have the most authority.

    AS   A   D   DS

20. A child should not obey his parents if he or she believes that they are wrong.

    AS   A   D   DS

21. It is more important to enjoy the present than to worry about the future.

    AS   A   D   DS

22. The best time in a child's life is when they are completely dependent on their parents.

    AS   A   D   DS

23. The teachings of religion are the best guide for living a good, moral life.

    AS   A   D   DS

24. We can attain our goals only if it is the will of God that we do so.

    AS   A   D   DS

25. A child should be taught to be ambitious.

    AS   A   D   DS

26. Fathers should always be respected regardless of any personal problems they might have.

    AS   A   D   DS

27. A husband should take over some of the household chores and childrearing duties if his wife wants to develop her career interests.

    AS   A   D   DS

28. A teenage boy needs to be protected just as much as a teenage girl.

    AS   A   D   DS

29. Being born into the right family is as important for achieving success as is hard work.

    AS   A   D   DS

30. A person should be satisfied with what he or she has without always wanting to achieve more.

      AS   A   D   DS

Total Traditionalism Score _____
Total Atraditional Score   _____
Balance Score   _____

Appendix D

Therapist's Cognitive Styles Observation Checklist

Communication Style

Field Sensitive	Field Independent
___ 1. The therapist does more talking than the client during the session.	___ 1. The therapist talks less than the client during the session.
___ 2. The therapist personalizes communications, is self-disclosing.	___ 2. The therapist remains a "blank screen" for the client.
___ 3. The therapist uses both verbal and nonverbal modes of communication.	___ 3. The therapist emphasizes verbal communication.

Interpersonal Relationship Style

Field Sensitive	Field Independent
___ 1. The therapist is informal and establishes a close personal relationship with the client.	___ 1. The therapist is formal and maintains "professional" distance.
___ 2. The therapist focuses on the nature of the therapist–client relationship in therapy.	___ 2. The therapist emphasizes self-reliance and is problem-focused.

Motivational Styles

Field Sensitive	Field Independent
___ 1. The therapist gives social rewards to the client.	___ 1. The therapist emphasizes self rewards.
___ 2. The therapist emphasizes achievement for others as one of the goals of therapy.	___ 2. The therapist emphasizes achievement for self.

Therapeutic–Teaching Styles

Field Sensitive	Field Independent
___ 1. The therapist becomes a model for the client in teaching new behaviors, values, and perspectives.	___ 1. The therapist uses the discovery approach.
___ 2. The therapist uses direct interpretation.	___ 2. The therapist uses reflection, encouraging the client to arrive at his or her own interpretations.
___ 3. The therapist uses deductive approach (global-to-specific) to teaching in therapy.	___ 3. The therapist uses an inductive (specific-to-global) approach to teaching in therapy.

Appendix E

Client Preferred Cognitive Styles Observation Checklist

Field Sensitive	Field Independent
____ Self-disclosing	____ Depersonalizes problems
____ Shows interest in personalizing relationship with therapist	____ Relationship with therapist secondary to focus on problems to be addressed in therapy
____ Indicates that social rewards from therapist will be important to progress	____ Indicates that increase in personal well-being will be important to progress
____ Global focus and deductive learning style	____ Detail-focused and inductive learning style

Appendix F

Client Preferred Cultural Styles Observation Checklist

Traditional	Modern
____ Behaves deferentially toward the therapist	____ Seeks to establish equal status with therapist
____ Expects the therapist to do most of the talking	____ Does most of the talking
____ Appears shy and self-controlling	____ Appears assertive and self-confident
____ Is observant of social environment	____ Seems to ignore social environment
____ Focuses on important others in relating reasons(s) for seeking therapy	____ Focuses on self in relating reasons(s) for seeking therapy

Appendix **G**

Bicognitive Orientation to Life Scale

SCORING PROCEDURE

Twelve of the Bicognitive Orientation to Life Scale (BOLS) items express a field sensitive (FS) orientation in the areas of: interpersonal relationships, leadership style, learning style, attitudes toward authority, and interest and natural ability in physical and math sciences versus humanities and social sciences. Twelve corresponding items express a field independent (FI) orientation in the same areas of behavior. Subjects express the extent of their agreement with each statement on a four-point Likert scale. Each item is subsequently scored on a scale from 1 to 4, with higher scores indicating greater agreement with the statements. Items 3, 7, 8, 9, 11, 14, 15, 16, 19, 20, 22, and 23 reflect an FI orientation, while items 1, 2, 4, 5, 6, 10, 12, 13, 17, 18, 21, and 24 reflect an FS preference.

Separate field sensitive and field independent scores are obtained for each subject. The bicognitive score is then calculated by taking the absolute difference between the two scores. The closer a respondent's score is to zero, the more bicognitive the respondent is judged to be. The further the score is from zero, the greater the degree of either field independence or field sensitivity.

RELIABILITY

Cronbach alphas were .85 and .82 for FS and FI items, respectively.

VALIDITY

Total scores were correlated with leadership behaviors of monocultural and multicultural Latino college students. Correlation coefficients with effective leadership behaviors in mixed ethnic groups under conditions of conflict (mediation, ensuring that all members were able to express their opinions, seek compromises, and so on) ranged from .65 to .77.

BICOGNITIVE ORIENTATION TO LIFE SCALE

After each statement, indicate whether you: Strongly Agree (SA), Agree (A), Disagree (D), or Strongly Disagree (SD). Please circle your choice.

1. I have always done well in subjects such as history or psychology.

   SA   A   D   SD

2. I prefer parties that include my parents and other family members.

   SA   A   D   SD

3. An individual's primary responsibility is to himself or herself.

   SA   A   D   SD

4. I learn best by working on a problem with others.

   SA   A   D   SD

5. I like a leader who is primarily concerned with the welfare of the group, even if it means that the job takes a little longer.

   SA   A   D   SD

6. When learning something for the first time, I prefer to have someone explain it to me or show me how to do it.

   SA   A   D   SD

7. What my professors or job supervisors think of me is never as important as feeling that I am really making progress in my studies or in my job.

   SA   A   D   SD

8. Math has always been one of my favorite subjects.

   SA   A   D   SD

9. Some persons do not deserve respect even though they are in positions of authority.

   SA   A   D   SD

10. Whenever I experience some failure or let-down, the encouragement of my family helps me get going again.

    SA   A   D   SD

11. I enjoy living alone more than living with other people.

    SA   A   D   SD

12. I like to get suggestions from others and frequently ask my family for advice.

    SA   A   D   SD

13. It is less important to achieve a goal quickly than to make sure no one gets their feelings hurt in the process.

    SA   A   D   SD

14. When I look at a mural or large painting, I first see all the little pieces and then, gradually, I see how they all go together to give a total message.

    SA   A   D   SD

15. I have always done well in courses such as chemistry or physics.

    SA   A   D   SD

16. One of the greatest satisfactions in life is the feeling of having done better than others.

    SA   A   D   SD

17. I learn better from listening to a teacher than from reading a book.

    SA   A   D   SD

18. History and social studies, in general, have always been among my favorite subjects.

    SA   A   D   SD

19. I give people honest criticism even though it might hurt their feelings.

    SA   A   D   SD

20. Getting individuals to compete with one another is the quickest and best way to get results.

    SA   A   D   SD

21. I like to read biographies and autobiographies.

    SA   A   D   SD

22. I prefer to learn things on my own, even if I make repeated mistakes before finally understanding.

    SA   A   D   SD

23. I learn better by reading about something myself than by listening to a teacher lecture about it.

    SA   A   D   SD

24. When I look at a photograph of someone, I am more aware of the total person than of the details such as hair color, facial expressions, or body type.

    SA   A   D   SD

Total FI Score   = _____
Total FS Score   = _____
Balance or Bicognitive Score = _____

Appendix **H**

Homework Effectiveness Assessment Instrument

Name _____   Date _____

Rating Effectiveness of Diversity Experience

1. How would you rate the conditions in which the diversity experience was tried?

1	2	3	4	5
Very negative	Mostly negative	Some positive and some negative	Mostly positive	Very positive

2. How confident were you when you attempted the diversity experience?

1	2	3	4	5
Not at all confident	Mostly not confident	Some lack of confidence and some confidence	Mostly confident	Very confident

3. How receptive was (were) the target person(s) or group(s)?

1	2	3	4	5
Very unreceptive	Mostly unreceptive	Some lack of receptiveness and some receptiveness	Mostly receptive	Very receptive

4. How closely did you follow the plans?

1	2	3	4	5
Total improvisation	Mostly improvisation	Some improvisation and some adherence to plan	Followed most of plan	Total adherence to plan

5. How successful was the diversity experience in achieving your goal(s)?

1	2	3	4	5
Total failure	Mostly a failure	Some failure and some success	Mostly successful	Very successful

6. If you feel that you need to change the plan and try another diversity experience of this type, indicate what you think should be done.

Appendix I

Figures and Tables for Introducing Flex Theory

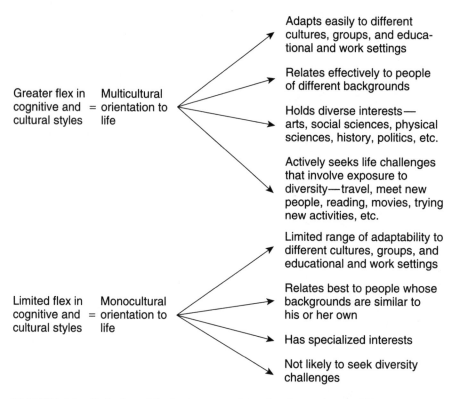

Greater flex in cognitive and cultural styles

Multicultural = orientation to life

Adapts easily to different cultures, groups, and educational and work settings

Relates effectively to people of different backgrounds

Holds diverse interests— arts, social sciences, physical sciences, history, politics, etc.

Actively seeks life challenges that involve exposure to diversity—travel, meet new people, reading, movies, trying new activities, etc.

Limited flex in cognitive and cultural styles

Monocultural = orientation to life

Limited range of adaptability to different cultures, groups, and educational and work settings

Relates best to people whose backgrounds are similar to his or her own

Has specialized interests

Not likely to seek diversity challenges

FIGURE I.1 **Relationship between cultural orientation to life and flexibility of personality**

FIGURE I.2   **Relationship between cultural style, socialization—life experiences, and cognitive styles**

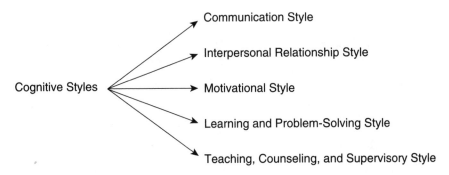

FIGURE I.3   **Components of cognitive styles**

Personality Characteristics of Field Sensitive and Field Independent People

Communications

Field Sensitive	Field Independent
___ 1. Tends to personalize communications by referring to personal life experiences, interests, and feelings.	___ 1. Tends to be impersonal and to-the-point in communications.
___ 2. Tends to focus more on nonverbal than on verbal communication.	___ 2. Tends to focus more on verbal than on nonverbal communication.

Interpersonal Relationships

Field Sensitive	Field Independent
___ 1. Open and outgoing in social settings.	___ 1. Reserved and cautious in social settings.
___ 2. Presents as warm and informal.	___ 2. Presents as distant and formal.

Motivation

Field Sensitive	Field Independent
___ 1. Values social rewards that strengthen relationships with important others.	___ 1. Seeks nonsocial rewards.
___ 2. Motivation is related to achievement for others (family, team, ethnic or racial group, etc.)	___ 2. Motivation is related to self-advancement.

Teaching, Parenting, Supervisory, and Counseling Relationships

Field Sensitive	Field Independent
___ 1. Focuses on relationship with student, child, supervisor, or client.	___ 1. Focuses on task or goal.
___ 2. Is informal and self-disclosing.	___ 2. Is formal and private.

Traditional and Modern Cultural Styles

Traditional	Modern
1. Typical of rural communities and poor neighborhoods in urban communities and of conservative religions.	1. Typical of urban and suburban communities and of liberal religions.
2. Emphasizes strictness in childrearing and separation of gender roles.	2. Emphasizes egalitarianism in childrearing and in gender-role definition.
3. Emphasizes cooperation and group competition.	3. Emphasizes individual competition.
4. Emphasizes lifelong identification with family, community, and culture.	4. Emphasizes separation from family and community early in life.
5. Spiritualism emphasized when explaining "mysteries of life."	5. Science emphasized when explaining "mysteries of life."

Appendix J

Rating the Effectiveness
of the Script

Name _____   Date _____

1. How would you rate the conditions in which the script was enacted?

1	2	3	4	5
Very negative	Mostly negative	Some positive and some negative	Mostly positive	Very positive

2. How confident were you when you enacted the script?

1	2	3	4	5
Not at all confident	Mostly not confident	Some lack of confidence and some confidence	Mostly confident	Very confident

3. How receptive was (were) the target person(s) or group(s)?

1	2	3	4	5
Very unreceptive	Mostly unreceptive	Some lack of receptiveness and some receptiveness	Mostly receptive	Very receptive

4. How closely did you follow plans for the script?

1	2	3	4	5
Total improvisation	Mostly improvisation	Some improvisation and some adherence to plan	Followed most of plan	Total adherence to plan

5. How successful was the script in achieving your goal(s)?

1	2	3	4	5
Total failure	Mostly a failure	Some failure and some success	Mostly successful	Very successful

6. How would you change the script to make it more effective?

FEEDBACK SUMMARY SHEET FOR CLIENTS

FAS–R	T Score	AT Score
Gender roles	—	—
Familism	—	—
Male superiority	—	—
Time orientation	—	—
Childrearing	—	—
Respect for adults	—	—
Balance score	—	—

TMI	M Score	T Score
Gender-role definition	—	—
Family identity	—	—
Sense of community	—	—
Family identification	—	—
Time orientation	—	—
Age status	—	—
Importance of tradition		
Spirituality and/or religion		
Subservience to convention and authority	—	—

MEI	Scores
Historical development pattern	—
CMI	—
Degree of comfort items	—
Total Score	—

BOLS	FS Score	FI Score
Interpersonal relationships	—	—
Leadership style	—	—
Learning style	—	—
Attitude toward authority	—	—
Interest and natural ability in physics, math, sciences, humanities and social sciences	—	—
Biocognitive score	—	—

Appendix **K**

Imelda's Response to TMI and Session Notes

Name: *Imelda M.*

Please express your true feelings about each statement below by indicating whether you Strongly Agree (SA), Agree (A), Disagree (D), or Strongly Disagree (SD).

1. Husbands and wives should share equally in housework.

   (SA) A   D   SD

2. All institutions should follow a democratic decision-making process.

   SA   A   (D)   SD

3. I prefer to live in a small town or a friendly neighborhood where everyone knows each other.

   SA   (A)   D   SD

4. Women with children at home should not have a full-time career or job outside of the home.

   SA   A   D   (SD)

5. Students should not question the teachings of their teachers or professors.

   SA   A   D   (SD)

6. I prefer to live in a large city.

   SA   (A)   D   SD

7. Husbands and wives should share equally in childrearing and child care.

   (SA) A   D   SD

8. In industry or government, when two persons are equally qualified, the older person should get the job.

   (SA) A   D   SD

9. It's hard to meet and get to know people in cities.

    (SA)   A   D   SD

10. Women should assume their rightful place in business and in the professions along with men.

    (SA)   A   D   SD

11. Laws should be obeyed without question.

    (SA)   A   D   SD

12. You should know your family history so you can pass it on to your children.

    (SA)   A   D   SD

13. In general, the father should have greater authority than the mother in bringing up children.

    (SA)   A   D   SD

14. Students should have decision-making power in schools and universities.

    SA   (A)   D   SD

15. It does not matter to me if my job requires me to move far away from the place where I have my roots.

    SA   A   D   (SD)

16. Husbands and wives should participate equally in making important family decisions.

    (SA)   A   D   SD

17. With institutions, the amount of power a person has should not be determined by either age or gender.

    SA   (A)   D   SD

18. I prefer the excitement of a large city to the relaxed living in a small town.

    SA   A   (D)   SD

19. Children should always be respectful of their parents and older relatives.

    (SA)   A   D   SD

20. Traditional observances, such as church services or graduation ceremonies, add meaning to life.

    (SA)   A   D   SD

21. Adult children should visit their parents regularly.

    (SA)   A   D   SD

22. We should not let concerns about time interfere with our friendships and interactions with others.

    (SA)   A   D   SD

23. Children should be taught to be loyal to their families.

    (SA)   A   D   SD

24. The Biblical version of the creation of the universe should not be taught in schools.

    SA   A   D   (SD)

25. Children should be encouraged to be independent of their families at an early age.

    SA   A   D   (SD)

26. If you are not careful, people can cause you to waste your time and you will never get anything accomplished.

    SA   A   D   (SD)

27. Most traditional ceremonies are outmoded and wasteful of time and money.

    SA   A   D   (SD)

28. There is no doubt that the universe was created by a supreme being.

    (SA)   A   D   SD

29. Children should be taught to always feel close to their families.

    (SA)   A   D   SD

30. We get into such a hurry sometimes that we fail to enjoy life.

    (SA)   A   D   SD

31. Everything a person does reflects on her or his family.

    (SA)   A   D   SD

32. Eventually, science will explain all the mysteries of life.

    SA   A   D   (SD)

33. A person should only be responsible to himself or herself.

    SA   A   D   (SD)

34. No matter how many advances we make through science, we will never be able to understand many important things in life.

    (SA)   A   D   SD

35. Most religions are primarily folklore and superstition.

    SA   A   D   (SD)

36. When making important decisions about my life, I always like to consult members of my family.

    (SA)   A   D   SD

37. Religion adds meaning to our mechanized and impersonal lives.

    (SA)   A   D   SD

38. If my family does not agree with one of my major life decisions, I go ahead and do what I think is right anyway.

      SA   A   (D)   SD

39. Tradition and ritual serve to remind us of the rich history or our institutions and our society.

      (SA)   A   D   SD

40. Traditions limit our freedom.

      SA   A   D   (SD)

Total T Score = +74

Total M Score = −40

Balance Score = +34

Therapist's Ratings and Notes on Preferred Cultural Styles Observation Checklist for Imelda

Initial Session

Traditional	Notes
_x_ Behaves deferentially	"Sir" and "Doctor"
_x_ Expects therapist or counselor to do the talking	Quiet, does not initiate interactions
_x_ Appears shy and nonassertive	Avoids eye contact, looks at floor
_x_ Observant of physical and social environments	Said she liked office as she was leaving
_x_ Focuses on important others when discussing presenting problem(s)	Focuses on relationship with grandparents, parents, teachers, and boyfriend

Modern	Notes
___ Seeks to establish equal status with therapist or counselor	
___ Does most of the talking	
___ Assertive and self-confident	
___ Ignores environment	
___ Focuses on self in discussing presenting problems	

Appendix L

Harold's Response to BOLS and Session Notes

Name: *Harold H.*

After each statement, indicate whether you: Strongly Agree (SA), Agree (A), Disagree (D), or Strongly Disagree (SD). Please circle your choice.

1. I have always done well in subjects such as history or psychology.

   SA　　　A　　　(D)　　　SD

2. I prefer parties that include my parents and other family members.

   SA　　　A　　　D　　　(SD)

3. An individual's primary responsibility is to himself or herself.

   (SA)　　　A　　　D　　　SD

4. I learn best by working on a problem with others.

   SA　　　A　　　(D)　　　SD

5. I like a leader who is primarily concerned with the welfare of the group, even if it means that the job takes a little longer.

   SA　　　A　　　(D)　　　SD

6. When learning something for the first time, I prefer to have someone explain it to me or show me how to do it.

   SA　　　A　　　D　　　(SD)

7. What my professors or job supervisors think of me is never as important as feeling that I am really making progress in my studies or in may job.

   (SA)　　　A　　　D　　　SD

8. Math has always been one of my favorite subjects.

   (SA)　　　A　　　S　　　SD

9. Some persons do not deserve respect even though they are in positions of authority.

    (SA)   A   D   SD

10. Whenever I experience some failure or let-down, the encouragement of my family helps me get going again.

    SA   A   (D)   SD

11. I enjoy living alone more than living with other people.

    SA   (A)   D   SD

12. I like to get suggestions from others and frequently ask my family for advice.

    SA   A   D   (SD)

13. It is less important to achieve a goal quickly than to make sure no one gets their feelings hurt in the process.

    SA   A   (D)   SD

14. When I look at a mural or painting, I first see all the little pieces and then, gradually, I see how they all go together to give a total message.

    (SA)   A   D   SD

15. I have always done well in courses such as chemistry or physics.

    (SA)   A   D   SD

16. One of the greatest satisfactions in life is the feeling of having done better than others.

    (SA)   A   D   SD

17. I learn better from listening to a teacher than from reading a book.

    SA   A   D   (SD)

18. History and social studies, in general, have always been among my favorite subjects.

    SA   A   D   (SD)

19. I give people honest criticism even though it might hurt their feelings.

    (SA)   A   D   SD

20. Getting individuals to compete with one another is the quickest and best way to get results.

    (SA)   A   D   SD

21. I like to read biographies and autobiographies.

    SA   A   (D)   SD

22. I prefer to learn things on my own, even if I make repeated mistakes before finally understanding.

    (SA)   A   D   SD

23. I learn better by reading about something myself than by listening to a teacher lecture about it.

    (SA)   A   D   SD

24. When I look at a photograph of someone, I am more aware of the total person than of details such as hair color, facial expression, or body type.

    SA   A   (D)   SD

Total FI Score = -47

Total FS Score = $+19$

Balance or
Bicognitive = -29
Score

Therapist's Ratings and Notes on Preferred Cognitive Styles Observation Checklist for Harold

Initial Session

Field Independent	Notes
_x_ Depersonalizes presenting problem(s)	Focuses strictly on communication style—no feelings discussed, "business-like," no attempt to personalize; "I want to be as effective and efficient as I used to be."
_x_ Relationship to therapist is secondary to problem(s)	
_x_ Improvement in personal effectiveness is primary concern	Notes he made on pad were very detailed; goes from specific to global.
_x_ Detail-focused and inductive	

Field Sensitive	Notes
_x_ Self-disclosing	Seems to value close relationships with managers, supervisors, and employees.
___ Personalizes relationship with therapist	
___ Values social rewards	
___ Global-focused and deductive	

Appendix M

Traditionalism–Modernism Inventory (Pre-Revised)

Please express your feeling about each statement below by indicating whether you Agree Strongly (4), Agree Mildly (3), Disagree Mildly (2), or Disagree Strongly (1).

1. Husbands and wives should share equally in housework.

   4   3   2   1

2. All institutions should follow a democratic process of decision-making.

   4   3   2   1

3. I prefer to live in a small town or a friendly neighborhood where everyone knows each other.

   4   3   2   1

4. Women with children at home should not have a full-time career or job outside of the home.

   4   3   2   1

5. Students should not question the teachings of their teachers or professors.

   4   3   2   1

6. I prefer to live in a large city.

   4   3   2   1

7. Husbands and wives should share equally in childrearing and child care.

   4   3   2   1

8. In industry or government, when two persons are equally qualified, the older person should get the job.

   4   3   2   1

9. It's hard to meet and get to know people in cities.

    4   3   2   1

10. Women should assume their rightful place in business and in the professions along with men.

    4   3   2   1

11. Laws should be obeyed without question.

    4   3   2   1

12. You should know your family history so you can pass it on to your children.

    4   3   2   1

13. In general, the father should have greater authority than the mother in bringing up children.

    4   3   2   1

14. Students should have decision-making power in schools and universities.

    4   3   2   1

15. It does not matter to me if my job requires me to move far away from the place where I have my roots.

    4   3   2   1

16. Husbands and wives should participate equally in making important family decisions.

    4   3   2   1

17. With institutions, the amount of power a person has should not be determined by either age or gender.

    4   3   2   1

18. I prefer the excitement of a large city to relaxed living in a small town.

    4   3   2   1

19. Children should always be respectful of their parents and older relatives.

    4   3   2   1

20. Traditional observances, such as church services or graduation ceremonies, add meaning to life.

    4   3   2   1

21. Adult children should visit their parents regularly.

    4   3   2   1

22. We should not let concerns about time interfere with our friendships and interactions with others.

    4   3   2   1

23. Children should be taught to be loyal to their families.

    4   3   2   1

24. The Biblical version of the creation of the universe should not be taught in schools.

    4   3   2   1

25. Children should be encouraged to be independent of their families at an early age.

    4   3   2   1

26. If you are not careful, people can cause you to waste your time and you will never get anything accomplished.

    4   3   2   1

27. Most traditional ceremonies are outmoded and wasteful of time and money.

    4   3   2   1

28. There is no doubt that the universe was created by a supreme being.

    4   3   2   1

29. Children should be taught to always feel close to their families.

    4   3   2   1

30. We get into such a hurry sometimes that we fail to enjoy life.

    4   3   2   1

31. Everything a person does reflects on her or his family.

    4   3   2   1

32. Eventually, science will explain all the mysteries of life.

    4   3   2   1

33. A person should only be responsible to himself or herself.

    4   3   2   1

34. No matter how many advances we make through science, we will never be able to understand many important things in life.

    4   3   2   1

35. Most religions are primarily folklore and superstition.

    4   3   2   1

36. When making important decisions about my life, I always like to consult members of my family.

    4   3   2   1

37. Religion adds meaning to our mechanized and impersonal lives.

    4   3   2   1

38. If my family does not agree with one of my major life decisions, I go ahead and do what I think is right anyway.

       4   3   2   1

39. Tradition and ritual serve to remind us of the rich history of our institutions and our society.

       4   3   2   1

40. Traditions limit our freedom.

       4   3   2   1

Total T Score   = _____

Total M Score = _____

Balance Score = _____

Appendix N

Record of Match and Mismatch

Name _____

	Description of Incident	Date and Time	Situation and Setting	How I Reacted (Include verbal and nonverbal behaviors)	How My Partner Reacted (Include verbal and nonverbal behaviors)	Describe Areas of Cultural and Cognitive Styles Match	Positive Effects on Relationship
Match							
Mismatch	Description of Incident	Date and Time	Situation and Setting	How I Reacted (Include verbal and nonverbal behaviors)	How My Partner Reacted (Include verbal and nonverbal behaviors)	Describe Areas of Cultural and Cognitive Styles Mismatch	Negative Effects on Relationship

213

GLOSSARY

Attitude of Acceptance   a nonjudgmental, positive, accepting atmosphere devoid of conformity or assimilation pressures. In therapy this enables the client to express his unique, or true, self.

Bicognitive Orientation to Life Scale (BOLS)   a personality inventory composed of items that reflect the degree of preference for field sensitive or field independent cognitive styles in different life domains. Assesses cognitive flex by determining the degree of agreement with items that reflect preference for either field independent or field sensitive cognitive styles. A balance or bicognitive score is also attained.

Bicognitive Style   a cognitive style characterized by an ability to shuttle between the field sensitive and field independent styles. Choice of style at any given time is dependent on task demands or situational characteristics. For example, if a situation demands competition, the bicognitive person usually responds in a field independent manner. On the other hand, if the situation demands cooperation, the bicognitive individual behaves in a field sensitive manner. People with a bicognitive orientation also may use elements of both the field sensitive and field independent styles to develop new composite or combination styles.

Bicultural/Multicultural Style   a cultural style characterized by an ability to shuttle between the traditional and modern cultural styles. Choice of style at any given time is dependent on task demands or situational characteristics.

Change Agent   a person who actively seeks to encourage changes in the social environment in order to ensure acceptance and sensitivity to all cultural and cognitive styles.

Cognitive and Cultural Flex Theory (or Theory of Multicultural Development)   the theory that people who are exposed to socialization agents with positive attitudes toward diversity, participate in diversity challenges, interact with members of diverse cultures, maintain an openness and commitment to learning from others, and are more likely to develop multicultural patterns of behavior and a multicultural identity. People who have developed a multicultural identity have a strong, lifelong commitment to their groups of origin as well as to other cultures and groups.

Cognitive Style   a style of personality defined by the ways in which people communicate and relate to others; the rewards that motivate them; their problem-solving approaches; and the manner in which they teach, socialize with, supervise, and counsel others. There are three types of cognitive styles: field sensitive, field independent, and bicognitive.

Cultural and Cognitive Flex (Personality Flex)   the ability to shuttle between field sensitive and field independent cognitive styles and modern and traditional cultural styles.

Cultural Democracy   (1) a philosophy that recognizes that the way a person communicates, relates to others, seeks support and recognition from his environment, and thinks and learns are products of the value system of his home and community; (2) refers to the moral rights of an individual to be different while at the same time be a responsible member of a larger society.

Cultural Style   an orientation to life related to or based on traditional and modern values or a combination of these values. Assessed by the Traditionalism–Modernism Inventory and the Family Attitude Scale.

Diversity Challenges   a catalyst for multicultural development such as cultural and linguistic immersion experiences, new tasks, and activities that encourage the process of synthesis and amalgamation of personality building blocks learned from different cultures, institutions, and peoples.

Empathy Projection   the process whereby a person tries to understand the point of view and feelings of others whose cognitive styles and values are different from his own.

False Self   the identity developed as a result of attempts to conform to cultural and cognitive styles of authority figures, institutions, and majority cultures.

Family Attitude Scale   a personality inventory to assess a person's degree of agreement with traditional and modern family values.

Field Independent   a cognitive style characterized by independent, abstract, discovery-oriented learning preferences, an introverted lifestyle, a preference for verbal communication styles, and an emphasis on personal achievement and material gain. People with a preferred field independent orientation are likely to be analytical and inductive and focus on detail. They also tend to be nondirective and discovery-oriented in childrearing, and in teaching, supervising, and counseling others.

Field Sensitive   a cognitive style characterized by interactive personalized learning preferences, an extroverted lifestyle, a preference for nonverbal communication styles, a need to help others. People with a preferred field sensitive orientation tend to be more global, integrative, and deductive in their thinking and problem-solving styles, and they tend to be directive in childrearing, and in teaching, supervising, and counseling others.

Life History Interview   focuses on the development and expressions of cultural flex during different periods of life: infancy and early childhood, early school and elementary school years, middle school years, high school years, and post–high school period. The life history interview also focuses on the extent of an individual's actual participation in both traditional and modern families, cultures, groups, and institutions. The life history identifies the type of cultural flex by examining the degree to which a person has been able to combine modern and traditional values and belief systems to arrive at multicultural values and worldviews.

Match and/or Mismatch refers to person–environment fit with respect to the degree of harmony or lack of harmony between cultural/cognitive styles and environmental demands. Two types are cognitive mismatch and cultural mismatch.

Mismatch Shock an extreme case of the mismatch syndrome.

Mismatch Syndrome a lack of harmony between a person's preferred cultural and/or cognitive styles and environmental demands. This occurs when people feel at odds to the important people and institutions in their lives. They feel alone, hopeless, and misunderstood; they may exhibit a number of symptoms, including self-rejection, depression, negativity, rigidity, and attempts to escape reality.

Model a person whom the client admires and who is dominant in the cultural/ cognitive styles the client wants to learn.

Modeling the process whereby people learn unfamiliar cognitive and cultural styles through imitation and observation of others, through reading and through travel.

Modern a value orientation that emphasizes and encourages separation from family and community early in life. It is typical of urban communities, liberal religions, and of North American and Western European cultures. People who are identified as having a modern value orientation tend to emphasize science when explaining the mysteries of life; they have a strong individualistic orientation; they tend to deemphasize differences in gender and age roles; and they emphasize egalitarianism in childrearing practices.

Multicultural Ambassador a multicultural person who promotes the development of multicultural environments which encourage understanding (multicultural education) and cooperation among different people and groups.

Multicultural Educator a multicultural person who educates others about the advantages of cultural and cognitive diversity and multicultural orientations to life.

Multicultural Experience Inventory (MEI) an inventory that assesses historical and current experiences. It focuses on personal history and behavior in three areas: demographic and linguistic, socialization history, and degree of multicultural participation in the past as well as the present. The MEI consists of two types of items: historical (reflecting historical development pattern—HDP) and contemporary functioning (reflecting contemporary multicultural identity—CMI). Includes items that deal with degree of comfort and acceptance.

Multicultural Model of Psychotherapy a model of therapy that emphasizes multicultural development by maximizing the client's ability to flex between cultural and cognitive styles when faced with different environmental demands and development of a multicultural orientation to life characterized by serving as a multicultural educator, ambassador, and peer counselor.

Multicultural Peer Counselor a multicultural person who provides emotional support and facilitates change and development of empowerment in those of his or her peers who are suffering from mismatch.

Multicultural Person–Environment Fit Worldview a worldview that is based on the following assumptions: (1) There are no inferior people, cultures, or groups in terms of gender, ethnicity, race, economics, religion, physical disabilities, region, sexual orientation, or language; (2) problems of maladjustment are the result of mismatch between people, or between people and their environments rather than of inferior people or groups; (3) every individual, group, or culture has positive contributions to make to personality development and to a healthy adjustment to life; (4) people who are willing to learn from others and from groups and cultures different from their own acquire multicultural building blocks (coping techniques and perspectives), which are the basis of multicultural personality development and multicultural identity; (5) synthesis and amalgamation of personality building blocks acquired from different people, groups, and cultures occur when the person with multicultural potential works toward the goals of understanding and cooperation among diverse groups and peoples in a pluralistic society; and (6) synthesis and amalgamation of personality building blocks from diverse origins contribute to the development of multicultural personality development and psychological adjustment in a pluralistic society.

Preferred Cultural and Cognitive Styles Observation Checklists   observational rating scales that list field sensitive and field independent behaviors in five domains: communications; interpersonal relationships; motivation; teaching, parenting, supervising, and counseling; learning and problem solving. The checklists can be used to assess modern and traditional cultural styles and values.

Preferred Styles   the dominant cultural and cognitive styles of a person.

Scriptwriting   a therapy strategy used, along with role-playing, to promote cultural and cognitive flex development by matching the cultural or cognitive styles of a person or institution.

Theory of Multicultural Development   *see* Cognitive and Cultural Flex Theory.

Traditional   a value orientation that emphasizes close ties to family and community throughout life. It is typical of rural communities, conservative religions, and of minority and developing cultures. People identified as having traditional value orientations tend to have a spiritual orientation toward life, are strongly identified with their families and communities of origin, usually believe in separation of gender and age roles; and typically endorse strict approaches to child-rearing.

Traditionalism–Modernism Inventory (TMI)   a personality inventory that assesses the degree of identification with traditional and modern values and belief systems. The instrument yields scores indicating the degree of agreement with items reflecting traditionalism or modernism. The degree of flex can be determined by examining the differences between the total traditionalism and total modernism scores (balance score) as well as by looking at the degree of agreement with the traditional and modern items across the different domains of life: gender-role definition; family identity; sense of community; family identification; time orientation; age status; importance of tradition; subservience to convention and authority; spirituality and religion; attitudes toward issues such as sexual orientation, the death penalty, the role of federal government in education, benefits to single mothers and noncitizens, and abortion. Type of flex can be determined by examining the degree of flex within each domain.

Tyranny of the Shoulds   an individual's perception of the self based on what she believes others expect the person to be like. The pressure to conform could contribute to psychological maladjustment—the individual develops a false self based on the "shoulds" of parents, important others, and societal institutions.

Unique Self   a person's preferred cultural and cognitive styles before he has been subjected to the pressures of conformity.

REFERENCES

Adler, A. (1931) *What life should mean to you.* Boston: Little, Brown.

Adler, P.S. (1974). Beyond cultural identity: Reflections on cultural and multicultural man. In R. Brislin (Ed.), *Topics in cultural learning: Vol. 2.* Honolulu, HI: University of Hawaii, East–West Culture Learning Institute.

Almeida, E., and Sanchez, M.E. (1985). Cultural interaction in social change dynamics. In R. Diaz-Guerrero (Ed.), *Cross-cultural and national studies in social psychology.* Amsterdam: North Holland.

American Psychiatric Association (1994). *Diagnostic and statistical manual of mental disorders,* 4th ed. Washington, DC: American Psychiatric Association.

Aponte, H.J. (1974). Psychotherapy for the poor: An ecostructural approach to treatment. *Delaware Medical Journal,* March, 1–7.

Ardila, R. (1986). *La psicologia en America latina. Pasado-presente y futuro.* Mexico, D.F.: Siglo Veintuno Editores.

Atteneave, C.L. (1969). Therapy in tribal settings and urban network intervention. *Family Process, 8,* 192–210.

Auerswald, E. (1968). Interdisciplinary versus ecological approach. *Family Process, 7,* 204.

Beck, A.T. (1976). *Cognitive therapy and the emotional disorders.* New York: International Universities Press.

Bond, H.M. (1927) Some exceptional Negro children. *The Crisis, 34,* 257–280.

Bowen, M. (1976). Theory in the practice of psychotherapy. In P. Guerin (Ed.), *Family therapy: Theory and practice.* New York: Gardner Press.

Boyd-Franklin, N. (1987). The contribution of family therapy models to the treatment of Black families. *Psychotherapy, 24,* 621–629.

Brink, T.L. (1984). *The middle class credo: 1,000 all American beliefs.* Saratoga, CA: R and E Publishers.

Bulhan, H.A. (1985) *Franz Fanon and the psychology of oppression.* New York: Plenum Publishing.

Buriel, R. (1981). *Acculturation and biculturalism among three generations of Mexican American and Anglo school children.* Unpublished paper. Pomona College, Claremont, CA.

Castaneda, A. (1984). Traditionalism, modernism, and ethnicity. In J.L. Martinez and R.H. Mendoza (Eds.), *Chicano psychology,* 2nd ed. Orlando, FL: Academic Press.

Cervantes, J.M., and Ramirez, O. (1995). Spirituality and family dynamics in psychotherapy with Latino children. In K.P. Monteiro (Ed.), *Ethnicity and psychology.* Dubuque, IA: Kendal/Hunt.

Cohen, R.A. (1969). Conceptual styles, culture conflict and nonverbal tests of intelligence. *American Anthropologist, 71,* 828–856.

Collins, M. (1954). *Cortez and Montezuma.* New York: Avon Books.

Cox, B., Macaulay, J., and Ramirez, M. (1982). *New frontiers: A bilingual early childhood program.* New York: Pergamon Press.

Crevecoeur, J.H. St. J. (1904). *Letters from an American farmer.* New York: Fox, Duffield.

Cubberly, E.P. (1909). *Changing conceptions of education.* Boston: Houghton Mifflin.

Darder, A. (1991). *Culture and power in the classroom: A critical foundation for bicultural education.* New York: Bergin and Garvey.

DuBois, W.E.B. (1989). *The souls of Black folks.* New York: Bantam Classic.

Ellis, A. (1970). *The essence of rational psychotherapy: A comprehensive approach in treatment.* New York: Institute for Rational Living.

Fanon, F. (1967). *Black skin, white masks.* New York: Grove Press.

Freire, P. (1970). *Pedagogy of the oppressed.* New York: Seabury Press.

Freud, S. (1961). Some psychological consequences of the anatomical distinction between the sexes. In J. Strachey (Ed. and Trans.), *The standard edition of the complete psychological works of Sigmund Freud: Vol. 19.* London: Hogarth Press. (Original work published in 1925.)

Garza, R.T., Romero, G.J., Cox, B.G., and Ramirez, M. (1982). Biculturalism, locus of control and leader behavior in ethnically mixed small groups. *Journal of Applied Social Psychology, 12*(3), 227–253.

Giroux, H. (1981). *Ideology, culture, and the process of schooling.* Philadelphia: Temple University Press.

Guthrie, R.V. (1976). *Even the rat was white: A historical view of psychology.* New York: Harper & Row.

Hale-Benson, J.E. (1986). *Black children: Their roots, culture and learning styles.* Baltimore: Johns Hopkins University Press.

Herrnstein, R.J., and Murray, C. (1994). *The bell curve: Intelligence and class structure in American life.* New York: Free Press.

Ho, M.K. (1987). *Family therapy with ethnic minorities.* Newbury Park, CA: Sage.

Horney, K. (1937). *The neurotic personality of our time.* New York: W.W. Norton.

Horney, K. (1950). *Neurosis and human growth.* New York: W.W. Norton.

Johnson, D.J. (1994). Developmental pathways: Toward an ecological theoretical formulation of race identity in Black-White biracial children. In M.P.P. Root (Ed.), *Racially mixed people in America.* Newbury Park, CA: Sage.

Katz, P.A., and Taylor, D.A. (Eds.) (1988). *Eliminating racism: Profiles in controversy.* New York: Plenum Publishing.

Levitsky, A., and Perls, F. (1970). The rules and games of Gestalt therapy. In J. Fagan and I. Shepherd (Eds.), *Gestalt therapy now.* New York: Harper & Row.

Lubrosky, L., McClellan, A.T., Woody, G.E., O'Brien, C.P., and Auerbach, A. (1985). Therapist success and its determinants. *Archives of General Psychiatry, 42*(June), 602–611.

Mahoney, M.J. (1995). The modern psychotherapist and the future of psychotherapy. In B. Bongar and L.E. Beutler (Eds.), *Comprehensive textbook of psychotherapy.* New York: Oxford University Press.

Malgady, R.G., Rogler, L.H., and Constantino, G. (1987). Ethnocultural and linguistic bias in mental health evaluation of Hispanics. *American Psychologist, 42*(3), 228–234.

Mannoni, O. (1960) Appel de la federation de France du FLN, *El Moudjahid, 59,* 644–645.

Marin, G. (1975). *La psicologia social en latino Americana.* Mexico, D.F.: Trillas.

McGill, D.W. (1992). The cultural story in multicultural family therapy. *Families in Society: The Journal of Contemporary Human Services,* June, 339–349.

Minuchin, S. (1974). *Families and family therapy.* Cambridge, MA: Harvard University Press.

Minuchin, S., Montalvo, B., Guerney, B., Roman, B., and Schumer, F. (1967). *Families of the slums.* New York: Basic Books.

Montero, M. (1979). *Aportes metodologicos de la psicologia social al desarolllo de comunidades.* Paper presented at the XVII Congress of the Inter-American Society of Psychology, Lima, Peru, July.

Norcross, J.C., Alford, B.A., and DeMichele, J.T. (1992). The future of psychotherapy: Delphi data and concluding observations. *Psychotherapy, 29,* 150–158.

Panday, A.K., and Panday, A.K. (1985). A study of cognitive styles of urban and rural college students. *Perspectives in Psychological Research, 8*(2), 38–43.

Ramirez, A. (1972). Chicano power and interracial group relations. In J.L. Martinez (Ed.), *Chicano psychology.* New York: Academic Press.

Ramirez, A. (1988). Racism toward Hispanics: The culturally monolithic society. In P.A. Katz and D.A. Taylor (Eds.), *Eliminating racism: Profiles in controversy.* New York: Plenum Press.

Ramirez, M. (1983). *Psychology of the Americas: Mestizo perspective on personality and mental health.* Elmsford, NY: Pergamon Press.

Ramirez, M. (1987). The impact of culture change and economic stressors on the physical and mental health of Mexican Americans. In R. Rodriguez and M.T. Coleman (Eds.), *Mental health issues of the Mexican-origin population in Texas.* Austin, TX: Hogg Foundation for Mental Health.

Ramirez, M. (1998). *Multicultural/Multiracial psychology: Mestizo perspectives in personality and mental health.* Northvale, NJ: Jason Aronson.

Ramirez, M., and Carrasco, N. (1996). Revision of the Family Attitude Scale. Unpublished manuscript. Austin, Texas.

Ramirez, M., and Castaneda, A. (1974). *Cultural democracy, bicognitive development and education.* New York: Academic Press.

Ramirez, M., Cox, B.G., and Castaneda, A. (1977). *The psychodynamics of biculturalism.* Unpublished technical report. Office of Naval Research, Arlington, VA.

Ramirez, M., Cox, B.G., Garza, R.T., and Castaneda, A. (1978). *Dimensions of biculturalism in Mexican-American college students.* Unpublished technical report. Office of Naval Research, Arlington, VA.

Ramirez, M., and Doell, S.R. (1982). *The traditionalism–modernism inventory.* Unpublished manuscript, Austin, TX.

Rappaport, J. (1977). *Community psychology: Values, research, and action.* New York: Holt, Rinehart, and Winston.

Raven, J.C., Court, S., and Raven, J. (1986). *Manual for Raven's Progressive Matrices and Vocabulary Scales.* San Antonio, TX: The Psychological Corporation.

Rodriguez, R. (1983). *Hunger of memory: The education of Richard Rodriguez.* New York: Bantam.

Ryan, W. (1971). *Blaming the victim.* New York: Random House.

Salazar, J.M. (1981). *Research on applied psychology in Venezuela.* Paper presented at XVII Inter-American Congress of Psychology, Dominican Republic, June.

Sanchez, G.I. (1932). Group differences and Spanish-speaking children—A critical review. *Journal of Applied Psychology, 16,* 549–558.

Snowden, L., and Todman, P.A. (1982). The psychological assessment of Blacks: New and needed developments. In E.E. Jones and S.J. Korchin (Eds.), *Minority mental health.* New York: Praeger.

Spanier, G.B. (1976). Measuring dyadic adjustment: New scales for assessing the quality of marriage and similar dyads. *Journal of Marriage and Family, 38*(1), 15–28.

Speck, R., and Atteneave, C.L. (1974). *Family networks.* New York: Vintage Books.

Stodolsky, S.S., and Lesser, G.S. (1967). Learning patterns in the disadvantaged. *Harvard Educational Review, 37*(4), 546–593.

Sue, D.W., and Sue, D. (1990). *Counseling the culturally different: Theory and practice,* 2nd ed., New York: John Wiley and Sons.

Sue, S., and Zane, N. (1987). The role of culture and cultural techniques in psychotherapy: A reformulation. *American Psychologist, 42,* 37–45.

Szapocznik, J., Scopetta, M.A., Kurtines, W., and Arnalde, M.A. (1978). Theory and measurement of acculturation. *Interamerican Journal of Psychology, 12,* 113–130.

Terman, L.M. (1916). *The measurement of intelligence.* Boston, MA: Houghton Mifflin.

Tharakan, P.N. (1987). The effect of rural and urban upbringing on cognitive styles. *Psychological Studies, 32*(2), 119–122.

Torrey, E.F. (1973). *The mind game: Witchdoctors and psychiatrists.* New York: Bantam Books.

Witkin, H., and Goodenough, D. (1977). Field dependence and interpersonal behavior. *Psychological Bulletin, 84,* 661–689.

SELECTED READINGS

Angelou, M. (1973). *I know why the caged bird sings.* New York: Bantam.

Beck, A.T. (1989). *Love is never enough: How couples can overcome misunderstandings, resolve conflicts, and solve relationship problems through cognitive therapy.* New York: HarperCollins.

Bellow, S. (1947). *The victim.* New York: Penguin.

Coles, R. (1968). *The old ones of New Mexico.* Albuquerque: University of New Mexico Press.

Ellison, R. (1947). *The invisible man.* New York: Vintage.

Estes, C.P. (1995). *Women who run with the wolves: Myths and stories of the wild woman archetype.* New York: Ballantine Books.

Fowles, J. (1977). *Daniel Martin,* New York: Signet.

Gray, J. (1992). *Men are from Mars, women are from Venus: A practical guide for improving communication and getting what you want in your relationships.* New York: HarperCollins.

Haley, A. (1964). *The autobiography of Malcolm X.* New York: Ballantine.

Houston, J.W., and Houston, J.D. (1974). *Farewell to Manzanar.* New York: Bantam.

McMillan, T. (1994). *Waiting to exhale.* New York: Washington Square Press.

Momaday, N.S. (1968). *House made of dawn.* New York: Perennial.

Norwood, R. (1991). *Women who love too much: When you keep wishing and hoping he'll change.* New York: Mass Market Paperback.

Quinn, A. (1972). *The original sin.* New York: Bantam.

Quinn, S. (1987). *A mind of her own: The life of Karen Horney.* New York: Summit.

Ramirez, M., and Castaneda, A. (1974). *Cultural democracy, bicognitive development and education.* New York: Academic Press.

Silko, L.M. (1977). *Ceremony.* New York: Signet.

Tan, A. (1992). *The kitchen god's wife.* New York: Ivy Books.

Tan, A. (1994). *The Joy Luck Club.* New York: Ivy Books.

Ullman, L. (1974). *Changing.* New York: Bantam.

AUTHOR INDEX

A
Adler, A., 77
Adler, P. S., xi, 30
Alford, B. A., 152
Almeida, E., 162
Aponte, H. J., 131
Aranalde, M. A., 131
Ardila, R., 16
Atteneave, C. L., 131
Auerswald, E., 131

B
Beck, A. T., 124
Bond, H. M., 15–16
Bowen, M., 132
Boyd-Franklin, N., 132
Brink, T. L., 160
Bulhan, H. A., 16, 109
Buriel, R., 26

C
Castaneda, A., 13, 20, 21, 23, 24, 25, 26, 27, 29, 161, 162, 165
Cervantes, J. M., 132
Cohen, R. A., 13
Collins, M., 11
Constantino, G., 13

Court, S., 13
Cox, B., 141, 162
Cox, B. G., 23, 24, 25, 29
Crevecoeur, J. H. St. J., 11
Cubberly, E. P., 12

D
Darder, A., 162
DeMichele, J. T., 152
Doell, S. R., 27
DuBois, W. E. B., 14, 16, 17

F
Fanon, F., 16, 17, 109
Freire, P., 162
Freud, S., 13, 15, 16

G
Garza, R. T., x, 29, 30
Giroux, H., 162
Goodenough, D., 55
Guthrie, R. V., 12

H
Hale-Benson, J. E., 13, 162
Herrnstein, R. J., 12

225

SUBJECT INDEX